GIFT

from

THE USF CENTER

for

CONTEMPORARY

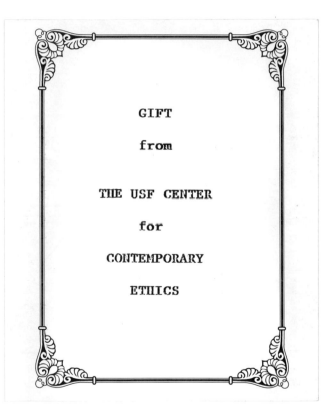

ETHICS

Durable Goods

Soundings

A Series of Books on Ethics, Economics, and Business

Thomas Donaldson, *Editor*

Durable Goods

A Covenantal Ethic for Management and Employees

Stewart W. Herman

University of Notre Dame Press
Notre Dame, Indiana

Designed by Wendy McMillen
Set in 11.5/14 Perpetua by The Book Page, Inc.
Printed in the U.S.A. by Edwards Brothers, Inc.

Library of Congress Cataloging-in-Publication Data

Herman, Stewart W., 1948–
Durable goods : a covenantal ethic for management and employees / Stewart W. Herman.
p. cm. — (Soundings)
Includes bibliographical references (p.) and index.
ISBN 0-268-00884-1 (alk. paper). — ISBN 0-268-00885-X (pbk. alk. paper).
1. Management—Religious aspects—Christianity. 2. Covenants—Religious aspects—Christianity. 3. Business ethics. 4. Christian ethics. 5. Interpersonal communication—Religious aspects—Christianity. I. Title. II. Series: Soundings (Notre Dame, Ind.)
HD31.H4736 1998
174'.4—dc21 97-17271
CIP

∞ *The paper used in this publication meets the minimum requirements of the American National Standard for Information Sciences—Permanence of Paper for Printed Library Materials, ANSI Z39.48-1984.*

To my father

&

mother

Contents

Acknowledgments

Business practitioners rightly exhort ethicists to dirty their hands and clarify their thinking with real-world experience, and so it is important to note that this study has a modest grounding in the workplace. Between 1973 and 1978, I closely observed industrial research and federal environmental policy, visiting corporate labs throughout the United States. This work, which resulted in several books and articles, gave me a feel for the world of values and pressures in which business management operates, and it has been reinforced since then by contacts through various academic forums. The world of collectively organized employees I experienced as a member of an urban transit-workers' union for several months in 1981. Yet for better or for worse, my knowledge of the employment relation in the private sector has been mediated primarily through texts.

I have incurred substantial debts in developing this project, debts which reach back to my graduate study at the University of Chicago Divinity School. Years ago, Robin Lovin introduced me to Christian realism as a means of gaining cogent critical leverage on the dialectic of ideal possibilities and realistic limitations on human action. From James M. Gustafson, and his mentor and colleague H. Richard Niebuhr, I have absorbed the imperative to integrate disciplines as a means of yielding insight in ethical analysis. Paul M. Hirsch, now of the Kellogg Graduate School of Business, helped me think sociologically about the employment relation. Franklin I. Gamwell imparted a sense of the heuristic power of moral principles for analyzing social relations. William J. Buckley gave, and continues to provide, invaluable practice in framing abstractions and analyzing arguments; both William C. French and he have continually sharpened my sensitivities to issues raised in this study.

This book began three years ago as a single chapter in an as yet unfinished manuscript on covenantal business ethics. Ronald M. Green originally put me on to the idea of covenant, while Paul F. Camenisch, Christine Firer Hinze, Hugh Wilson, and Max L. Stackhouse helpfully jarred my thinking at certain points subsequently. Series editor Thomas Donaldson believed in the project long before this particular germ had sprouted. I am grateful that he kept my ideas and energies focused with timely interventions. I owe thanks to him, and to David P. Schmidt, Donald W. Shriver, Jr., Hugh Wilson, and Ron Green for reviewing all or parts of the manuscript at critical moments. Responsibility for any errors of fact or interpretation lies entirely with me, of course. Over the years, Jennifer Ristau invested the project with dozens of hours of careful and good-humored research and editing; H. Robert Homann, Concordia's academic dean, graciously provided financial support for the final portion of that work. Finally, as the chapters of the manuscript were fissioning repeatedly during the past three summers, my wife and colleague, Linda Johnson, gave me the benefit of her shrewd insight and expressed a patience which surpassed all understanding.

There is a last, specifically theological set of debts which need to be acknowledged. Although this study betrays few signs of my Lutheran confession, it is parasitic upon one of Martin Luther's grander projects, which it aspires to extend. In Lutheran thinking, the conviction that God is the sole agent of human salvation authorizes and encourages us creatures to articulate and pursue a sense of vocation strictly on the "horizontal" plane. This conviction suggests that an important task of Lutheran ethics is to make claims about precisely what it is God wants us to do within our roles, as Luther himself sometimes attempted to do. The best scholars in the Lutheran tradition are therefore not shy about tracking historical patterns, drawing upon scholarly and other resources, forming hypotheses, and even drawing conclusions. My mentors at the Lutheran School of Theology at Chicago, Joseph Sittler, Philip Hefner, and Bob Benne, imparted to me their zest for doing theology through interdisciplinary conversation. Throughout the project, I have benefited from the stringent prophetic tutelage practiced by my brother Nicholas. And finally, in pursuing this adventurous and bumpy track, I owe much to my parents, Stewart W. and Ethelyn C. Herman, and my brother Christopher, who always have encouraged me to stay the course on long and risky explorations.

PART 1

Constructing a Covenantal Narrative

CHAPTER 1

Why a Covenantal Theory of the Employment Relation Is Needed

More than 90 million men and women in the United States work in the private sector of the economy, in for-profit enterprises. They are embedded in the "employment relation"—an arrangement which requires management and employees to coordinate their efforts in service of economic production. It is a relation in which cooperation and conflict historically have become deeply intertwined. On the one hand, management and employees have developed ways to accommodate the needs and interests of each other in times of both prosperity and adversity. On the other hand, they frequently have struggled with each other over the past two hundred years to define the terms—wages, conditions, and job security—of the employment relation. Since the 1970s these contradictory tendencies have only intensified. While management now is making unprecedented efforts to secure the willing cooperation of employees, tens of millions of jobs have been destroyed and replaced, if at all, by positions much inferior in wages and security. This "restructuring" of the employment relation has yielded important competitive gains for the U.S. economy, but enormous dislocation and suffering as well. Perhaps no other aspect of business ethics is now so germane to Christian belief and practice as the quality of relationship between management and employees. It is here that the raw forces of the global market and the more subtle currents of power relations within corporations have tangible impacts upon millions of lives.

The Argument

This study seeks to explain how the employment relation in modern business enterprises might be covenantal. Because I aspire to a

Christian realism which avoids both the easy optimism of managerial ideology as well as the dismissive pessimism of radical critics, I emphasize what is perhaps the most intractable issue: the long struggle between management and labor over the right of management to run its enterprises as it sees fit, and the right of labor to achieve a collective voice through unions. To interpret this often conflicted history, I use another history, of God's efforts to sustain covenantal relations with Israel and with the followers of Jesus. I connect these two histories by developing a theory of what it means to covenant within business enterprises as networks of functional interdependence.

According to my model, the occasion for covenanting arises when two parties decide to cope with the durable or ineradicable contingencies they present to each other by making durable commitments. To covenant, I suggest, is to cope with durable contingencies by making enduring commitments, just as God in the biblical narratives copes with durable human contingencies by making durable commitments. Extended to the employment relation, covenanting is a process for creating a community of mutual accountability by engaging the wills of management and employees in the making and fulfilling of commitments oriented to shared goals and self-restraint in the use of power. As will be seen, covenanting seen as a process is a uniquely appropriate vehicle for interpreting the actions of management and employees who, being constituted of will and spirit, present ineradicable contingencies to each other.

The history of management-labor relations yields a succession of strategies and tactics through which each side has sought to bend the other to its will. I will argue that two kinds of durable covenantal goods have emerged, however haltingly, in this history. First, at certain points, management and employees have sought to enlist the willing cooperation of each other, rather than to frustrate the troublesome agency of each other. In so doing, they have achieved an enlarged freedom particularly appropriate to the nature of business corporations as networks of densely interdependent human action. Second, at certain points and in various ways in this history, both sides have bound themselves, through self-obligating gestures, to acknowledge and respect the moral principle central to the action of each other: whether the "managerial prerogative" claimed by management or the "self-representation" sought by employees, or most recently, the "self-direction" of employee work sought sometimes by both sides.

I aspire here to a Christian realism which hews a middle way between the optimism of those ethicists who think that management alone can define and achieve genuine cooperation and moral community within firms, and the pessimism of dissenting voices who believe that management can achieve nothing of the sort. As this chronological narrative makes clear, the rudiments of covenanting have become evident not in a steady evolutionary march from conflict to cooperation but in a turbulent and tragic intertwining of achievement with failure. Nevertheless, the gains should not be dismissed out of hand as too modest when measured against the high aspirations of the covenantal love and justice commended by the biblical prophets. The two goods delineated in the paragraph above may be modest, but they are of covenantal value precisely because they are forged out of the very contingencies which the biblical witness sees as enduring, and even ineradicable, within human history: the will and spirit identified by Reinhold Niebuhr as crucial to the biblical image of human nature.[1] This study therefore closes not with the ebullient confidence of managerial ideology nor the unbudgeable suspicion of radical critics, but with a cautious analysis and appraisal of the potential for genuine cooperation between management and employees.

Towards Realism: Explaining Covenanting under Conditions of Conflict

Five years ago, Max L. Stackhouse and Dennis P. McCann challenged the guild of religious ethicists to envision the corporation as a "secular form of covenantal community"[2]. Though their proposal met with considerable skepticism in some quarters, it underscored a swelling chorus of efforts to interpret modern business enterprise through this venerable biblical symbol. Indeed, there appears to be a latent consensus among religious ethicists as to what it means to covenant in a corporate context. Business enterprises are "covenantal communities," it seems, when management acknowledges responsibilities radiating out to various "stakeholders," which comprise that community of beings (including now the natural environment) affected by the operations of the enterprise. As far as the employment relation is concerned, covenanting involves making and keeping promises; respecting the dignity of all participants; and aiming at a common good of the firm as expressive of some larger social good.[3] A corporation becomes covenantal insofar as management and employees see their relationship to each other and to the wider community in terms of mutual service and responsibility, rather than become enmired in conflict and short-sighted selfishness.[4]

The obvious procedure for talking about covenanting therefore seems to be to discuss contemporary success stories—exemplary cases of managerial promise-making and promise-keeping. Indeed, there have been corporations where management and employees have achieved an enviable harmony in the pursuit of economic goals, such as the often-praised Herman Miller furniture company of Michigan. But this broadly affirmative approach, as encouraging and illuminating as it might be, sidesteps the more difficult problem: to explain what it means to covenant in the context of conflicting interests, especially conflicting collective interests. The questions to be answered therefore include: how might management and employees achieve anything approximating covenantal justice when their interests diverge? And how might they achieve anything approximating covenantal love when they seek to control each other, or more pointedly, to insulate themselves against control by the other?

In this study, I examine the efforts of employees to organize themselves collectively in labor unions, as met by the countervailing initiatives of management to thwart such efforts, or more subtly, to render unions unnecessary.[5] I explain what it means to covenant in the context of a business enterprise by developing a formal, abstract theory in conversation with organization theory in chapter 3, and then drawing its normative content from the biblical history of God's covenant-making in chapter 4. The balance of the book (chapters 5–17) fleshes out this still rather abstract definition by interpreting the history of labor-management relations in the United States, which I divide into four distinct eras during the past two centuries. I relate this history in outline, following each stage of narration with reflections upon the covenantal elements raised up therein. (Readers interested in a summary of the historical argument might want to turn to chapter 4.) As can be seen from the table of contents, these elements point successively to dimensions of conflict, contracting, and cooperation in the employment relation. I argue that covenanting in a business corporation means striving for a genuine cooperation—one founded not upon sentiment or ideology but upon a realistic awareness that the employment relation places management and employees in a position of divergent and even conflicting interests.

Even if the need is acknowledged for explaining covenant under conditions of conflict, it still might be asked, why is a *theory* needed? What might a theory add to the compelling moral visions already articulated by religious ethicists? Why bother to develop such a bulky apparatus of interpretation for such a familiar symbol as covenant—especially when the idea of covenant already presents such a clear and salutary challenge to the stereotypical business ethos of self-interest narrowly understood? A theory of covenanting is needed for two reasons. The first is to connect biblical visions of covenanting with the business corporation as a fundamentally new form of human association; the second is to ensure that any covenantal construal of the employment relation will be fair in balancing the commitments it asks of management and employees.

Functional Interdependence as the Context

Christian business ethics, as a recent field of inquiry, needs to connect its prescriptions on how a business corporation ought to function with a description of how business corporations actually do function. (By "Christian business ethics" I mean nothing more here than texts on business ethics written by ethicists who by religious background or chosen competence are deeply familiar with the Christian tradition.) Christian business ethicists are heirs to a potent moral vision—epitomized in the symbol of covenant—but need to develop the theoretical apparatus to connect that vision with the employment relation as it is experienced by management and employees.

The symbol of covenant is packed with the prophetic vision of God's justice and righteousness, and this content offers a transcendent platform from which to evaluate the moral tone of any given employment relation. Its moral meanings have been unpacked by H. Richard Niebuhr in terms of unlimited commitment,[6] Paul Ramsey in terms of God's righteous love and sovereignty,[7] Douglas Sturm in terms of peace, righteousness, and loving-kindness,[8] and Joseph Allen in terms of a steadfast, inclusive, and need-centered communal love.[9] There is little moral substance to add to these powerful visions from biblical theology. But simply using these norms to judge organizational arrangements results in "thin prescription": evocative and visionary, but not viscerally connected with organizational realities, and as a result not terribly useful to management and employees seeking to respond faithfully to the challenges they face. With few exceptions, the brief invocations of covenant in current Christian business ethics all have this quality of abstractness. When applied to business, the norms of covenantal love, promise-keeping, and justice intersect organizational practice as external ideals, foreign to the specific dynamics of business organizations. These ideals need to be mediated by a descriptive theory which explains how in fact they illuminate the employment relation. As the ancient Hebrew prophets redescribed the lives of their fellow Israelites by drawing upon concrete imagery of broken pots, ravenous beasts, trees, and fruit, so a covenantal ethic needs to develop a terminology which expresses the context in which management and employees negotiate their relationship.

In this study, I will draw upon a generalized social-scientific explanation of how business corporations function in order to connect the symbol of covenant with the lived experience of management and employees with the employment relation. A business corporation differs fundamentally from other modes of human association more familiar to Christian social ethics in that it is a dense, designed network of intentional human interaction oriented to producing goods and services. This distinctive kind of collectivity was largely unfamiliar before the mid-nineteenth century, whatever roots it may have in monastic orders, joint-stock companies, and other earlier forms of organization.[10] The interactivity of management and employees, mediated by roles, supervisors, and the other apparatus of bureaucratic organization, fosters functional interdependencies between management and employees. This in turn generates and accentuates mutual vulnerabilities of each side to the nonperformance of the other. Such vulnerabilities prompt management and employees to shape the thinking and action of each other, which in turn fosters complex and often asymmetrical flows of power. In essence, a corporation might be said to consist less of whole human persons than of the strategies and tactics, authorized or not, which are intentionally applied by human actors to shape thinking and action of other human actors, in a dense network of reciprocal actions.

To the extent that this description encapsulates the nature of the business enterprise, it draws attention to the quality of interactivity as a key moral dimension of the employment relation. The relations between management and employees range along a spectrum from conflict through passive compliance to full-hearted cooperation—with every degree imaginable of intertwining among these three formally differentiated alternatives. The past two hundred years of management-employee relations in the United States reveal all three in abundance. The task of Christian business ethicists is to sort out which alternative is appropriate in a given situation. Sometimes it may be appropriate for management and employees to take an oppositional posture, as when employees resist a management that presents patently unjust contract terms in collective bargaining, or when a management resists employees who obstinately nurture a culture of destructive opposition. At other times, passive acquiescence may be warranted.

Yet most Christian business ethicists rightly have intuited that in the absence of compelling reasons for conflict or withdrawal, a covenantal construal of the employment relation calls both management and employees to nourish relations of genuine cooperation with each other. Genuine cooperation, as will be seen, is the covenantal goal appropriate to the specific nature of the business corporation. More than eighty years ago, Walter Rauschenbusch sounded a clarion call for "cooperation," by which he meant the self-management of workers as an alternative to the excess of power and cupidity which owners enjoyed over workers by virtue of the exploitative competition fostered by capitalism.[11] This study revises that long-neglected call by asking what genuine cooperation might look like today. It will not do simply to revive Rauschenbusch's proposals for economic democracy and worker-controlled cooperatives, for the overwhelming triumph of the business corporation mandates a focus on the covenantal potential of the employment relation as it is now experienced by tens of millions of managers and employees.

Fairness as a Goal

The second reason for a theory of covenanting is to establish moral objectivity or fairness as the methodological and substantive commitment of Christian business ethics as a field of inquiry. While establishing fairness might seem an obvious and unproblematic goal, achieving it actually requires considerable effort. Christian business ethics has been taking shape not on some Olympian summit of disinterested inquiry but in close conversation with the realities of business. Two kinds of ideology compete for the attention of ethicists, and critical leverage needs to be developed against both. First, according to radical critics, genuine cooperation between management and employees is a simple impossibility, due to the unredeemably exploitative nature of the employment relation as it has taken shape in the modern business corporation. These voices are too pessimistic, and generally have been ignored in Christian business ethics, but fairness requires attending to them by virtue of their keen moral sensitivity to injustices experienced by employees.

Second, as ethicists have sought to make the Christian tradition alive to executives and managers, they have come within the powerful gravitational field exerted by what I call the "ethical managerialism" of enlightened U.S. management, an ideology which embraces the overly optimistic conviction that cooperation can be engineered by management.[12] This ideology strongly colors contemporary interpretations of the employment relation in business ethics. As such, it has been variously absorbed or rejected by Christian ethicists (see chapter 2). What is needed at this point is neither uncritical acceptance nor prophetic denunciation of ethical managerialism itself, which would be tedious and pointless, but attention to a more basic task: a reflective analysis of the basic moral components of the employment relation. Unlike this moral impulse in management thought, covenantal realism recognizes that there is a tragic element in the employment relation: management and employees, as evidenced by the testimony of their two-hundred-year struggle, base their actions upon moral principles that are not simply convergent. Covenantal theory can provide a useful service to ethical managerialists by making room for the perspectives of employees while continuing to emphasize, as does management ideology, that genuine cooperation is the norm by which the employment relation in any given business is to be assessed. Indeed, such evenhanded and critical scrutiny is crucial to establishing Christian business ethics as a field in its own right.

In short, this study aspires to a realistic appraisal of the possibilities for genuine cooperation between management and employees. As Robin Lovin recently has argued, Reinhold Niebuhr answered both the idealisms and disillusionments of his day with interlocking moral, political, and theological "realisms"; he aimed to reach behind nihilistic despair and sentimental hopes to a faith that could appraise social achievements in light of an ultimate social harmony known only to God.[13] The point of such realism is to search for the very real goods that emerge from conflictual social processes, all the while correcting the ideologies which falsely absolutize partial and biased interpretations of those goods.

The lure of ethical managerialism

To appreciate the difficulty of achieving a fair description of genuine cooperation, a brief excursus on the nature of ethical managerialism is needed. Within the guild of Christian ethics, it is probably fair to say that the role of management as a social function has been regarded with considerable suspicion. Rarely does such distaste find expression in texts specifically about the employment relation, but when it surfaces, it is categorical, uncompromising—and quite wide of the mark. A decade and more ago, for example, Alasdair MacIntyre, Robert Bellah, and colleagues dismissed the function of management as amoral and technocratic, while condemning the role of managers in the employment relation as unredeemably manipulative.[14] Such prophetic dismissals may apply to some kinds of managerial ideology, but they fail to connect with *ethical* managerialism. What distinguishes ethical managerialism as an ideology is that it frames the function of management within a moral purpose oriented to cooperation within the enterprise and to the common good with reference to the environing society. Ethical managerialism, at its core, is the deeply held conviction that management has a moral obligation to maximize the value of the business enterprise for its employees, customers, suppliers, and other stakeholders. Peter Drucker, dean of business consultants and a social philosopher as well, has done more than anyone to establish this sense of professional vocation and to spell it out in practical advice.[15] Ethical managerialists assume that the interests of the enterprise and of the larger society converge, and see a special role for management in providing a fiduciary service for the utilitarian benefit of society. They see this ideology of service as effectively legitimating the power and control management wields over employees and other stakeholders. And so it is this moral argument, rather than simply the contemporary functioning of management, which needs to be assessed.

Within the emerging specialty of Christian business ethics, ethical managerialism appears to be accepted, implicitly if not explicitly, as the basic moral compass for steering the employment relation (for a map of the terrain, see chapter 2). After all, it is an intensely moral creed. Its broad utilitarian vision is reassuringly comprehensive. It embraces the mandate to make creation productive, offering a sorely needed organizational context in which to elaborate ideas of personal vocation and calling. Its vision of the common good compounds the realization of many individual goods. It resonates with the symbol of covenant, interpreted by Christian business ethicists as the ideal of mutual responsibility. It provides a reassuringly firm platform of good intentions and anecdotes upon which theologians can construct their own distinctive modulations upon managerialist themes. And it has survival value, for to achieve its self-proclaimed mandate to make human and physical resources productive, ethical managerialism has been amazingly flexible and responsive. As Donald Shriver has pointed out, a humanitarian bent has progressively softened the authoritarian and paternalistic ring of early management ideology. As such, it has proven a powerful and continually evolving response by U.S. business to labor problems.[16] It is small wonder that ethical managerialism has been well received by those ethicists who have sought to explain how business enterprises can be covenantal communities. This powerfully adaptive ideology is a valuable resource and conversation partner for the doing of Christian business ethics, and merits more explicit attention than it has received.[17]

Two flawed assumptions

Yet there is a problem when the ethical managerialist viewpoint is absorbed uncritically by Christian business ethicists. This ideology is deeply flawed with regards to the employment relation, in that it rests upon a biased viewpoint which is morally questionable, and a further assumption which is empirically dubious. These two problems do not warrant prophetic dismissal of the ideology, but they suggest that a much more rigorous theory than ethical managerialism is needed to explain how the employment relation can be characterized by genuine cooperation.

First, the ethical managerialism of Christian business ethics simply swallows the bias of managerial ideology generally, that management is the creative and driving force within business enterprise. This partial viewpoint encourages us to ignore what employees do of their own initiative to define and establish their own visions of moral order within their workplaces.[18] (If this formulation sounds presumptuous, it certainly is no more so than the paternalistic claim of ethical managerialism to define what is good for employees.) The power of this bias can be gauged by noting how rarely Christian business ethicists consider employees to be independent agents with their own moral viewpoints on organizational affairs, and with collective and individual interests distinct from those of management. Rarely do ethicists violate the managerialist creed by endorsing unionization, let alone discussing labor-management conflict, or bringing up labor history. These oversights appear to stem from the failure to see employees as significant actors, engaged in influencing managerial thinking and action.

The right of management to define every aspect of an enterprise, including appropriate values and virtues, simply is assumed rather than raised for critical discussion. As will be seen in later chapters, there is some descriptive merit to this bias, in that management has been a more dynamic force than employees in shaping the employment relation during the past several decades. Nevertheless, ethical managerialism alone does not present the whole story, for this ideology itself is more a tool for containing labor problems than a disinterested heuristic tool for adjudicating the employment relation. It was and remains a means for management to avoid or overcome adversarial relations with employees, by imposing its own vision of cooperation upon captive or suspicious employees.[19] The result is that Christian business ethics lacks, as a matter of simple descriptive adequacy, any conscious development of the dialectic involved between managerial and employee expectations. A theory is needed which takes account of the initiatives and responses of both sides. Here Protestant ethicists might take a leaf from official Roman Catholic social teaching, which for the past century has developed an ethical framework for taking seriously the claims of both employees and management.

Second, the moral legitimacy of ethical managerialism for defining the employment relation rests upon a questionable empirical assumption: that the interests of managers—to sustain and enhance their enterprises, particularly their own role in directing the work of their enterprises—are materially congruent with the interests of their employees. There arguably was such a congruence during the post–World War II decades of U.S. hegemony in the world marketplace. But the loss of millions of manufacturing jobs during the 1970s and 1980s wedged apart the interests of white-collar management and blue-collar workers. And during the 1980s and 1990s, waves of corporate "down-sizing" have made it clear to equal numbers of suddenly unemployed middle managers that their interests are not simply congruent with those of senior management. Between 1979 and 1993, for example, the Fortune 500 shed some 4.4 million positions, amounting to one-quarter of their total employment. By 1996, the rate of job destruction was averaging more than 3 million per year (up from 1.5 million in 1980), evenly divided between managerial and production or service jobs.[20]

This is not the whole story, of course. According to Labor Department numbers compiled by the *New York Times,* while 43 million jobs were erased between 1979 and 1996, even more jobs were created, for a net gain of 27 million positions. And the competitive position of the U.S. economy has improved dramatically since the stagnation of the 1970s. But even if management may take justifiable pride in this work of regeneration, a covenantal ethic cannot let measures of aggregate utility outweigh concern for the material and moral destruction wreaked upon the lives of millions of individuals. A Christian ethic can never stray too far from its primary concern for the welfare of concrete individuals, no matter how alluring or compelling are the larger economic arguments in favor of restructuring whole economies.

As far as the employment relation within business enterprises is concerned (as opposed to collateral effects upon communities), the principal problems concern the quality of the new jobs created and the impact of restructuring upon the bonds between management and employees. Only one-third of the laid-off individuals are finding work that pays as well as their former positions. At least one-fifth of the new jobs are "contingent," for a 1993 total of 21 million part-timers, of which at least 6 million would prefer to have full-time jobs. The nation's largest employer is now Manpower, Inc., with 767,000 temporaries that it rents out to businesses. This churning of employment is unprecedented in U.S. business history. Welcomed by some and deplored by many, it has shattered the comfortable convergence of interest between employees and management. Such a convergence, after all, was the basis for the trust and loyalty which ethical managerialism seeks to foster. What politically minded organization theorists have termed the "coalition" of interests which enable enterprises to grow and prosper—and lends descriptive plausibility to "stakeholder" theory—has become deeply problematic.[21] The loyalty of tens of millions of employees has been sacrificed to the legal and economic power of management to streamline its enterprises in the name of efficiency and managerial control. A *New York Times* poll in late 1995 found that the vast majority of respondents experienced a marked decline in the loyalty formerly reciprocated between management and employees, while competition and anger among coworkers had increased.[22] The comfortable "social contract" established between management and employees after World War II is collapsing, with incalculable ripple effects into surrounding communities. What this destruction of jobs demonstrates is that the interests of a corporation, as defined by its management, are not and probably cannot be fully expressive of employee interests. As a result, the ideal of cooperation espoused by ethical managerialism has become deeply problematic, however necessary and successful has been the restructuring of U.S. business for a truly global environment.

Towards an Enlargement of Ethical Managerialism

The ideology of ethical managerialism likely will adapt to accommodate the massive dislocations now occurring, just as it has adapted to earlier changes in the management-employee relation. Such adaptation is needed, because a broad acceptance of management's moral legitimacy is an important lubricant of the American business machine. As Max Stackhouse and Dennis McCann have argued so vigorously, there simply is no widely accepted moral alternative to the modern corporation as a vehicle for organizing economic activity.[23] As a result, there appears to be no alternative to the moral leadership which enlightened managements have claimed. Ethical managerialism is likely to remain the gravitational field of meaning in which Christian ethicists operate. In fact, it is difficult even to imagine a Christian ethic for doing business in the U.S. which does not draw its vision from or connect it with the ethical managerialist creed.[24] The challenge therefore is to enlarge ethical managerialism, to articulate a vision of cooperation which is genuinely covenantal, rather than one which is partial to the perspective of management. To meet this challenge, a covenantal ethic needs to articulate a theory which is fair to the perspectives of both management and employees. To avoid sentimentality or cynicism, a sense of the realistic possibilities for and constraints upon genuine cooperation needs to be developed relative to both the long history of struggle between management and employees, and to the nature of business enterprises as tightly interlinked systems of human action. Michael Keeley defines the justice achievable by organizations primarily as safeguarding the rights of their participants.[25] More is needed than a keen libertarian sense of justice, however. Business enterprises require the structured interaction and interdependence of individuals, and therefore some positive vision of appropriate interrelatedness is needed, beyond the criterion of nolo maleficare—do no harm.[26] For modern business enterprises, then, fairness requires a vision of genuine cooperation—and assessing the realism of this prescription for management and employees tempted to revert to patterns of authority and obedience, or domination and resistance. The last four chapters of this study attempt to develop a realistic assessment of the possibilities for genuine cooperation.

A Methodology for Achieving Fairness

To support a vision of genuine cooperation, a methodological commitment is needed to "moral objectivity" in interpreting and appraising the employment relation. It involves first of all being equally affirmative of the goals and interests of management and employees: employees have a legitimate interest in retaining their jobs, earning a comfortable living, and achieving some considerable degree of control over the conditions of their work; management has a legitimate interest in retaining control of business decisions while eliciting a maximum of reliable work from employees. Moreover, achieving relative neutrality requires acknowledging the divergence as well as congruence of managerial and employee interests—something which the dominant tendency in Christian business ethics is unwilling to do. It means recognizing that the employment relation, far from expressing a fundamental harmony, has evolved over the past two hundred years into a complex blend of convergent and conflicting interests. The employee relation is neither essentially cooperative, as ethical managerialists assume, nor essentially conflictive, as radical critics assume, but it intertwines irreducible elements of both conflict and cooperation.

How to account for this complexity while being fair to both sides? It involves somehow connecting moral vision to the lived experience of management and employees. To date, philosophers and social scientists in the budding applied field of business ethics have made great strides in connecting moral norms with organizational practice. While they have developed their theories and models largely within the orbit of ethical managerialism, they possess potent methods for enhancing moral objectivity, were they to turn their attention to issues such as collective bargaining and unions.[27] Indeed, nowhere in Christian business ethics is a passion for fairness so evident as in the philosophical business ethics textbooks authored by figures such as Ronald M. Green and Manuel Velasquez.[28] The task for Christian business ethicists is to develop theories or models which present covenant-making as an open-ended process which intertwines cooperation and conflict. Where narratives are conflictual, it involves representing and interpreting the differing perspectives. The aim is to discern and express more encompassing wholes of meaning in which the contending perspectives each have their place. This work requires a methodological commitment to listen to all voices, especially those of the excluded or oppressed. Such empathic, inclusive listening attends to the interplay of contending moral claims, generating a more inclusive picture than if only one side were consulted, no matter how morally holistic it claims to be. A truly interactive ethic seeks a more complete perspective than the ethical managerialism of management, the claims of employees, or the analyses by radical critics, for that matter.

The covenantal approach developed here invokes the biblical covenantal norms of justice, righteousness, and lovingkindness, not as abstract and irrelevantly general prescriptions but as concrete aspirational standards organically linked to organizational processes. Following H. Richard Niebuhr and his pioneering integration of theology with social science around the image of human beings as "responders,"[29] I treat the interaction of social actors as the genesis of moral meaning and seek to explain the actions of contending parties in a manner empathic to each side, such that prescription emerges naturally and obviously from such holistic description. Such "thick prescription" involves attending to the thinking and gestures of individuals over time. It involves working complexes of dialogue and action into narratives that draw attention to the salient moral issues, perspectives, convictions, and principles operative in those histories. Theological claims are introduced in order to identify and illuminate the moral goods at stake rather than simply to assert a priori standards to which the parties are to be held accountable.[30] Explaining comes before prescribing, and indeed, prescriptions grow from carefully crafted explanations.[31] Such methodological humility is called for by the novel nature of the business corporation as an interactive network of functional dependencies oriented to the production of goods and services.

This thick prescription, as a model of religious moral reasoning in business ethics, differs sharply from the deontological or teleological models of philosophers in that it finds moral claims incarnated less in formal arguments than in the expectations, actions, and reactions which constitute the ongoing history of conflict and cooperation between two parties. The history of interactive behaviors itself generates its own argument, as H. Richard Niebuhr brilliantly demonstrated. Seen in such a light, the strategies and tactics of resistance and counterresistance practiced by management and employees themselves constitute a two-century-long moral argument as to what the shape of the employment relation should be. The issue is: what promises should management and employees make to each other, and what commitments should they keep? The actions of both sides, traced across decades, constitute a perhaps more vivid argument than moral claims abstracted from this contentious history and tailored to fit precisely crafted deontological, teleological, or utilitarian arguments.

Three resources

To generate the "thick prescription" constitutive of a covenantal ethic, I marshal three kinds of resources. The first is a narrative of labor-management relations, here compiled from a variety of primary sources. This material, of course, is not theologically self-explanatory, nor does it take seriously enough the perspective of management, with its mandate to keep business enterprises running and profitable.

To interpret the history of the employment relation presented by the primary sources, I deploy a second kind of resource: a set of ideas derived loosely from the applied social-scientific field of organization theory. The most salient insight yielded by organization theory, outlined above and developed in chapter 3, is that business enterprises are systems of densely interdependent human actions. This abstract model provides me some tools to sift labor history for the covenantal dynamics it discloses. A few years ago, I argued that business organizations are covenantal in that participants become enmeshed in patterns of mutual vulnerability which defy being contained within the exacting stipulations of contracts.[32] Here I develop that line of thinking. In business enterprises, as tightly interlinked systems of coordinated action, management and employees present manifold contingencies to each other, within an environment of uncontrollable and often unpredictable external pressures and constraints. I describe the array of strategies and tactics that both sides have used to shape the thinking and action of each other (chapters 6, 8, 11, 13, 14). In effect, these strategies and tactics constitute an ongoing conversation about what management and employees are willing or able, or not, to promise each other. They express the moral principles basic to the action of each side: the prerogative claimed by management, and the self-representation and self-direction claimed by employees.

The third resource used in this study, the Bible, provides a normative focus for interpreting this interplay of strategies, tactics, and principles. The historical literature of the Old and New Testaments offers profound insights into how God and God's people, as active agents, cope with the contingency they present to each other (chapter 4). Both conflictual and cooperative elements are interwoven, yielding a picture of human nature which illuminates the complex history between management and employees. In the view afforded by the biblical histories, covenanting is primarily an interactive process rather than a fixed quality of relationship. The covenants established by God initiate dialectics of promise and fulfillment, obedience and reward, disobedience and punishment, despair and affirmation, learning and hardening, recruitment and apostasy, and so forth. The relationships evolve as both sides seek to shape the responsiveness, and indeed the character, of each other. The biblical narratives emphasize—as did Augustine, Luther, and

Reinhold Niebuhr subsequently—that human will and spirit are the engines of both conflict and cooperation. The biblical witnesses, in their unsentimental view of human capacities, envision only a provisional and limited harmony between God and God's creatures within the eschatological horizon assumed in the later parts of the Old Testament and in the New.

The Covenantal Dynamic of the Employment Relation

The quality of a covenant turns, of course, upon the nature of the commitments made and kept. A covenantal ethic will put tough questions to both parties in their long history of tangled antagonisms and collaborations: to what moral principles have you committed yourself through your actions? And in hewing to those principles, have you refrained from abusing the power you hold over each other? What durable goods, in the sense of mutually intertwined, trustful expectations of just and benevolent behavior, have you established and reinforced through the promises you have made and kept?

The next three chapters develop the covenantal theory sketched above. It is only a model; to illuminate a history, one must flesh it out with the narrative of that history—the work which occupies most of this study. Chapter by chapter, the covenantal model highlights revealing tragedies and redeeming moments in the long history of struggle between management and employees. A measure of progress is discernible, as signaled in the succession of headings under which the narrative is pursued: conflict, contracting, and cooperation. Two hundred years of struggle have moved management and employees in the direction of making particular durable commitments to each other. In those eras when they have sought to recruit rather than control the energies of each other, they have achieved an enlarged sense of freedom through cooperation. And when they have bound themselves not to exploit the advantages they hold over each other, they have committed themselves to the moral core of covenantal love and justice. But these goods are not indestructible; the progress is hardly irreversible. The harsh managerial tactics of the 1980s and 1990s have called forth a revival of confrontational labor activism, and the cooperation now sought so fervently by management may be an illusory hope.

The thick texture of the argument developed here precludes simple and easy solutions to the recurrent struggle between management and employees. The succession of strategies and tactics used by management and employees raises difficult questions about the place of coercion, conflict, consent, and active cooperation in the employment relation. As a result, the study ends less on a note of idealistic hope than of realistic caution about the conditions and limits of genuine cooperation. Management and employees, as creatures of will, present ineradicable contingencies to each other. The strategies and tactics of each side echo moral principles which are exceedingly difficult to reconcile. There is no magic bullet, no foolproof formula for each side to use in suppressing or controlling the contingency presented by the other. Rather, there is only the endless adjustment of strategies and tactics in light of transcendent goods imperfectly embodied in actual relations. The aim of this study therefore is to provide tools for further analysis rather than to stand as an exhaustive prescription for how to make and keep covenants in business enterprises.

CHAPTER 2

Christian Business Ethics and the Corporation as a Moral Community

During the past century, the internal operations of business enterprises have attracted only occasional theological scrutiny. Most recent Christian reflection about economic matters has been maddeningly silent, vague, general, or abstract about the concrete relations between management and employees within business corporations.[1] A few Christian ethicists have discussed what working individuals experience—the dynamics of what happens on a daily basis within business enterprises. In their treatments, the central question has emerged with clarity: is it possible for a business enterprise to be a moral community?

While this question does not connect directly with the nature of business corporations as productive enterprises, it provides a helpful point of departure for achieving moral impartiality between management and employees. It encourages intense scrutiny of the employment relation. Indeed, there is more than one way to frame this question, given the variety of theologies which have been brought to bear upon it. From a prophetic Protestant standpoint: can Christian love and justice be achieved meaningfully in organizational settings? From the viewpoint of Roman Catholic social teaching, can business enterprises protect human dignity and foster social solidarity? From the perspective of narrative ethics: can a business enterprise provide a setting in which the virtues and character appropriate to fully human ends can be cultivated? Finally, from the specifically covenantal viewpoint developed here, can management and employees merit the entrustment and loyalty of each other? To what truly common goal can they demonstrate a commitment through their actions? Can both sides be confident that their basic interests and moral principles will be respected, at the same time that their energies will be applied to the pursuit of constructive purposes?

The debate has not been, and perhaps cannot be, resolved simply by the evidence of social facts. With more than a million business enterprises in existence at any given moment, the record of the present yields no definitive answer to the moral question. On the one hand, there are the dismal current trends in downsizing and layoffs, as described in chapter 1. On the other, there remain many "great places to work," as author Robert Levering said a decade ago in popularizing the search for satisfying relations of employment.[2] And of course, there are also many miserably awful places to work, to say nothing of every shade in between. Business enterprises are protean. Today's model business corporation might decline rapidly tomorrow, or even pass out of existence. In 1982, for example, Thomas J. Peters and Robert H. Waterman, Jr., published a runaway best-seller extolling the virtues of some forty-three companies which paid special attention to their employees and customers. Two years later, an unsparing analysis by *Business Week* magazine found that fourteen had slipped badly.[3]

At issue is less the flux of the present than the potentialities resident in the employment relation. Potentiality is the question because modern business enterprise is founded upon a historically novel element: the idea of "management." Management is a function whose moral implications we still are attempting to unfold. The debate about the potential of business enterprises to be moral communities turns largely upon two questions, affirmative answers to which are key to the credibility of ethical managerialism. First, does management have the will to establish moral community with employees? Second, does it possess the power to do so?

The ethical managerialism sketched in chapter 1 answers in the affirmative to both these questions as a dogma of faith—even if the experience of individual executives may not square with the optimism of this ideology. Among those few Christian ethicists who have addressed the employment relation, three distinct schools of thought are taking shape in response to the strong gravitational pull of managerial ideology. At one end are the "ethical managerialists" who embrace the ideology and optimistically believe that the moral climate of business enterprises can be shaped by management around appropriate values and goals. At the other extreme are the "prophetic" voices who implicitly or explicitly reject the ideology, doubting that management espouses constructive goals, and more to the point, doubting that the dynamics of business enterprise permit management much effective latitude to engage in such moral shaping in the first place. And finally, staking out the middle ground are those managerial "realists" who affirm the vocation of management to exercise moral leadership but are acutely conscious of the conflicting interests and moral considerations which make it difficult for managers to shape their enterprises into moral communities.

The balance of this chapter takes up these three perspectives, pointing out where ground has been broken for the covenantal ethic laid out here, and also where further development is needed. In general, these perspectives helpfully acknowledge the centrality of influence strategies and tactics in shaping the relationship of management and employees; they affirm the importance of history in explaining how character is shaped in such settings; and they explore some of the harmful effects of managerial structures and policies upon employees and managers themselves. Yet such accounts are one-sided. They would gain more descriptive cogency and normative power if they took account of the expectations, tactics, and strategies of employees as well as management. It is simply odd to speak of building moral relations, as some of these authors do, while ignoring how the expectations and actions of management and employees react back upon each other.

Ethical Managerialists

Ethical managerialists often address their texts to managers and use case studies drawn from the ranks of management, for they assume that managers are the principal agents for bringing about a healthy moral environment within a business enterprise. Such a focus does not mean that they swallow managerialism whole, but simply that they see management as the primary shaper of the employment relation. This may be the most significant assumption within Christian ethics for conceptualizing how business enterprises can become moral communities. At the very least, it cuts across denominational lines, as evidenced by the following three illustrations.

A fervent belief in the power of management to be a force for good radiates from the practical manuals authored by evangelical Christians, whether of a Reformed or Baptist stripe. Perhaps the best of the evangelical genre is *Business Through the Eyes of Faith*, a thoughtful manual for business practice authored by Richard C. Chewning, John W. Eby, and Shirley J. Roels.[4] The authors see a close link between the functions of management and God's will that human and material resources be used to meet human need.[5] They seem to assume that the key to resolving conflicts between efficiency, justice, and mercy resides in the personal morality of managers. What managers need is a motivation purified of self-interest, where they attend carefully to the impact of decisions upon employees. As long as managers are acting from Christian motives, they may use the conventional devices of management with confidence that they are glorifying God.[6]

Among mainline Protestant business ethicists, Charles McCoy has published perhaps the most resounding statement of a managerialist ethic. His 1985 *The Management of Values* exuberantly expands the standard wisdom of business strategy. He asserts that management has not only the responsibility for developing goals and strategies for business performance but for mobilizing the moral will of subordinates. "The management of values means the conscious activity of recognizing the variety of values present, of undertaking to decide among them and develop a corporate culture on the basis of value commitments, and of integrating those values into the policy process and ensuring that they have a firm foundation in the corporate community."[7] A later essay of his outlines the decisive action needed. Drawing from his extensive experience in consulting with corporations in California, McCoy advises management to initiate and sustain a lengthy process of consultation aimed at uniting all layers of management and employees around a congruent set of understandings regarding the basic direction and values of the firm.[8]

Finally, during the past twenty years several Roman Catholic ethicists also have pressed the idea that managers ought to be engaged in shaping the moral character of their enterprises. While Charles McCoy deploys the rationalistic language of managerial planning and goals, Oliver Williams and Patrick Murphy apply Aristotelian "virtue theory" to business enterprises. They argue that management can inculcate laudatory habits in managers and employees by narrating, reinforcing, and living out those paradigmatic stories which invest their organizations with a collective moral identity. "Underpinned by a theory of virtue, an ethical corporate culture, through an ingrained set of habits and perspectives, trains all those in its purview to see things in a certain way and hence is likely to predispose [them] towards ethical behavior."[9] In a further step, Dennis McCann has sought to legitimate managerialism against the skepticism of Alasdair MacIntyre and other virtue theorists by arguing that management can be a "social practice," a cooperative effort with standards of excellence which provide a focus for the individual pursuit of virtue.[10]

Ethical managerialists push the work of a covenantal ethic forward in an important respect. They unflinchingly accept, as a basic datum, the fact that human behavior in a business environment is consciously shaped by deliberately chosen strategies and tactics. Business enterprises are intentionally designed, tightly interlinked assemblages of human action, as opposed to, for example, loosely knit networks of spontaneous expression. Employees are acted upon; their thinking and action is shaped by technological imperatives, market pressures, and other forces, particularly as mediated through managerial directives.

At the same time, this robust model of influence is one-sided. It needs to be rounded out, to recognize the fact that management also is acted upon. The lines of influence do not simply move downward, as it were, but upwards and sideways. In H. Richard Niebuhr's terms, management and employees are "responders," engaged in interpreting each other's action, and acting in accord with their interpretations. Ethical managerialists need to offer some account of how employees respond to and even shape managerial initiatives, a possibility for which organization theorists and behaviorists long since have made room in their models.[11] Here the idea of covenanting can provide an interactive model. A covenant involves more than a sense of obligation which management harbors towards employees[12] or the uncodified expectations society has of corporations.[13] It is a device through which both sides seek to render each other worthy of trust and loyalty. As will be seen in the next chapter, covenantal relationships are shaped by the initiatives and responses of two parties, as they seek to define and enforce the basis upon which they can repose confidence in the reliability of each other. Any comprehensive vision of what a business enterprise should be needs to refer to the moral vision, claims, and tactics of employees as well as to that of management.

In the absence of some interactive theory, ethical managerialism will be tarred by a partiality to management. For example, managerialists are fond of pointing to Johnson and Johnson's risky but successful recall of Tylenol as the result of decades-long executive efforts to implant in employees a corporate commitment to the well-being of customers.[14] Covenantal relations indeed are built over time, as parties gain confidence in each other. But how are such mutual understandings built up? Ethical managerialists will be unable to provide a full answer until they critically examine two ideological assumptions which undergird their work. First, they assume management is the moral leader in business enterprise and, second, that management exercises effective control over organizational events. McCoy, for example, only suggests that management elicits the "suggestions" of employees in a process to be initiated and driven by management. "The approach we favor involves cascading the discussions down through the entire organization, with the culture and values statement being talked about in every workplace in a session led by the line manager in charge."[15] As illustrated by celebrations of the Tylenol episode and other managerialist anecdotes and case studies, management is assumed to have the starring role; employees are not recognized to have an independent role of their own. But why is management assumed to be best equipped to define the values that will serve to shape the enterprise into a moral community? Management of course has a legal obligation to advance the interests of stockholders, which employees do not. Management therefore operates within a legal framework which protects its right to take action for the good of the business, as it defines that interest. But a certain skepticism is called for. Why, as a matter of descriptive adequacy, are the values which really drive a business enterprise assumed to be chosen and embedded by management? Indeed, why is management rather than employees assumed to be the principal agent in a business enterprise? Ethical managerialists use abundant anecdotes about courageous and humane executive leadership to support these two assumptions. The assumptions may be defensible, but they do need to be defended, and with evidence more satisfying than anecdotes.

Ethical managerialists need to explain the moral ecology of business enterprises, to develop a theory that locates ethical managerial visions relative to the moral visions of employees, as well as to the perspectives of customers, suppliers, local communities, and all the other relevant actors. For example, the robust but one-sided vision outlined by Charles McCoy could benefit greatly by being enriched with the "federalist" covenantal theology he proposes elsewhere.[16] At present, employees are not seen as independent agents—individually or collectively—with their own agendas and influence upon managerial policy. Of course, to open up the question of employee perspectives is problematic, in that it inevitably opens up the complex and contentious history of unions, collective bargaining, and relations between management and employees more generally—which the ideology of ethical managerialism studiously avoids. Rarely if ever do ethical managerialists mention, let alone bless, the efforts by employees to organize their own values into the collective form of labor unions, even though unions historically have had a decisive influence upon the moral tone of business enterprises.[17] The cost of this silence is that it effectively limits the managerialist wing of Christian reflection to providing an ethic for management rather than an ethic for the whole business enterprise. Such partiality is not necessarily pernicious; no ethic can give every relevant actor or consideration the attention it deserves. But it is incomplete.

Prophetic Critics and Skeptics

Opposing the "ethical managerialists" are the "prophetic" voices, who position themselves better to emphasize the interests of employees. Here lies perhaps the major divide within the field of Christian business ethics. Managerialists take it for granted that management possesses both the capacity and the will (at least latent) to exert moral leadership. The prophetic critics, in contrast, hold modern management and corporations up to the light of covenantal justice, or its secularized moral counterparts, and find them woefully deficient. Interestingly enough, they rarely attack management for lacking the moral will to establish and safeguard the basic elements of moral community within its enterprises. Rather, they seem to doubt whether management possesses the effective power to do so. This distinction between willingness and ability divides prophetic "critics" from "skeptics." The dividing line is fuzzy, however, since few of the prophetic voices explicitly take up the distinction between managerial intentions and effective managerial power, and so no hard-and-fast distinctions will be drawn here.

The prophetic critics and skeptics include, first of all, those Roman Catholic and Protestant ethicists—often women, interestingly enough—who consciously adopt the perspective of employees and gather their stories. They see these employees as victims who experience business enterprises principally in terms of domination, exploitation, rejection, and exclusion. These terms suggest a moral failure upon the part of management. Nevertheless, these ethicists tend not to attack managers as persons: they see more complex dynamics at work than the personal moral failures of sheer greed or insensitivity. Five years ago, Barbara Andolsen found the world of clerical workers cursed by a historical weight of gender stereotypes and shrinking under the powerful, seemingly inevitable dynamic of automation. She questioned whether justice is even possible within the present economic system.[18] At the same time, Karen Bloomquist reported similarly impersonal dynamics from within the threatened world of blue-collar work. She argued that pervasive managerial controls served to induce a sense of powerlessness and alienation in employees, while the class-stratified enterprises reinforced a sense of inferiority as well. She reported how employees strive to compensate by pursuing the American dream outside of work, only to have this cruel illusion ripped from their grasp as they were laid off.[19] A few years earlier, John Raines and Donna Day-Lower sketched the consequences of unemployment in similarly dire terms.[20] Like Andolsen and Bloomquist, Raines and Day-Lower do not hold managers as individuals responsible for the nefarious dynamics which propel employees out of their jobs.[21]

Wherever the responsibility lies, the obvious remedy would begin with management committing itself to offer secure, well-paying employment to employees. Interestingly enough, none of the authors calls for a commitment of that sort or of any kind. Perhaps they assume that management simply does not have the effective power to establish the kind of community where the interests of employees might be safeguarded. Indeed, the continuing drama of job destruction in the U.S. provides prophetic skeptics with powerful evidence of managerial impotence: how can a business enterprise be a moral community when management—whatever its moral values—is effectively forced by market pressures to terminate employees in large numbers?

The question is sharpened by a skepticism with different roots: philosophical or sociological claims about the pernicious effects of bureaucratic organization as an issue distinct from the intentions of management. Alasdair MacIntyre and Robert Bellah and colleagues have argued for years that management as an institution is essentially manipulative.[22] Twenty-five years ago Douglas Sturm argued that business enterprises are caught in an inexorable logic of growth which resists both the rule of law and the "peace, justice and steadfastness" integral to covenantal relations.[23] Prentiss L. Pemberton and Daniel Finn claim that larger organizations render their participants "less fully human": more likely to manipulate others, more detached from their work, and more numbed to the effects of their actions upon others.[24] In various ways, these observers question whether management has the effective power to nurture communities of morally responsible beings within business enterprises.[25]

The prophetic voices offer a helpfully cautious counterpoint to the ebullient optimism of the ethical managerialists. While the latter embrace business enterprise as an arena where management can recruit employees to some form of moral cooperation, the critics and skeptics find work in business enterprises to be cursed by impersonal forces not readily subject to intentional human control. The critics and skeptics in effect undermine the managerialist assumption that management is the cardinal agent for defining moral values and initiating moral behavior in business enterprises. Yet the pessimistic notes sounded by critics and skeptics also ring curiously hollow. They fail to devote much attention to the workplace strategies and tactics of employees as agents in their own right, establishing their own vision of moral order. If labor historian Peter Rachleff is right in his analysis of the bruising 1984 Hormel strike in Minnesota, this image of victimhood works powerfully against the efforts of employees to claim an effective moral agency.[26] The critics and skeptics also fail to make room for the capacity and ingenuity of management to ferret out new resources—including the moral energies of employees—to adapt to changing circumstances. In short, the prophetic critics and skeptics also are in need of an interactive theory.

Realists for Ethical Management

Between the ethical managerialists and the prophetic voices lies the proverbial middle ground, occupied by those ethicists who construe the role of management primarily in terms of conflicting obligations or moral claims. These "realists for ethical management" span denominational lines. Sometimes they employ a philosophical vocabulary of morally weighty principles to express the tensions management faces. Among Roman Catholic ethicists, Gerald F. Cavanagh and Arthur F. McGovern contrast the "traditional business values" of individual freedom, responsibility, and economic growth with the "social values" of human dignity, common good, and justice, while Cavanagh, Dennis J. Moberg, and Manuel Velasquez apply an irreducible quartet of utility, rights, justice, and care to the complex choices which bedevil managers.[27]

Velasquez and Ronald M. Green separately have authored detailed textbooks which apply their chosen blends of Kantian and utilitarian thinking to reconcile the conflicting interests and perspectives which management must adjudicate.[28] Their philosophical approaches represent the most systematic recognition by religious business ethicists of the conflicting imperatives which render business morally so complex. Other rigorous approaches are available. On the Protestant side, James M. Gustafson and Elmer W. Johnson discuss three kinds of conflicts: preserving hierarchy vs. engaging initiative, long-term stewardship vs. short-term self-interest, and efficiency vs.

equity.[29] In a more critical vein, William F. May argues that organizational bureaucracies can obstruct the cultivation of professional, caring management by emphasizing profit rather than service to the public, hierarchy rather than collegiality, office routines rather than the pursuit of excellence.[30]

Less formally, David Krueger examines the external pressures which impose limits upon the moral intentions of managers.[31] James M. Childs, Jr., proposes a dialogical model which he uses to bring Lutheran theology to bear upon the vocational conflicts managers face.[32] Laura Nash contrasts an enterprise run on the "self-interest model" and one run on a "Covenantal business ethic." She voices the tensions managers face in the choice to create value or maximize return; to seek a mutually beneficial exchange or look no farther than the legal requirements; and to integrate self-interest with service to others or to wedge them apart.[33]

Common to all these discussions is what might be termed a chastened or realistic managerialism. The authors assume that management has an obligation to exercise moral leadership, but that its capacity to create moral community is circumscribed severely by a complex array of pressures, external and internal to its enterprises. These pressures are seen to permit management a modest but significant degree of discretion to shape the working environment of employees.

Most of the Christian business ethicists presented above as ethical managerialists likely would claim to be realists, if asked. And they would qualify for this middle ground to the extent that they treat the conflicts and paradoxes facing management. The difference between ethical managerialists and realists is a matter of emphasis. Realists tend to be less interested in motivating management than in guiding it through dilemmas.[34] They are less interested in articulating expansive visions of managerial virtues and obligations than mapping the welter of claims and pressures through which management must muddle.

Despite these differences, realists share with ethical managerialists the same basic assumption: that management is the most significant moral actor, even the sole protagonist worthy of discussion, within its enterprises. Here the realism of their descriptions falls short and could be enhanced by the same corrective applied to the ethical managerialists above: the acknowledgment that business corporations are shaped by the interaction of management and employees, that is, the mutual influence which occurs up and down the hierarchy, and laterally. Even the most demoralized, passive, and compliant subordinates become a factor affecting decisions, while even the most aggressive, morally righteous management has to cope with the divergent and recalcitrant expectations of its subordinates.

Needed: An Interactive Approach

Contemporary relations between management and employees express a tangle of interests, motives, and purposes. This tangle is the legacy of two hundred years of struggle. I use the term "struggle" in a more Augustinian than Marxist sense, to point to the contest among creatures endowed with will. "Struggle" here encompasses the ensemble of efforts by management and employees to define and control their relationship. The historical record includes elements of both conflict and cooperation, rigid will and flexible accommodation. To date, ethical managerialists have emphasized the cooperation which can be accomplished in the future, paying insufficient attention to the uncomfortable legacy of past conflicts which burden the present. The prophetic voices, in contrast, have been more open to the past but find within it a history mainly, if not exclusively, of conflict and exploitation.

A fully realistic perspective involves paying attention equally to the moral vision, claims, and tactics of the perspectives of both management and employees. It involves excavating the historical legacy and attending particularly to the processes by which relationships are constructed: the tactics and strategies used by both management and employees. It involves consulting both poles of the relevant literature: labor history and business history; oppositional polemics and managerialist thought; radical sociology and the applied management-oriented fields of organization theory and organizational behavior. These perspectives are often incommensurable, if not mutually hostile, but all are necessary points of departure in the search for relative objectivity and fairness.

To date, a comprehensive vision for such an interactive approach has been provided mainly by Roman Catholic social teaching. Since the groundbreaking 1891 *Rerum Novarum* of Leo XIII, papal encyclicals about economic life have provided grounds in natural law and scripture for regarding management and employees as interactive and interdependent contributors to their enterprises. Of course, the purpose of these encyclicals, with their global audience, is to provide general moral guidance rather than a theory of the interdependence between management and employees in Western business enterprises. More development is needed. If Roman Catholic ethicists were to work labor history, the organizational fields of social science, and other relevant disciplines into a theory of the employment relation with the same enthusiasm that, for example, Catholic biblical scholars in the twentieth century have appropriated modern tools of biblical study, a remarkable blossoming might occur.[35]

In Protestant ethics, a resolutely interactive perspective has appeared only in the work of James W. Kuhn and Donald W. Shriver, Jr. These authors envisage management as surrounded by a variety of constituencies (employees, customers, institutional investors, social activists), each with its own distinct vision of justice. The usefulness of their analysis for this study is limited by the fact that their concern is primarily with external constituencies rather than the employment relation internal to the enterprise. Yet they helpfully model some of the elements needed in covenantal ethical analysis. They argue that historical perspective is needed, and they trace how managerial values have evolved under pressure.[36]

Conclusion

The budding field of Christian business ethics has much to gain by listening to all strata of business enterprises. At present, the field is dominated by ethical managerialism, a deeply moral impulse firmly rooted in U.S. business history. Ethical managerialism seeks to overcome labor conflicts by nourishing cultures of cooperation. My project shares that impulse, for genuine and active cooperation appears to be the highest expression of a covenantal ethic within business enterprises as densely interactive networks of mutual dependence. Similarly, I share the assumption of ethical managerialists and realists that management has an obligation to exercise moral leadership. But the cooperation sought by managerialists is unsatisfying, if not illusionary, when defined by a monologue of managerial intentions. Chapters 6 through 16 initiate a dialogue, seeking to present past history from the perspective of both management and employees, in order to give fair play to the claims and initiatives of both sides. Covenantal leadership, as will be seen by the end of the book, involves shouldering the considerable costs of cooperation; it involves accepting rather than vanquishing elements of contingency, risk, and vulnerability in the employment relation.

Contingency, risk, and vulnerability are key terms in a covenantal ethic. The next chapter begins the work of constructing this ethic by tapping some insights from organization theory.

chapter 3

Durable Interdependence as the Occasion for Covenant-Building

Roman Catholic social teaching has enshrined the adage that capital cannot do without labor, nor labor without capital.[1] This basic formula for cooperation is true as a statement of enduring fact as well as a matter of moral conviction. As such, it provides a key to combining the perspectives of management and employees into a single narrative, and to understanding why their relationship both is covenantal, and can become more covenantal. It is this interdependence which provides the key to explaining how durable goods can be generated within the employment relation.

Management and employees have had to find ways to get along with each other because, to put it bluntly, they are stuck with each other. This claim might seem preposterous for two reasons. First, tens of millions of jobs in business enterprises have been destroyed during the past hundred years, whether rendered obsolete by the technologies of automation or eliminated by executive fiat. But management is stuck with employees in the sense that tens of millions more jobs have been created because they are needed—even if the positions are often of a lower caliber, and even if haunted at the margin by what Karl Marx referred to as the "reserve army" of the unemployed. Second, the boundaries between management and employees have become quite blurred in recent decades, which leads some managers and observers to hope that the traditional tensions might be transcended in new partnerships. And to be sure, in recent decades, management has delegated an array of traditional managerial functions to employees. As will be seen in chapter 14, management is engaged in a remarkable bid to tap the full resources of employees as a means of increasing their productive efficiency.[2] But despite the blurring of the boundaries, management and employees have remained distinct enough in a larger sense: management establishes and sustains the conditions for employee work, including setting the terms for the employment relation, while employees carry out the assigned work. These functions are complementary, and there are major shifts of power, whether towards more direct control by management or more self-direction by employees. But the basic division of labor is likely to persist as long as management is legally vested with the right to shape the employment relation in pursuit of its goals.

This basic complementarity of function, a hallmark of modern business enterprise, forces both parties into a mutual dependence. Modern business organization in the U.S., since its artisanal beginnings in small Philadelphia manufacturing concerns two centuries ago, enmeshes management and employees in a tightly interlinked system of coordinated actions. The tighter the linkages, the greater the vulnerability of each to the other. "Vulnerability" has a particular meaning in this study. The vulnerability of management and employees is what might be termed "external" in the first instance, having to do with economic liability and mutual reliability in work performance. Employees always have been vulnerable to being underpaid, overworked, laid off, or fired, to working in dangerous or unhealthy conditions or under incompetent management. Management always has been vulnerable to various kinds of costs employees might impose upon the work process: organized resistance, carelessness, reduced effort, absence, substance abuse, absentmindedness, theft, sabotage, espionage, and the like. External vulnerability likely is compounded by vulnerability in the common "internal" or psychological sense. Internal vulnerability has to do with the fear of abandonment or loss which accompanies a profound sense of attachment. Some of the Christian business ethicists reviewed in the previous chapter, particularly the prophetic critics, have explored how work in organizational settings can engage this internal dimension of vulnerability.[3] Surely this is of immense and growing significance in our era of massive layoffs. Few ethicists, however, have attended to the external dimension, which in its own way is just as important, because it bears directly upon how business enterprises function.

Mutual Vulnerability and Human Will

Management and employees are vulnerable because they present "contingencies" to each other. By "contingencies" I mean intentions and actions that do not lend themselves to being controlled, let alone predicted, by other actors. The term commonly is used to refer to the kind of unpredictability generated by the sheer complexity of elements contributing to outcomes. In this broader sense, the management and employees of business enterprises face manifold contingencies having to do with impersonal technological, economic, political, social, and other factors. This study addresses only one kind of contingency which operates between management and employees: the kind arising from the domain of human intentions, specifically the intentions of management and employees towards each other.[4] The notion of a contingency acquires a special bite when restricted to what philosophical action theorists label "actions" rather than "events"—those behaviors explainable in terms of human purposes rather than as the mechanical working out of blind forces.[5] Here relationships among intentional actors are of special interest.

The contingency facing managers and employees derives from the fact that they are continually and perhaps inescapably present to each other as beings endowed with will: they both possess the capacity to define and pursue purposes, particularly against resistance.[6] Management wants employees to function efficiently in pursuit of managerial goals; it seeks to preserve its prerogative to determine how products and services are generated, at what cost in labor. Employees, for their part, want management to provide steady work, high wages, and a variety of other benefits. They seek to exercise some control over their labor and the conditions under which they work.[7]

These aims are reflected in the strategies and tactics both management and employees apply to each other. They seek to shape each other's expectations regarding how much work can be done, and for what return. On the one side, management has devised ever more ingenious means to elicit compliance and an extra margin of attentiveness and effort from employees. These strategies and tactics range from outright coercion and violence, through more subtle inducements, to devices for "empowering" employees to join management in decision-making. None has served as a magic key to unlock the motivation of employees and channel their will and energies precisely along the lines management hopes for. On the other side, employees have devised potent means of collective, group, and individual resistance. They always have been able to resist yielding up everything that management wants. But none of their initiatives has ever thwarted the ability of management to devise ever more ingenious countertactics. For more than half a century, social scientists have studied this struggle, coining such intriguing terms as the "effort bargain," "withdrawal of effort," "engineering of consent," and the like to describe how both sides cope with their vulnerability to each other.[8] Here I will employ the political vocabulary of strategies and tactics, using the first to point to larger aims or programs of action, and the latter to specific gestures or initiatives.

The Intertwining of Conflict and Cooperation

It would be erroneous to conclude that all management and all employees are stuck with the same struggle. Technologies, ranging from plant-wide automation to individual drug-testing, have profoundly shaped the relationship between employees and management. In ways too various to be included in this study, management has used technologies to contain its vulnerability to employees. Such technical tactics have served variously to resolve or rechannel and exacerbate the struggle. Assembly lines, for example, have paced the output of workers with a regularity no foreman ever could hope to achieve through personal supervision, but at the cost of more profound kinds of alienation, leading to massive resistance during the middle decades of the twentieth century.[9] Perhaps no two kinds of manufacturing or business are alike in the profile of contingencies which management and employees present to each other. At the same time, the experience of earlier industries has been recapitulated in later ones, as the horrors of midwestern meatpacking described so vividly by Upton Sinclair almost a century ago have found a new roost in the chicken-processing plants of the South.[10]

Nor would it be correct to assume that friction is always present. Perhaps a majority of the managers and employees in the U.S. enjoy relatively amicable, constructively purposeful relations with each other most of the time, at least when insulated from the cutthroat competition of the market, the catastrophic effects of hostile takeovers, and job-eating advances in technology. After all, contemporary management rarely celebrates conflict and domination as desirable aspects of its organizations, while employees rarely seek to pick fights which might cost them their jobs. Here they benefit from a deposit of experience derived from accomodations achieved over decades. This deposit of experience supports that complex blend of conflict and cooperation which here is denominated as "struggle," for lack of a more comprehensive term to describe the relationship between management and employees.[11]

The struggle need not be vocal, flagrant, or even visible. It occurs most constructively, perhaps, when employees are convinced they possess more expertise about their work than does management, even as management seeks to redefine the content of their jobs. It occurs more conflictually wherever management and employees are engaged in seeking to influence each other's perceptions and actions about the conditions of work, or unilaterally renegotiating what they will require of and provide to each other. It occurs regrettably when employees steal paperclips in a symbolic effort to rectify unjust pay scales, or when management permits such behavior in order to defuse discontent. It occurs when management revokes privileges, and employees respond by carving out new perquisites for themselves. It occurs more jarringly when management calls in consultants to deprogram employees of comfortable assumptions about job security, and when employees respond by conspiring to obstruct the layoffs management intends to institute.[12] Moreover, the struggle is durable. Indeed, it is virtually built into the nature of business enterprise. Business organizations are not "natural" but artificial creations, constructed by the initiatives and responses of both sides. Business enterprises are defined and driven by the wills of participating individuals. Tasks and roles are invested with expectations which are constantly being evaluated and altered.

To the extent that this depiction of business enterprises is accurate, it calls for a sharpened theological conception of human action in organized settings. Thirty years ago, H. Richard Niebuhr coined the term "responder" to account for the essentially relational character of human thinking and action.[13] This image has become widely influential in Christian ethics and is a key resource for interpreting the human dynamics of business enterprises. Management and employees are engaged in interpreting the actions of each other and responding in light of their interpretations and anticipations of how the other will respond. But this image needs to be intensified. "Responding" appears simply too passive and bland to capture the cold-blooded strategies, the ingenious tactics, the forceful confrontations, and the sheer volatility of the conflict between employers and workers. The tactics narrated in later chapters of this study suggest that both sides are endowed with the capacity to initiate and react aggressively. The "interaction" of employers and workers is characterized by a hard edge of purposefulness in the face of external obstacles and resistance—what I mean by "will." For two hundred years, management has been searching for magic bullets to neutralize the resistance and enlist the energies of employees; for two hundred years, employees have negotiated and renegotiated their compliance with management wishes. The fact that the struggle has not been resolved by a permanent victory of the one side over the other implies that neither side can be controlled completely and contained by the other. In short, both sides are likely to remain vulnerable to each other indefinitely.

Covenants as Devices for Coping with Durable Contingencies

It is the very durability of the struggle that makes the idea of covenant so relevant to explaining management-employee relations. During the past two hundred years, management and employees have developed mutual arrangements for reducing their vulnerability to each other. Most common are contracts, whether bargained collectively through unions, or negotiated individually with employees. Christian ethicists often view contracts as inferior to covenants, in that they provide social actors a means to limit their obligations to each other. From the pragmatic perspective of management and employees, contracts have a very different liability: their incompleteness. No contract signed in a personnel office has been able to contain all the contingencies which employees present to management. Similarly, no thick union contract, saturated with work rules, has been able to foresee and regulate every eventuality management might present to employees. If contracts sufficed to align the wills of management and employees reliably and exhaustively around a set of common interests, there might be no need for covenants.

Contracts belong to a class of behavioral devices through which social actors reduce their vulnerability to each other. This genus includes treaties, nonaggression pacts, licenses, and other arrangements which enable actors to *cope with contingency by making commitments*. In effect, the actors commit themselves to fulfill certain stipulations as a means of neutralizing the suspect contingencies they present each other.[14] But where these devices are not self-sustaining, as in the long struggle between management and employees, something more is needed. Human relationships stray into the domain of covenant-making as the two parties encounter *durable* or *ineradicable* contingencies in each other, and seek to cope with them *by making enduring commitments.*[15] The tactic may seem obvious to Christians steeped in the history of God's efforts to nourish the faith of God's people: God is understood to express flawless covenantal fidelity by sticking with a stubborn people through thick and thin, even to the point of self-sacrifice in Jesus Christ. Christianity long has celebrated agape as that kind of love which does not coerce, yet neither gives up in the face of continuing resistance. But the idea of making enduring commitments as a means to contain durable contingencies is far less obvious in business enterprises. What kind of durable commitments can management and employees realistically offer to each other?

A covenantal interpretation of the employment relation suggests that genuine cooperation, as the appropriate expression of covenant in business corporations, is founded upon two generic commitments from both parties.

> First, the parties must be united around some common interest or purpose; there must be some aim shared by both parties.
> Second, in pursuit of this aim, the parties must bind themselves not to abuse or exploit the advantages they hold over each other.[16]

As formal elements, these commitments are hardly unique to covenants; contracts, treaties and other contingency-coping devices all require some shared aim, however limited or evanescent, and some kind of self-binding, however shallow. Moreover, as generally stated, they would be embraced without hesitation by ethical managerialism. What makes these two conditions uniquely covenantal can be stated parsimoniously as a further requirement: *the shared cause that links management and employees must be forged out of the very contingencies that push them to covenant in the first place, and the self-limitations to which they commit themselves must also derive from these contingencies.* In other words, a relationship becomes covenantal in the degree that the parties convert the hold which they have over each other into a resource for the benefit of each other. Later chapters develop the covenantal content of these two formal conditions.

The moral requirement of durable commitment can be stated in the imperative mode, following the common practice in Christian ethics. Management may not be able to promise employees lifetime employment in a fluid, market-driven economy, but it can promise to apply its will to sustaining conditions of employment. Employees may not be willing to promise compliance with every managerial wish but can commit themselves to work for the best interests of the firm. A covenantal bond will develop as both sides refrain from taking advantage of their power over each other: as they keep their promises despite adverse conditions; as they engage in nonobligatory concessions or spontaneous gestures of good will; as they adhere to unwritten as well as written norms of procedural justice; as they avoid manipulating and deceiving each other; and so forth. As such, a covenantal ethic can provide a grid for evaluating the moral adequacy of the tactics and strategies management and employees apply to each other.

Covenanting as Common Human Experience

These prescriptions commend themselves to common moral sense and certainly express what I mean by covenanting. Yet a foundation is needed for a covenantal ethic to be persuasive. Why should management and employees even want a covenantal quality of relationship? If faith is what grounds us in a conviction that the world makes sense, faith must be able to discern that covenanting is what is already going on. The burden lies upon the ethicist to show that covenanting is grounded in the realm of fact as well as of wish; that it is "really real" in the world, as well as desirable. The point to be proven is not just that management and employees ought to covenant but that they already are covenanting—and breaking covenants—because making and breaking promises of all kinds is the best way they pragmatically have discovered of coping with the kind of contingency they present to each other. The ethicist must search for seeds of genuine cooperation which already are evident in the employment relation as it has developed, rather than simply impose a requirement from out of the blue.

In short, the role of the ethicist is to describe before prescribing. For such explanation, I turn first to the Bible as a resource for explaining how covenanting already is occurring in the employment relation. The biblical history yields clues as to where to find evidences of covenanting in the contentious history of business enterprise. In essence, covenanting as a process is anchored in the nature of God and of God's creatures. The Bible reports a struggle between God and God's people, a struggle which resonates with the common human experience of individual wills intertwined in conflict and cooperation. The long struggle by God to shape Israel and the Christian church into faith-full communities is driven by the same basic endowment of capacities which also energizes the struggle between management and employees, and so yields the faithful hope that God is at work in the same way in both histories.

This vision of covenanting may seem overly conflictual, based as it is upon ideas of contingency, vulnerability, strategies, and tactics. It lacks the serene unity of imperatives such as the common good, dignity, love, justice, vocation, virtue, and other important symbols of human flourishing which have been worked into contemporary treatments of Christian business ethics. Yet if the managerial realists are right, that to work as a manager (or employee, presumably) is to be exposed to conflicting obligations, the basic metaphor upon which an ethic is constructed must be ample and manifold enough to contain the idea of conflict within it. The symbol of covenant and the process of covenant-building are capacious enough to encompass both God's unified aim for humanity as well as the struggle through which that aim is accomplished.

But how indeed are conflict and cooperation integrated within the biblical symbol of covenant? The next chapter sketches the complex of strategies and tactics which express how the tension between these two elements is both sustained and resolved in the Bible.

CHAPTER 4

A Trajectory of Covenant-Building in the Bible

Few attempts have been made to derive practical moral guidance for modern business enterprise from the Bible, and even fewer attempts have been made to use the Bible to explain "what is going on" in the relationship between management and employees. This reticence is not surprising. The biblical writers had no experience with enterprises consciously designed and constructed to achieve economic interests through closely coordinated human action. Nevertheless, the sheer strangeness of the modern business enterprise need not render the Bible irrelevant. The biblical narratives offer fascinating glimpses of how God and God's people seek to shape the characters of each other. God is understood anthropomorphically in the Bible as an intentional being in struggle with emphatically intentional human beings. The lessons to be derived from this struggle carry the weight of many centuries—now, almost three millennia—worth of experience. In this chapter I describe some of these mechanics, sketching the strategies and tactics through which covenantal relations are constructed, destroyed, and renewed between God and the people of the Old and New Testaments.

If in the following history I lay too heavy an accent upon the problem of containing contingency and resolving conflict, it should be remembered that my aim is not a definitive or exhaustive account of what it means to covenant. I am not attempting here to generate a single ethical model which can be applied generically to any human situation; that would be a futile exercise in universalistic theorizing. Rather, my intention is to provide an account of what it means to covenant which is specifically appropriate to relationships of functional interdependence. I assume that different facets of this history open up as God's people have sought instruction for how to conduct themselves in different spheres of social activity. The intense and often conflicted history of management and employees draws attention specifically to the practical mechanics of conflict and cooperation evident in these narratives, and it is to these realities that an interpretation of the Biblical narratives needs to be addressed.

Covenant-Building in the Bible

A biblical covenant generally is understood to be similar to a contract in that it is an implicit or explicit agreement with some specified stipulations, such as the covenant at Mount Sinai. Two major types of covenants are evident between God and the people in the Old and New Testaments, as well as several other varieties among human partners.[1] All involve specific agreements determined, and renewed, at particular identifiable points. All involve a dialectic of commitment and fulfilment. Yet when seen in longitudinal perspective, such formal or informal agreements might be better understood as discrete points punctuating the ongoing biblical narrative of how covenantal relations are sustained or undermined. The agreements are preceded by a "prehistory" of how God and the people have sought to cope with each other (either to neutralize a threat or actualize a potential which each presents to the other). And the agreements are followed by what might be termed a "posthistory" of efforts to render each other more reliable and trustworthy covenant partners within the terms the covenant sets for their ongoing relationship. In essence, covenants are devices for building the relationship between God and God's people. They license both parties to shape each other in the direction of remaining faithful to the terms they have established with each other. This expanded view of covenant-building opens up the whole narrative for inspection. In addition to asking, "What have both parties agreed to?" and "Have they lived up to their promises?" a covenantal theorist will want to know, "What tactics and strategies are the parties using to shape the action, thinking, and character of each other?" It is these tactics and strategies reported in the Bible which can shed some light on the struggle between management and employees.

The struggle between God and the people

Business enterprises, caught in the flux of a market system, constrain management and employees to think in terms of goals and means, contingencies and contingency plans. Many of the covenants drawn up between individuals in the Old Testament echo this practical perspective. The "parity" or "suzerainty" covenants between human actors appear oriented to containing contingency. Jacob sought to elicit binding commitments from a slippery Laban, Abraham from a powerful King Abimelech, the weak Gibeonites from a triumphant Joshua.[2] Sometimes the practical reasons are unspoken, as when David and Jonathan pledge an undying friendship, at least in part, it would seem, to preclude a bloody rivalry for Saul's throne.[3] These and other "human" covenants are transparently devices which enable parties to cope with their vulnerabilities to each other by making binding commitments to each other.

Less obvious is the fact that the covenants "cut" (to use Old Testament terminology) by God with the people also are devices for coping with contingency. On the one side, God has a project, a goal: to fashion the people of Israel, and later the church, into a moral community faithful to this one God alone. This aim renders God vulnerable to the failure of the people to respond appropriately. Now, if the materials God had to work with were inert and unresistingly plastic, building and sustaining a covenant would be no more difficult than throwing a pot, in that memorable biblical metaphor.[4] But the people God has to work with are anything but predictably cooperative or compliant. They are prone to misunderstanding, forgetfulness, waywardness, and rebelliousness—as well as capable of expressing wisdom, single-mindedness, courage, and loyalty in pursuit of God's project. These contradictory elements are the chief elements of the contingency the people present to God.

On the other side, the people hardly find in God a guarantee that sovereign divine power will be used reliably to fulfill their wishes. The people are seen to be prey to a host of vicissitudes. In roughly chronological order, from the Old Testament through the New, they experience slavery, hunger and thirst, tribal warfare, economic exploitation, personal enmities, invasions, deportations, religious oppression, diseases, and "evil spirits." The people covenant with God and periodically renew their covenant as a means of coping with their vulnerability. Through these covenants they seek deliverance from infertility, landlessness, lawlessness, and enemies. The people seek to secure the favor and power of God. But behind all the threats that the people face stands a God who is anything but a reliable tool of their desires, anything but a powerful provider molded in their image. God chastises their waywardness with afflictions of the flesh and spirit, raising up powerful enemies from afar, as well as permitting cruel despotisms within. A recurring fear of this people, conveyed most vividly in intercessory prayers or laments, is that they might be destroyed or abandoned by this powerful deity.[5]

A struggle rooted in spirit and will

The sheer vulnerability of God and God's people to each other has two deep roots in a character that both sides share; the people, after all, are understood to be made in the image of God. First, they are endowed with "spirit," which is the capacity of indefinite transcendence, as Reinhold Niebuhr put it.[6] God's spirit cannot be captured within any construction of human understanding. The people, for their part, are empowered by their spirit to envision great evil as well as great good. But spirit alone does not explain the durable contingency which God and God's creatures present to each other. There is a second feature of biblical psychology at work. Both God and the people are understood to express will—the capacity to pursue and realize intentions, even in the face of resistance. Compounded by spirit, this will works variously for destructive, punitive ends, or for more creative, redeeming ends. Like God, we are creatures endowed with will, capable of devising our own initiatives in response to action upon us. More specifically, we not only seek to interpret action upon us but to guide and even control how others will interpret our action upon them. This capacity is evident in the biblical narratives as well as in the complex relationship between management and employees. It explains why H. Richard Niebuhr's image of human agents as "responders" needs to be amended, as proposed in chapter 3.

The result of this twofold endowment is a durable struggle by God and God's people to shape the action and character of each other. How the God of the Bible would envy the God of Deists, who had nothing more challenging to do than design and set in motion a world conceived as a mechanism! The work of God begins, rather than ends, with the formal covenants ratified by the people. The biblical God cannot walk away, leaving the covenant to sustain itself, but rather is faced with the often thankless work of fashioning the people of Israel, the church and the whole world, into a community faithful to this one God alone. This struggle, endless within history, is what I mean by "covenant-building."

The Biblical History

Following mainstream biblical scholarship, I will describe the struggle between God and the people as moving through four distinct phases: from the time of the patriarchs through the exodus and wandering; the conquest of Canaan and the monarchical period; the exile in Babylon; and the Roman occupation of New Testament times.[7] Here, as in the chapters to follow, I will focus solely upon the strategies and tactics which the two parties use to bend the will of each other. These strategies and tactics (printed in italics for emphasis) express the intentions of each side in a way which is more concrete and less problematic than any modern psychological claims about the motivation of God and God's people. All the strategies and tactics are evident at each period, but shifts in emphasis occur. These shifts turn upon the difference between strategies and tactics intended to suppress conflict and those intended to elicit cooperation. Viewed along this axis, the biblical history offers important insights as to how, in a contested history, progress in achieving covenantal relations is measured.

The history of building covenants between God and God's people begins on a potentially cooperative note. From the time of the patriarchs through the exodus and the wandering, God applies a dialectic of *promising* and *testing* to establish and sustain covenantal relations with Abraham and Moses. Moses and Abraham respond with *questioning* of their own, to determine the degree of God's commitment and power.[8] After a covenant is "cut" at Sinai, the struggle commences in earnest.[9] God uses *miracles, discipline* and *punishments* to evoke, quite forcibly, the faith of the people during their wandering in the wilderness.[10] Moses and the people respond to God's initiatives by *questioning* and *bargaining* with God. Moses intervenes as necessary to *negotiate* for the survival of the people from God's destructive wrath.[11]

Between the conquest of Canaan and the end of the monarchical period, Israel becomes increasingly stubborn and rebellious, in part due to overconfidence invested in God's promise of eternal kingship to the Davidic dynasty. The people *apostasize*, following other gods and *flouting* or *ignoring* stipulations of the Sinai covenant.[12] These tactics on both sides presuppose conflict. By this point, God has *delegated* effective power to kings of Israel and other nations, and effective authority to the prophets. Through the first God *punishes*, and through the second, God seeks to *deter* abuses of kingly and priestly power.[13] These tactics are not the only alternatives; sometimes God *forbears* carrying out announced punishments.[14] Occasionally the people respond with *repentance* or a turning of their own.[15] The liturgical *sacrifices* of the people are seen to be insufficient; what God wants is genuine *obedience*—which is rarely forthcoming.[16]

The third stage, the exile, costs the people their political sovereignty and their complacent confidence that God never would abandon the covenant. Their despair prompts a radical redirection of divine will. God initiates tactics of *reassurance* and *affirmation* which presuppose a cooperative will upon the part of the people. Prophets during the exile apply the tenderest terms of intimate sympathy to comfort the people.[17] Prior covenants with Noah and Abraham are revised into promises binding God to Israel in perpetuity.[18] Wholehearted *learning* and punctilious *obedience* to the law become the means for the people to bind themselves to God, as the character of the Jewish people comes to be defined around fidelity to the written covenant.[19] Yet despite prophetic visions of an end to conflict between God and God's covenant partners, the practical reconstruction of Jewish life elicited the dialectic of promises, deterrent threats, and even punishment once again.[20]

During the Roman occupation (New Testament), the struggle forks, as it were. On the one hand, God *hardens* the hearts of those deemed lost, threatening damnation at the end of history, answering the murderous *opposition* of the religious authorities.[21] On the other hand, God through Jesus seeks the lost sheep (those deemed saveable), even to the point of *self-sacrifice*.[22] Jesus assumes a readiness on the part of his listeners, or at least select followers, to renew the covenant. He *recruits* disciples to be willing instruments of the Kingdom, encouraging them to see God as a benign father.[23] He applies *teaching* to elevate and refine their understanding of covenantal law (Matthew), of God's partiality to the vulnerable (Luke), and of God's universal covenant-building mission (Luke-Acts).[24] Jesus invites his followers to influence God by making requests through *prayer*.[25] Finally, he offers a new covenant, sealed by his own self-sacrifice. The disciples, for their part, *hear* and *follow;* their misunderstandings and failures are frequent, but willful disobedience is rare.[26]

The Logic of Covenanting in the Bible

There are four remarkable features about the biblical narratives, each of which can serve as a clue for interpreting the shorter but equally contentious history between management and employees.

First, the biblical writers accept the idea that *God's people not only do, but ought to participate actively in the making and breaking of covenantal relations with God*. God is not the only actor; divine tactics are answered by human tactics, while human tactics are answered by divine tactics. Covenant-building, as a process, is inherently interactive, in that covenants are constructed in the intersection of the expectations brought by both sides. There appears to be nothing wrong, in principle, with the fact that the people have expectations of God, which they seek to realize by influencing God's action, and that God responds by meeting or transforming those expectations.

Of course, the Bible contains a major internal debate about the propriety of specific human efforts to influence God. The biblical writers do not speak with one voice. They do not all see human agency as contributing constructively to the long historical process of covenant-building. In the Old Testament the tactics of testing God, questioning God, repenting, sacrificing, making requests, and obeying the minute stipulations of the Law are variously seen to be valid tactics for influencing God's action. The people, after all, may be clay in God's hands, but God is open to being influenced.

> Just like the clay in the potter's hand, so are you in my hand, O house of Israel. At one moment I may declare concerning a nation or a kingdom, that I will pluck up and break down and destroy it, but if that nation . . . turns from its evil, I will change my mind about the disaster that I intended to bring upon it. And at another moment I may declare concerning a nation or a kingdom that I will build and plant it, but if it does evil in my sight, not listening to my voice, then I will change my mind about the good that I had intended to do to it.[27]

Parts of the New Testament appear to be less open to such interactivity. In particular, the theology of Paul which has dominated Lutheran conceptions of the relationship between God and humanity asserts that God fulfills covenantal promises unilaterally—without the cooperation of, and indeed, against the opposition of—rebellious and wilfully ignorant covenant partners. According to this reading, the appropriate human response is surrender.[28] The Gospels generally appear to be much more open to the idea of believers seeking to influence God through prayer and right action.

The second remarkable feature of the biblical narratives is implied by the first: *God accepts, rather than suppresses, the durable human contingencies which impede consummation of the divine covenant.* Within the thought-world of the biblical writers, it was conceivable that God might either destroy or abandon the people; the absolute freedom to dispose of the people as God sees fit is rarely in question. But God is understood as making a durable commitment not to destroy the world, nor to let Israel wither away for lack of land, heirs (Abraham), or a legitimate ruling dynasty (David). The tactic of utter destruction is postponed until the end of history. More forcefully put, God chooses to accept the forgetfulness, waywardness, and outright rebellion of the people as recurring obstacles to the arduous work of creating faithful, reliable covenant partners. God chooses to use tactics which do not undercut the "moral freedom" of the people. They can respond as they will to God's initiatives.

Of course, the freedom of the people is not absolute. They have the liberty to behave uncovenantally, but not the power to place themselves beyond God's reach. They lack freedom in the sense of being able to insulate themselves against God's larger strategy of creating and sustaining a covenanted people. Yet despite this qualification, the implications of God's renunciation of absolute power are staggering. God chooses to preserve the irrepressible contingency of the people, even to render it ineradicable within history. The people retain the capacity to cooperate or not cooperate.[29] In effect, God turns the logic of covenant-building on its head: God's durable commitment to the moral freedom of the people creates a durable contingency, an option available only to an omnipotent agent. Still, God's project is to create a people of faith, and so God's durable commitment serves as a means of inspiring the people to channel their contingency along constructive and cooperative lines. God takes on vulnerability, as it were, as a means of urging the people to commit themselves in response. God's commitments to Noah, Abraham, David, all Israel, and the church through Jesus are best seen as bids to evoke a response, as strategies to elicit a commitment.

The third remarkable feature about the biblical narratives is *a studied ambiguity about the success of God's campaign to sustain the people in a covenantal relationship*. On the one hand, the full range of conflictual and cooperative tactics are in evidence across all four stages of the biblical history, implying that no progress has been made. On the other hand, a shift in emphasis is evident in divine tactics: from overpowering resistance to eliciting cooperation.

God's tactics can be ranged along three points of a continuum. First, when God and the people are understood to be in conflict, the biblical writers report coercive tactics—punishment or deterrent threats by God, disobedience by the people—through which both parties seek to thwart or bend the will of the other. Second, when their wills are seen not as in conflict, but not yet in agreement, both sides apply less coercive tactics, such as bargaining, testing, promises, and recruitment and obedience, to induce each other to cooperate. Finally, where a congruence of wills is assumed, what the parties communicate to each other has less the quality of inducement, let alone coercion, than instruction absorbed by already recruited and compliant wills. Here God through Jesus is engaged in teaching (occasionally in learning), and the people in hearing and following.[30] These three alternatives reflect the conflict-compliance-cooperation continuum mentioned in chapter 1 and developed in chapter 15.

But in what direction do the biblical narratives move along this continuum? On the one hand, a trajectory appears evident: from earlier to later texts the emphasis in divine tactics appears to shift from the conflictive towards the cooperative end. Jesus' efforts to recruit followers and teach them the ways of the Kingdom contrast starkly with the more threatening tactics of earlier prophets. (An argument about the superiority of Christianity to Judaism is not being made here; the shift in emphasis occurs within the Old Testament as well as between the Old Testament and the New.) By the time of the exile, God's tactics shifted from applying raw punishment via foreign kings, or deterrent threats via the prophets, towards encouraging the efforts of pious Jews to internalize the covenantal Law. As the prophet Ezekiel argues after Israel has gone into exile, the terrain of contest between God and the people moved into every individual heart.[31] The once proud spirits of the people, shattered by the exile, no longer are presumed to be reflexively hostile or indifferent as during the monarchy, but rather are seen as open to receiving the law as instruction.

On the other hand, God's tactics for eliciting cooperation always are admixed with more coercive tactics. In the Old Testament the postexilic prophets and the author of Nehemiah mince no words in chastising the people returning from exile to Jerusalem for their history of disobedience. Jesus sought to recruit and train some individuals as disciples for the building up of the Kingdom, but the Gospel of Mark is considerably more dubious than the Gospel of John about the capacity of disciples to understand Jesus' program, let alone commit themselves to it. All the major New Testament authors assume that God hardens the ears and the wills of those who are not favored. Further, these authors promise destruction at the end of time for those who have failed to commit themselves to God's covenant. Of course, the most coercive tactics are indeed deferred until then; there always remains time for repentance—except, presumably, for those who are hardened.

So the trajectory is ambiguous; right up until the end of history, God applies coercive threats as well as gentler tactics for eliciting and guiding cooperation. This ambiguity permits two interpretations of God's overall strategy. The first possibility is that the process of covenant-building is open-ended, or a permanent process within history. By this interpretation, the full range of tactics will be needed until the end of time; the process is more important than the goal, as God continues to tolerate the contingent responses of the people, who will be variously wayward, mistrusting, rebellious, but occasionally enthusiastic, trusting, and loyal covenant partners until the end of time. This appears to be the view of the synoptic Gospels, and is the view which informs my model of covenant-building.

The second possibility is that the goal, so to speak, is more important than the process of recruitment. The covenant is circumscribed more narrowly to encompass only those individuals whose wills already are aligned with the divine project; the others are written off as having rejected God's offer of covenantal partnership. God's shift towards more cooperative tactics, then, applies only to those who have subscribed to God's program, whom God teaches and caresses with the assurance of undying love. This appears to be the view of the Pharisees and perhaps of the Gospel of John.

It does not appear possible, on biblical grounds, to rule out either of these interpretations of God's larger strategy. This ambiguity serves to discourage extremes of optimism or pessimism in assessing how God's project is faring. While it is foolish to claim steady linear progress, it is equally foolish to deny that any progress is being made. As Reinhold Niebuhr observed, the possibilities for increasing both good and evil remain deeply intertwined within history. For this reason, my interpretation of the history of struggle between management and employees assumes that the "already" of God's project is intertwined with the "not yet." The idea of covenant remains both a description of what has been accomplished, in conflict and cooperation with the people of God, and a prescription for what yet must be strived for.

The fourth remarkable feature about the biblical narratives is that *despite repeated human failures God in no way relaxes stringent divine expectations for authentic covenantal relations*. God expects faith as utter trust and exclusive loyalty from God's people, while holding them to a high standard of love, justice, and fidelity in their relations with each other. The Bible defines no required level of attainment beyond which God's covenant partners are excused from striving. Beyond the needy Jew lies the Samaritan prostrate in the road; beyond the blind man stand the ten lepers; beyond the family and neighbors to whom one owes the duties of responsibility specified in the codes and case law of the Pentateuch and the "Haustafeln" of the New Testament epistles, there always lies the stranger in need of mercy.

What stands behind the inexhaustible demand for love and justice is not arbitrary divine will but the long and sometimes bitter experience of God as recorded from the beginning to the end of the biblical narratives. The hard-won lesson of this history is that mercy, forgiveness, and fidelity are the most durable, even if not obviously effective, tactics for coping with the ineradicable contingency presented by stubborn and wilful covenant partners. Where conflict dominates, these tactics serve as an antidote or balance for more coercive ones, keeping the relationship intact, even if unfulfilled. Where antagonists have become partners, these gentle tactics may serve to call out and reinforce the deepest gratitude and affection, and that prospect alone justifies God's continuing vulnerability to the error and malfeasance of the people.

Conclusion

God's inexhaustible demand for covenantal righteousness long has been recognized by Christian ethicists. Here I have tried to reach behind the moral standards of love and justice to outline the process by which God struggles to create and sustain covenantal relationships. The biblical narratives report how God and God's people have been engaged in shaping each other's expectations of what a covenantal relationship entails. God applies promises, tests, threats, punishment, the delegation of power and authority, affirmation, hardening, recruiting, teaching, self-sacrifice, and undoubtedly other tactics for eliciting and sustaining the fidelity of the people. The people, for their part, respond by questioning, testing, bargaining, disobeying, repenting, sacrificing, obeying, learning, following, and undoubtedly many other tactics.

Seen as only a raw list, this catalogue of tactics imparts little insight into the strategies of both parties. The tactics reported in the Bible were tailored to particular situations, and so derive their sense and value from where they are embedded in the biblical narrative. The long trajectory of the biblical history suggests that God's choice of tactics is shaped decisively by the people's response to the situations they find themselves in. Yet there are threads of consistency: each and every tactic and strategy is understood to be powered by inexhaustible love. And overall, God sustains the covenant as much or more by efforts to recruit and shape human energies as by tactics aimed at deterring or punishing human action. God's tactics shift, however ambiguously, towards accepting the will and spirit of the people as latently cooperative, even in the face of recurring resistance.

The tactics of the people suggest no such coherent overall strategy. The people make a succession of efforts to define their vision of the covenant, and to bend God to fit within it. What their tactics demonstrate is that the history of covenant-making never comes to a conclusion; the covenant never reaches its perfect consummation—except, according to some New Testament writers, in the all-sufficient sacrifice of Jesus. On the one hand, the people present an ongoing contingency to God characterized by sin, weakness, fear, pride, love, and all the drives and affections of which human character is compounded. No covenantal agreement, no strategy, no tactic by God serves to contain and channel that contingency exhaustively into the faith that God seeks to elicit. On the other hand, God presents to the people a contingency compounded of sovereign power, judgment, love, and often opaque purpose. No covenantal agreement, strategy, or tactic enables the people reliably to domesticate God—or each other—to their own particular expectations of what a covenant authorizes or demands.

By now the open-ended biblical struggle should seem very familiar as well as very strange. It is strange from the perspective of modern individualism: the mythic claim that social actors ought to stand alone, insulated by some sort of privileged vacuum against pressures upon them, free to choose whatever course of action they like. No vision of human selfhood could be farther from the biblical world, where the people of God are caught in a veritable pressure cooker of expectations and actions upon them, both human and divine. Surely the biblical view is more familiar; it lies closer to the the multiple interactive networks—of family, church, school, and organizations of all kinds—through which we make our way by negotiating the expectations of others, by anticipating and responding to the contingencies they present. Where durable, even ineradicable, contingencies are present in contemporary social life—and where are they not?—the human devices for coping with other human actors stray into the domain of covenant-making staked out in the biblical narratives. The task of the Christian ethicist is to interpret one complex blend of conflict and cooperation by means of the other.

chapter 5

Linking Biblical and Business History

The previous two chapters have described the struggle between God and God's people, and that between management and employees, in similar terms. The parallel cannot be pushed too far; whatever eager business consultants may say, management does not represent God to employees! Rather, the way that God copes with the enduring contingency presented by God's people serves as a guide for the way management and employees ought to cope with the contingencies presented by each other. The key term here is "enduring commitments." What kinds of enduring commitments are appropriate to the notorious flux of market-driven business enterprises? It would be altogether too easy at this point to unroll the biblical prophets' demand for love and justice, and then measure how far the attainments of management and employees fall short of this demand. More challenging and useful is the procedure of seeing how management and employees have sought to cope with each other, and to what extent their tactics express the basic ideas and logic of covenant-building. This study aspires to the standard of Christian realism in its appraisal of the possibilities for genuine cooperation between management and employees, and such realism involves working both aspirations and limitations into a matrix of achievable and discernible factuality.[1]

The next eleven chapters describe and interpret the two-hundred-year struggle between management and employees in considerable detail. I argue that when the four eras of this history are viewed through the lens afforded by the biblical history, the rudiments of covenant-making (and covenant-breaking) become visible—not simply as a matter of aspiration, but as a matter of fact. The biblical logic outlined in the previous chapter provides a filter for sifting what has been of covenantal value in this struggle from what has not. The struggle has been characterized by complex ebbs and flows, however. Since my larger argument is at risk of being overwhelmed by the details, this chapter links the claims abstracted from the biblical history of covenant-making with the arguments made throughout the rest of the book.

1. Discerning a covenantal history begins with identifying the contingencies which the two sides present to each other.

The early history of business and labor in the U.S. was characterized by protracted and widespread conflict, as described in chapter 6. Within a decade after the Republic was founded, journeyman artisans went on strike against Philadelphia manufacturers. The strike became the major tactic of employees, although bold efforts also were made over the course of the nineteenth century to counter the power of owners through other means. Workers organized political parties to gain control of the economy and cooperatives to foster economic self-sufficiency. The increasing radicality of these tactics illustrated how the gap between those who owned or managed business enterprises and those who worked for them was deepening into a chasm between social classes. By the late nineteenth century, the era of Leo XIII's *Rerum Novarum* and the heyday of the Social Gospel, the two sides had squared off as "capital" and "labor." Employees flirted with anarchism and violence; owners and management responded with coercive tactics of their own: court injunctions, lockouts, blacklisting, Pinkerton agents, and state militias.

Two mutually contradictory principles lay at the heart of this struggle, as explained in chapter 7. The tactics of management reflected a claimed right to direct its enterprises as it saw fit—what might be termed the principle of "managerial prerogative." The tactics of employees reflected a claimed right to represent their own interests in managerial decision-making—the principle of "self-representation." Management sought to break employees and their unions, while employees sought to escape managerial control. Each side effectively rejected the moral principle central to the thinking and action of its opponent.

Reconciling these two action-guiding principles is far more difficult in practice than resolving a logical contradiction. The basic problem is that the principles of managerial prerogative and employee self-representation, when each is pushed to an extreme, imply a rejection of the biblical insight that covenant-making is an inherently interactive process. This failure to acknowledge and legitimate processes of mutual influence between management and employees remains perhaps the greatest obstacle to covenant-making.

Nonetheless, this opening phase of the struggle was not devoid of covenantal value. The fact that neither side could vanquish the other demonstrated that they presented each other with ineradicable contingency, a contingency expressed in the tactics they used, and encapsulated in the contending moral principles which informed those tactics. The mutual frustration forced management and employees to find ways of working more productively with each other. Moreover, the century-long struggle demonstrated with unmistakeable clarity what was at stake for each side: managerial prerogative vs. employee self-representation. Any viable initiatives towards more covenantal relations would have to somehow affirm both of these implicitly contradictory moral principles.

2. Covenants are built through tactics which affirm the agency of one's antagonist.

By this light, little covenantal potential was visible during the nineteenth century. Management and employees used strategies and tactics which effectively implied a rejection of each other as legitimate actors. But some breakthroughs occurred during the period from 1898 to 1920, as reported in chapter 8. On the cusp of the twentieth century, both sides took a brief "honeymoon" from the brutal tactics of the previous century. This respite served to embed the idea of a trade agreement: contracts by which management and employees regulated their relations with each other according to the rule of law. Through such negotiated pacts, both sides took the first steps towards recognizing each other as legitimate actors. Moreover, some employers began seeking the cooperation of employees. The "corporate welfare" movement which peaked in the 1920s engaged hundreds of employers in providing housing, medical care, social facilities, and higher wages for their workers. These efforts were admittedly paternalistic, hardly reflecting a full acknowledgment of the employees' principle of self-representation. More significant were some efforts by employees and management to reorganize their work scientifically.

As explained in chapter 9, progress in constructing covenantal relations can be measured along two axes: first, that the parties move towards a shared cause, and second, that both sides bind or obligate themselves as a means of shaping the thinking and action of each other. According to these measures, management and employees made fitful but discernible progress. First, both sides began to understand that their freedom to act under conditions of mutual interdependence was contingent upon securing the cooperation of the other. From a biblical point of view, both sides were making the first tentative step towards seeing the contingency they presented each other as an asset rather than a liability; as a resource to be enlisted rather than suppressed. Second, management and employees then began to bind themselves to respect the principle of action most central to the action of the other, as a means of generating cooperation.

Subsequently, however, these two elements of covenant-building were obscured. As reported in the first half of chapter 11, increasingly aggressive and coercive tactics were adopted by management in the 1920s and 1930s, and by employees during the 1930s. Management sought to destroy unions through "open-shop," "American plan," and other campaigns, until such tactics largely were prohibited by the Wagner Act of 1935. Employees, for their part, engaged in enormous and successful strikes during the 1930s, winning the right to bargain labor contracts with management. The young Reinhold Niebuhr, caught up in the struggle of Henry Ford with Detroit autoworkers, was apparently unable to discern covenantal value in this "collective bargaining." Yet as argued in chapter 10, covenantal love takes a significant form in negotiated labor contracts. Both parties commit themselves not to undermine each other by abusing the power they possess to harm each other.

3. Building covenants involves enlisting rather than suppressing the contingency presented by the other party, through tactics which shift from suppressing conflict to eliciting cooperation.

After World War II, a fast-rising tide of labor unrest persuaded management to adopt "collective bargaining" on a large scale (chapter 11, second half). For a time, covenantal progress was evident, as hard confrontations yielded to hard bargaining during the 1940s and 1950s. The elements of a social contract began to become visible, as management obligated itself to recognize unions formed by workers and to apply ever more generous wages and benefits. Management saw the wisdom of negotiating contracts to define the terrain of collaboration with unions as legitimate representatives of employees. The efforts by both sides to coerce each other were offset by the contractual obligations they bound themselves to. But this social contract did not satisfy employees, who wanted more democracy and participation than permitted by management or by their own hierarchically organized unions, nor did it satisfy management, which wanted more flexibility than union-imposed work rules allowed. From the 1950s to the 1970s, employees used wildcat strikes, often against their unions, while honing the skills of individual and group resistance in "fractional bargaining." As argued in chapter 12, such power tactics run counter to the principal covenant-building strategy, which is to bind oneself as the most appropriate pathway to influencing the partner whom one is seeking to recruit.

The past three decades have intensified, if anything, the contradictory trends reported so far. On the one hand, management has deployed a variety of deplorable but effective means to discourage employees from creating or joining unions (chapter 13). They have used, abused, and simply flouted federal law. Or they simply have divested themselves of employees and plants, as a means in part to rid themselves of unions. On the other hand, management also has initiated bold strategies for eliciting cooperation from employees, even to the point of building whole new plants from ground up, as is the case with the enormous Saturn plant managed by employee teams in Tennessee (chapter 14). Management asserts that it wants to recruit and empower employees to join the management team, while employees have been battered by a decade of job insecurity and falling expectations into complying. Employees are just beginning to mount effective resistance against the first set of tactics, and have taken to the second with more or less enthusiasm, depending upon how genuinely committed management is to programs of cooperation.

From a covenantal perspective, cooperation is much to be preferred over conflict. The brilliant advantage of cooperative tactics is that they aim at harnessing the contingency of human will, rather than expending large quantities of energy in simply suppressing it. But there is a price. Genuine cooperation is costly to both management and employees, in terms of coercive power yielded up, informational demands added on, and burdens of mutual influence intensified (chapter 15). Perhaps Reinhold Niebuhr's "realist" skepticism has been vindicated. Yet the very costliness of cooperation is mirrored in benefits which add up to a kind of value which cannot be captured in economic terms (chapter 16). The value is poignantly evident where vibrant programs of cooperation have been destroyed, as at the Caterpillar company during the early 1980s.

Conclusion

The sheer complexity of the historical struggle between management and employees is daunting, but it should not be surprising. The biblical narratives, after all, report and anticipate a close and confusing intertwining of conflict and cooperation between God and God's people, right until the end of history. Nor should it be surprising that the struggle between management and employees has not generated some simple, obvious solution.

The biblical narratives offer not a blueprint for felicitous mutual manipulation but a deposit of solid wisdom gained over centuries of struggle. The best means to cope with an unpredictable and uncontrollable covenant partner is to make an enduring commitment to enlist the contingency presented by that party. As attested to by the long trajectory of divine tactics, an enduring covenantal commitment best finds expression in the use of tactics which assume that the will of the other is basically in agreement, and so aims at fostering cooperation rather than coercively containing visible conflict.

But how to gain that cooperation? The method of this study is not to develop moral ideals or abstractions but to search for durable goods within history. The history of management and employees yields two clues. First, when their struggle is viewed in a long historical perspective, it appears that both sides have been fumbling towards a shared cause. They have been attempting to work out a shared understanding of the freedom appropriate to their tight functional interdependence. To be durable, this common cause must incorporate and integrate the major contingencies—the principles of managerial prerogative, employee self-representation, and, most recently, self-management—which their tactics have been designed to protect. There appears to be no single, final philosophical formula for expressing this synthesis. In the practical world of business, visible tactics speak louder than voiced intentions or comprehensive plans. The shared cause may be defined most concretely in the endless adjustment of tactics, as a pragmatic array of measures serving to foster rather than undercut a spirit of cooperation.

There is a second clue expressive of the essence of covenant-building tactics. During the past two hundred years, the rudiments of covenanting have emerged as management and employees have discovered that binding themselves can be a more effective means of coping with their vulnerability to each other than seeking to coerce each other directly. At certain critical junctures, such as the turn-of-the-century "honeymoon" or the post–World

War II heyday of collective bargaining, management and employees have adopted tactics which acknowledged boundaries on the ways in which they could seek to shape the thinking and acting of each other. Not surprisingly, the commitments they made were modest and precarious, but they appear the indispensable foundations for a truly covenantal relationship. The commitment of management to the principle of managerial prerogative is too deeply embedded to be changed by the brute force of strikes or more covert tactics. Similarly, the will of employees to exert meaningful control over the conditions of their labor is too deeply embedded to yield to shallow managerial manipulations. What is needed, for the long haul, are tactics which demonstrate that both sides respect the moral freedom of the other.

These two clues point to moral goods which are durable, in the sense that they have recurred as tangible assets in the history narrated in this study. Of course, it would be foolish to term the historical struggle "progressive," as if there were some unambiguous goal to which both management and employees were firmly if haltingly bound. A dominant thread in the strategies and tactics of both management and employees has been the aim of each to insulate itself against vulnerability to the other. On the side of management, the right to manage as it sees fit remains deeply embedded; on the other side, employees have hung on just as doggedly to the conviction that they are authorized to limit the encroachment of managerial control. There is no obvious end in sight except more struggle; the challenge is to make that struggle covenantally viable, rather than destructive.

PART 2

Conflicting Principles and Covenanting Overtures

CHAPTER 6

The Nineteenth Century: Spiraling Conflict

For those who seek evidence of genuine cooperation in the employment relation, the first century of industrial history in the United States presents few points of light. To be sure, some employers evinced a stoutly paternalistic concern for their workers.[1] They sought to overcome or eliminate the labor strife which plagued their industries increasingly as the decades wore on. But overall, the nineteenth century was characterized by recurrent and escalating conflict. As narrated by scholars friendly to labor, this history consisted of ever-renewed campaigns by workers against onerous conditions imposed by employers, and the corresponding efforts by employers to frustrate those efforts by workers.[2]

The problem is, of course, that both sides were vulnerable to the economic pressures exerted by the other. On one side, workers were concerned about how much they would be paid, how long they would be made to work, at what pace, under what quality of supervision, at what risk to their health and safety, and with what security in their jobs. On the other side, employers worried about whether they could pay out the higher wages and concede the short hours and other conditions demanded by workers, and whether such demands would simply spiral upward endlessly; they were concerned with how to motivate workers to work hard and take responsibility for their work. Workers and employers, in short, presented significant contingencies to each other. Each was faced with essentially the same problem, as implied by the strategies and tactics they used: how to render the other a reliable and trustworthy instrument for gain. Workers had to devise strategies to secure the conditions of work they wanted from employers; employers had to devise strategies to ensure that the tightly coordinated and interdependent tasks required by their business enterprise would be accomplished.

Resistance and Counterresistance

From early on, workers adopted strategies of resistance. Here the term "resistance" points to more than the friction or blockage offered by something inert. It refers to the intentional efforts by workers to define the conditions under which they would work—in effect, to impose their interests and values upon employers. In this study, I focus upon resistance which is collective, as opposed to individual, "unorganized" tactics of resistance.[3]

The early era of labor history in the United States saw an efflorescence of collective tactics, not all of which have survived to the twentieth century. The most familiar and flamboyant tactic of resistance was the strike. The strike was and still is used against employers who refuse to recognize and negotiate with unions. This tactic is a major weapon in the labor strategy of trade-unionism. Invented in the nineteenth century, trade-unionism is the idea of organizing workers into an association, and using this solidarity to draw or force management into negotiating the conditions under which workers would continue to work. Important as it has been, the strategy of trade-unionism needs to be understood against the backdrop of two other major strategies—quitting the capitalist economic system or gaining control of it through the political process.

In pursuit of these three strategies, workers applied a variety of tactics during the nineteenth century. Not surprisingly, their efforts provoked a strategy of strong counterresistance by employers. In particular, when workers coalesced in trade unions to force their will upon management, management sought to evade, marginalize, or even destroy those unions. Owners and managers early began to cultivate a solidarity of their own, through employer associations and industry groups. During the nineteenth century, their collective tactics involved the use of force, in various guises, often in answer to the coercive tactics of workers. Employers obstructed the recruitment of workers into unions with blacklists and they fought strikes with lockouts, court injunctions, and other coercive means. As one might expect, unions rose and fell in every economic cycle of boom and depression.

Three Strategies of Worker Resistance: Idealistic, Political, and Opportunistic

The strategies and tactics used by workers and employers have been reported in detail by the academic field of labor history. For an outsider to the field, the past two hundred years present a dense and confusing patchwork of local episodes and larger initiatives, from which broad trends can be abstracted only with great caution. The following sketch of the nineteenth century draws principally from a detailed study by John Commons, an economist at the University of Wisconsin, and several of his colleagues.[4]

According to these economists, the labor movement pursued three broad strategies during the nineteenth century. First, workers and their allies sought to quit the system of for-profit enterprise. In their "idealistic" vision, they sought to extend the logic of the Declaration of Independence to include economic freedom.[5] Inspired by Robert Owens's 1826 experiment at New Harmony, Indiana, and figures such as Charles Fourier and Horace Greeley, they pursued a blend of self-employment and collaborative enterprise. They established producing cooperatives in order to compete with privately owned businesses.[6] In effect, they sought to develop their own means of production. Such co-ops appeared as early as 1791 and 1836.[7] They sprang up by the score either during deep recessions, when workers lost jobs, or during inflationary booms, when their wages lost purchasing power. The peak periods include 1848–55, 1866–70, and especially the mid-1880s.[8] The Knights of Labor, a broad coalition of workers which at its height reached into every county of the U.S., encouraged dozens of such experiments. But most co-ops perished within a year or two, due to pressure from either internal disorganization, private competitors, or the railroads needed to transport raw supplies and finished goods. Despite ardent later support by the Social Gospel movement, and a revival during the 1930s, the idea of cooperatively owned production never regained the peak of popular enthusiasm which it enjoyed in the mid-1880s.

A related stream of labor activism sought political representation, in order to tighten the framework of legal constraints in which business operated.[9] Throughout the nineteenth century, repeated efforts were made to organize a labor party, just as labor parties were being formed in Europe. The political campaigns were successful in generating major reforms such as public education and a workday shortened from twelve hours to ten and, later, to eight hours. But they were not successful in instituting a voice for labor in politics, especially when this political activism after 1850 grew into a more revolutionary strategy aimed at transforming the economic system.[10]

During the 1870s, Lasallean socialists and the openly Marxist International Workingmen's Association differed as to whether workers should seek economic power through unions and cooperatives or by gaining control of the state.[11] Attempts to unite these other labor factions failed during the great upheaval of 1886–87.[12] The American Federation of Labor, the principal association of skilled workers, within a decade or two decided to exert labor's political influence only through existing parties. By the twentieth century, proposals for securing control of the economic system were largely abandoned by the labor movement. The populist International Workers of the World were crushed after World War I, and socialist and Marxist parties revived only for a time in the 1930s before succumbing to the combined power of the state and employers.

The Opportunistic Strategy and Spiraling Conflict

By the end of the nineteenth century, workers were turning to a third strategy, which Commons and his colleagues unflatteringly term "opportunism."[13] They pressed collectively for agreements with employers, company by company and industry by industry. Rather than transform the rules of the system, they sought to win specific concessions regarding wages, hiring practices, working conditions and hours, and other issues defining their relationships with employers. Nevertheless, this strategy was hardly more palatable to management bent on retaining control over the workplace, because it emerged from a conflict which had descended into violence—on both sides—over the course of a century.

According to Commons, the conflict was caused by factors beyond the control of either side. At the end of the eighteenth century, the earliest U.S. manufacturers and their skilled journeymen workers in Philadelphia and other centers of commerce enjoyed an overlapping of economic interest sufficient to preclude major conflict. The relationship frayed as canals, turnpikes, and railroads increased the scope of markets, fostering the growth of wholesalers who effectively forced employers to cut both wages and the quality of workmanship expected of craftsmen.[14] The first unions were organized in Philadelphia, New York, and Baltimore during the 1790s, and the first strike, by Philadelphia shoemakers, occurred in 1799.[15] By the 1820s, unions—and strikes—were reported from skilled printers, shoemakers ("cordwainers"), tailors, carpenters, house painters, and other craftsmen.[16] The demonstrations tended to be orderly and peaceful, at least until the first factory strikes erupted at the textile centers of Paterson, New Jersey, and Lowell, Massachusetts, in 1828 and 1834, respectively.[17] By then, wage-earning workers realized that they were in a class with interests distinct from those of their employers. More than 170 strikes occurred between 1833 and 1837.[18]

This divergence of interests was not lost upon manufacturers. As early as 1810, Philadelphia employers had begun organizing their own association to resist the demands of journeymen. Employers along the East Coast initiated tactics which set a pattern that lasted, and indeed escalated, for more than a century. First, employers turned to the courts for help. They haled striking workers into court on charges of conspiracy—often successfully. In 1836, a New York court condemned unions formed for the purpose of raising wages as illegal "combinations."[19] In 1840, another court declared unions to be a legal form of association, but conspiracy and antitrust cases were decided in favor of employers well into the twentieth century. Second, employers organized their own means to discourage or break up unions. They refused to meet with representatives of workers, or subjected strikers to a "lockout," preventing them from entering the workplace. Third, employer associations funded joint campaigns against unions. They drew up and circulated "blacklists" in order to protect each other from known agitators. "The blacklist was the chief weapon of the employers."[20]

Workers, for their part, responded with more organization. By the 1830s, they were forming unions of national scope. Only a few national unions existed prior to 1860, but the boom following the Civil War drove up the cost of living, encouraging rapid growth. Membership almost doubled in ten years, to 300,000 by 1870.[21] Employers took advantage of the depression of 1873–79 to sweep away these unions as well as the wage gains they had achieved. "Employers sought to free themselves from the restrictions that trade unions had imposed upon them during the years preceding the crisis. They consequently added a systematic policy of lockouts, of blacklists, and of legal prosecution to the already crushing weight of hard times and unemployment."[22]

In response, workers turned first to violence and then to peaceful but equally aggressive mass protests and boycotts. The use of violence as a tactic was exemplified most notoriously by the "Molly Maguires," a movement planted in Pennsylvania during the 1850s and most active in the 1870s. Members of this Ancient Order of Hibernians intimidated and sometimes murdered mineowners. They also used the threat of violence against workers to enforce the strikes which were called. The Hibernian lodges numbered as many as 6,000 nationwide but were crushed through mass arrests and prosecutions in 1875–76.[23] As the depression deepened in 1877, East Coast railroad companies cut wages by 20 percent. This action ignited violence by mobs of strikers in Baltimore and Pittsburgh, and the violence spread nationwide. Federal troops were called out. The violent strikes failed to restore wages, and served to revive the charge of conspiracy as a legal weapon against labor. Further, the violence prompted state authorities to build armories, which stood as concrete symbols of the alliance between the state and employers against workers.[24]

The atmosphere of repression effectively drove another union, the Knights of Labor, underground until it emerged as a national organization in 1878.[25] The Knights were the most successful movement of the era. They drew in large masses of workers, and organized large-scale strikes. While the strikes often failed, due to disorganization, the Knights also popularized another tactic: enlisting sympathetic unions to boycott the products of a company being struck. Fully 59 of the 196 boycotts kindled by the Knights in 1885 were successful.[26] Employers, however, had boycotters prosecuted for extortion. And in 1886, a famous prosecution of workers for boycotting a Chicago beer garden effectively outlawed the tactic. The membership of the Knights peaked at 700,000 in 1886, and fell to 100,000 by 1890.[27]

Trade Unionism and Counteroffensives by Employers

During the late 1880s, the Knights lost members to a different kind of union applying a different kind of tactic. The Knights were a loosely organized, democratic mass movement, motivated by a hatred of capitalism and wishing to become independent of capitalism by organizing cooperatives. Individual trade unions, in contrast, excluded unskilled workers, organized only skilled workers in particular specialties ("trades"), and sought to gain leverage over work conditions affecting only themselves.[28] According to Commons and his associates, "It signified a labour movement reduced to an opportunistic basis, accepting the existence of capitalism and having for its object the enlarging of the bargaining power of the wage-earner in the sale of his labor."[29] These trade unions of "pure wage consciousness" proved more effective, however. While the Knights, in their enthusiasm for democratic action, often bungled the strikes they called, trade unions maintained tight control over their members, directing strikes from central offices.[30] After 1887, members of the Knights rushed to join national trade unions.[31]

Despite their acceptance of capitalism, the trade unions were no more acceptable to employers than the Knights. Employers relied increasingly upon the coercive power of the state to thwart union initiatives. The strategy of employers, quite simply, was to avoid making concessions by whatever tactic available. When in 1886 anarchists detonated a bomb in Chicago's Haymarket Square, the movement for reducing the working day from ten to eight hours was set back for years.[32] Employers signaled their unrelenting opposition to unions in two late nineteenth-century strikes which have become symbols of the conflict at its most fierce. An 1892 strike by skilled steelworkers in Homestead, Pennsylvania, was answered by employers with authorized and organized violence: armed Pinkerton guards and the state militia. The strike resulted in the elimination of unions from the steel industry.[33] An 1894 strike in Chicago illustrated a different, less violent, but equally effective weapon: the "injunction". Injunctions are legal orders secured by employers in order to require workers to refrain from striking, or to return to work.[34] The Pullman Company applied injunctions against the builders of its railroad cars in Chicago and prosecuted the strike leaders who violated the injunctions. Sympathetic strikers around the U.S. took the occasion to "rob, burn and blunder," imposing costs which amounted to the staggering sum of $80 million. Bereft of public support, and faced with a daunting alliance of railroad management and federal troops, the Pullman strike collapsed. Commons concludes: "The labour organizations were taught two important lessons. First, that nothing can be gained through revolutionary striking, for the government was sufficiently strong to cope with it; and second, that the employers had obtained a formidable ally in the courts."[35]

This alliance of employers with the legal system continued well into the twentieth century, as federal and state courts issued some 4,500 injunctions against strikers from 1877 through 1930.[36] Employers cleverly turned legislation intended to break up trusts into an instrument for breaking up strikes and thwarting union organizers. They persuaded courts to see labor unions as "malicious conspiracies" outlawed by antitrust legislation. Such coercive use of the law prompted unions to respond with their own lawsuits, of course, but the courts sided more often with employers. During a 1905 teamster strike in Chicago, an association of employers secured an injunction which enabled them to keep their operations going while they simply refused to negotiate with the strikers. The power of the striking teamsters, attenuated by their violent attacks on "scab" replacement workers, ebbed as union leaders were prosecuted for conspiracy.[37] Prosecutions for conspiracy effectively served to restrict the right of workers to strike. Use of this tactic peaked in 1908.[38]

Two other tactics of virulent counterresistance to unions continued from the nineteenth century well into the twentieth. First, employers sought to consolidate their legal victories in the political process. Many states, particularly in the South, legislated the "right to work" in laws which protected nonunion workers from recruiting pressure by union organizers. By 1904, the National Association of Manufacturers (NAM) effectively controlled both houses of Congress, as far as labor legislation was concerned.[39] Second, employers sought to turn the public against unions. The first nationwide campaign was the vigorous "open shop" movement sparked by small businessmen. The movement began with the successful 1900–1902 campaign by Dayton, Ohio, businesses to take back control of their workplaces from unions—they succeeded in driving unions out of the city. The "open shop" movement spread rapidly through the U.S. after 1903. Small businessmen formed secret "citizen alliances" which supplied interested cities both with strikebreakers and with guidance for swaying public opinion.[40] The movement waned after 1907, but it was reinvigorated a decade later. In 1921, employer associations launched an instantly and widely successful "American Plan," a campaign to affirm the hallowed individual liberty of every worker to sell his labor without interference by union organizers.[41] The campaign effectively set the individual property rights of workers (rights to their labor) against their right of representation. The campaign also set white Americans against racial and ethnic minorities, as employer groups allied themselves with the Ku Klux Klan and other nativist groups.[42]

Conclusion

I have related this tortuous history of struggle and stalemate in some detail in order to prepare the ground for a covenantal interpretation. My aim is to explain how covenantal elements have become manifest in the employment relation. This work begins with an unblinking narration, which here involves acknowledging that the coercive tactics recounted in this chapter were noticeably devoid of covenantal potential. That, however, is less significant than the fact that both sides failed. Neither employers nor workers were able to contain the contingency presented by each other. Nineteenth-century workers failed to sustain a political force, or to displace business corporations as the main engines of the economy. Despite recurrent spasms of labor militancy, employers enjoyed the upper hand. They were able to suppress the latent collective power of workers. They were able to call upon the court system and the military power of the state to force workers to labor longer, at lower wages, and under more onerous conditions than many workers freely consented to. Nevertheless, the tactics of employers also failed. They failed to contain the rising tide of trade unionism, which transposed larger issues of economic destiny into an increasingly effective struggle for control of the shop floor.

Interestingly enough, it is this failure of either side to vanquish the other which signaled the possibility that the employment relation might evolve in a covenantal direction. Because both sides continued to present a durable and perhaps ineradicable contingency to each other, both were faced with the necessity of devising some strategy and supporting tactics to render the other party reliable and trustworthy. And indeed, during the early twentieth century, employers began to experiment with tactics which suggested a tentative but important break with the nineteenth-century legacy of coercion. These tactics are taken up in chapter 8.

Before continuing the narrative, a pause is needed to explore what precisely was the nature of the contingency that employers and workers presented to each other. What was at stake in their conflict, and why was each side so unwilling to yield? If nothing more than their respective interests were at stake, the economic relationship which they coerced each other into would have nothing of covenantal value. A covenantal relationship, as Robin Lovin has argued, involves mutual "recognition."[43] Such recognition is the glue which obligates contending parties to acknowledge the claims they press against each other. The question is, what, if any, moral claim was implied by the tactics employers and workers used against each other? Did their admittedly coercive tactics imply a claim for "recognition"? This question is taken up in the next chapter.

CHAPTER 7

Two Contending Moral Principles

For a covenantal ethic, narrating and interpreting history is a theological procedure. The task is to attend to "what is going on," in H. Richard Niebuhr's famous phrase. Niebuhr was making a theological recommendation in suggesting that the ethicist should attempt to discern what God is bringing about through the densely interactive patterns of human action before making any ethical recommendations. For example, in 1942 and 1943, Niebuhr construed World War II as God's judgment upon all participants through the crucifixion of innocent victims—a morally loaded description which pointed decisively to appropriate human responses of repentance and sympathy for those victims.[1] Here, a broad argument about what God is accomplishing through the struggle between workers and management will be constructed, piece by piece. I will argue that God is moving both sides towards internalizing a covenantal relation in terms appropriate to business enterprises as networks of dense functional interaction. However, God does not appear as an actor with arms and legs in the following narrative. Rather, if I follow Niebuhr correctly, God's action is evident in the way human actors are called to interpret and evaluate events. More specifically, God acts when events are "transvalued" by being understood in the most capacious terms as expressing God's covenanting will.

Covenantal analysis engages the history of labor relations as what Niebuhr terms "inner" history, of what events mean for human actors, as opposed to the "external" history of inert, disinterested facts.[2] In the previous chapter, I focused selectively upon the strategies and tactics both sides applied to each other during the nineteenth century. To explore these actions as inner history requires making some inferences about what the strikes, lockouts, courtroom struggles, and other initiatives mean, in the larger whole of God's covenant-building. This is obviously a dangerous procedure, since these meanings may not correspond to the actual intentions of the human actors involved. Here I will distill the history of labor relations during the nineteenth century into a contest between two moral principles, one vitally important to employers and the other vitally important to workers. (A third and final principle will be introduced in chapter 14.) I follow the lead of the managerial realists described in chapter 2, who articulate moral principles as a conceptual shorthand for expressing the essence of conflicting interests and agendas. I assume that however venal or vindictive may have been the psychological motivations of employers and workers, the strategies and tactics they used reflected moral claims or principles central to their actions, and that it is through this moral dimension that God's particular will for business enterprises becomes visible.

The Bitter Conflict of Two Morally Weighty Principles

The struggle in the nineteenth century was so protracted and bitter because it pitted what here will be termed the workers' principle of "self-representation" against the employers' principle of "managerial prerogative." These principles were revealed by the tactics employers and workers used to elicit what they wanted from each other—to contain the contingency presented by each other. On the one side, workers pressed to have a collective voice, to represent themselves. Their campaigns to establish trade unions, political parties, and independent producing cooperatives expressed a demand for the right to participate in, if not control, economic decisions profoundly affecting their welfare. On the other side, employers deployed countertactics which effectively rejected this principle of self-representation. Blacklisting, lockouts, court injunctions, the open-shop campaign, and other such coercive tactics implied a claim of absolute freedom by employers to manage their enterprises as they saw fit. Employers asserted the right to immunize themselves against being influenced by workers, while workers asserted the right to shape the conditions under which they worked.

Of course, this analysis is oversimplified. The tactics used by employers and workers imply more than two moral principles. Many workers were motivated to resist out of the burning conviction that they were entitled to more, according to a distributive justice based upon need. Yet, as the tactics used by workers implied, self-representation was essential for achieving such justice. Walter Rauschenbusch, a firm partisan of labor, forcefully asserted the linkage between self-representation and justice in his 1912 *Christianizing the Social Order:*

> The grievances of the working class are mainly two. They feel that they are being deprived by the more powerful class of part of their just share in the proceeds of their joint labor, and in many cases are being compelled to labor too fast, too long and under conditions harmful to their physical and mental health. Therefore they raise the charge of injustice and exploitation. They also feel that they are not being treated as free men and of equal worth with the other class. Therefore they raise the charge of oppression. The two things are closely related. The weak have always been kept unfree in order that they might be exploited . . .
>
> Back of all material demands in the labor movement is the spiritual demand for a fuller and freer manhood. . . . The unrest of our American workingmen is in part at least the unrest of men who know liberty and are forced to live in unfreedom. Most of our relations in America are on a footing of democracy. . . . (T)he relation of employer and employee is still frankly undemocratic. Every business concern is a little monarchy. . . . In business the autocratic principle is still in full possession, unshaken and unterrified, with its flag flying from every battlement. Business is the last entrenchment of autocracy, and wherever democracy is being beaten back, the sally is made from that citadel.[3]

Employers, for their part, were concerned with efficiency, as a practical and moral imperative, as well as with retaining their freedom unfettered. They likely were motivated to combat the unions springing up in their midst out of a fear that collectively organized workers might detract from the economic efficiency of their enterprises. Yet, just as workers assumed that self-representation was essential for achieving justice, owners appear to have assumed that managerial prerogative and control were indispensable for achieving economic efficiency and the utilitarian benefits it brings. Only in the early twentieth century did a few employers choose to sacrifice some significant degree of autonomy as a means of improving the efficiency of their enterprises. These "scientific" experiments were significant forerunners of the kind of cooperation management seeks today.

Here, the principles of self-representation and managerial prerogative will serve as a shorthand for explaining the conflict between employers and workers. It was the contradiction between these two principles, posed so starkly in the nineteenth century and continuing today, that explains why it is so difficult to construct and sustain covenantal relations.

A Covenantal Evaluation

Of the three strategies pursued by labor in the nineteenth century, the idealistic and political pathways have fallen far behind trade-unionism. Of course, these strategies are hardly dead. The AFL-CIO invested millions of dollars during the 1970s and 1980s to influence congressional legislation. And the idealist strategy revived in the same time period as workers and communities have gained control of dozens of ailing or abandoned companies and made them profitable again.[4]

These two strategies epitomize the principle of self-representation, which is essential to a covenantal vision of workplace relations. Yet from a covenantal perspective, the fact that they were largely abandoned in favor of trade-unionism by the end of the nineteenth century appears to have been necessary, even if regrettable. These strategies, at least as defined in the nineteenth century, avoid the basic issue, which is how to reconcile the deeply tensive principles of worker self-representation and managerial prerogative. The political strategy, particularly in its revolutionary extreme, laid exclusive emphasis upon the principle of representation and simply rejected the property rights exercised by employers altogether, although with perhaps some compensation for the owners of to-be-nationalized property. Workers first sought to found political parties in order to gain control of the means of production—hardly a reassuring tactic for owners. The idealistic strategy aimed to enable workers to escape the oppressive conditions under which they worked, rather than to change them from within. In the compact vocabulary of economist Albert O. Hirschman, it expressed "exit" rather than "voice."[5] As such, both strategies failed to engage the problem of building a covenantal relations at its most problematic center: who was going to control the employment relation within the large, powerful modern corporation of the early twentieth century? Both strategies opted out of achieving a working synthesis of worker self-representation (or self-direction) with managerial prerogative.

In retrospect, the labor movement's retreat from the idealistic and revolutionary strategies in favor of trade-unionism may have been a necessary precondition for establishing more covenantal relations between employers and workers. In theory, trade-unionism offered more promise, in that it formally eschewed any categorical rejection of managerial prerogative. Against Marxists and socialists, trade-unionists loudly trumpeted their acceptance of the capitalist system, insisting that they wanted only to secure their share of the wealth it generated. In practice, of course, this concession hardly reassured employers. Trade-union activists hammered away with strikes, boycotts, and violence which elevated the aim of self-representation above all other considerations. Such tactics offered employers little evidence that workers respected the right of employers to manage their firms without interference. Their tactics still assaulted the indispensable basis for a viable employment relationship: respect for private property and managerial prerogative.

On the other hand, the counterresistance by employers inspired just as little confidence on the part of workers. The strategies and tactics of employers directly contradicted the principle of self-representation. Employers pressed their rights of property and managerial prerogative to an extreme, measuring the reliability of workers by their simple obedience to managerial wishes—and any resistance was simply to be crushed. Blacklists, court injunctions, lockouts, the open-shop movement and other such tactics were aimed directly at destroying the efforts of workers to represent themselves collectively. As pressed to an extreme in these tactics, the principle of managerial prerogative invited and merited little support from workers. Workers not surprisingly saw themselves as excused by their lack of self-representation from any obligation to refrain from using tactics which would impede or obstruct management from attaining its own goals. In sum, both sides used tactics which effectively pressed their moral principles to an extreme unacceptable to the other side.

Perhaps the coercive tactics were unavoidable and necessary, to demonstrate beyond a shadow of a doubt that neither side could yield up the principle most central to its own action. Yet the problem remains: neither principle could provide both employers and workers with the means to develop confidence in the contingency they presented to each other. On the one side, workers used tactics which suggest they considered employers to be tyrannical. Workers hardly would be motivated to concede significant moral weight to the principle of managerial autonomy when employer tactics reflected little more than an interest in maintaining an unimpeded field of action. On the other side, employers used tactics which suggested they thought workers to be irresponsible. Employers hardly would be motivated to concede significant moral weight to the principle of self-representation when the tactics of workers appeared to reflect little more than the pursuit of narrow self-interest.

The Moral Grounding of Each Principle

The tension between the principles of managerial prerogative and worker self-representation sparked fierce conflict because both principles are deeply grounded and enjoy considerable moral weight. The principle of self-representation has roots which are both republican and biblical, in the terminology used by Robert Bellah and his colleagues.[6] The demand for self-representation reaches back before the American Revolution, to struggles between kings and parliamentary government, and was established in the Constitution. Biblically, the right of the people to be represented before God reaches back to the origins of Judeo-Christian community at Mount Sinai, where Moses and a caste of Levite priests intercede with God on behalf of the people. As elaborated in the Christian tradition, this principle authorizes and encourages all believers to use prayer and worship as a means of making themselves present to God, as well as acknowledging God's presence to them. While the idea of modern democratic self-representation nowhere is suggested in the Bible, a related idea is firmly embedded: that the covenant confers upon God's people a claim to be heard and responded to.

Similarly, the principle of managerial prerogative has a solid, if different, political anchoring in the right of private property and general social utility. The sanctity of private property historically rests upon the social-contract theory of John Locke which informed interpretations of Anglo-American law. Legally, employers long have asserted the right to use the assets of their companies without interference from workers, and this right only recently has been challenged successfully in courts. The ongoing legitimacy of private property and managerial prerogative as institutions rests upon their enormous utilitarian value. The right of entrepreneurs and management to use company assets as they see fit has made possible the relentless "creative destruction" of jobs and products in order to generate the wealth that is the chief moral argument in favor of capitalist economic organization. On the biblical side, these utilitarian arguments may mean little, and the right of private property receives little if any direct attention. Yet no denominational strands of U.S. Christianity are willing to abandon the right to private property, however much they might qualify it. In Roman Catholic social teaching, Leo XIII asserted—against socialism—that private property had a firm basis in natural law, and this teaching has been reaffirmed for a century, even if strongly tempered by holding management accountable to the norms of common good and common access.[7]

Conclusion

Given the firm moral anchoring of both principles, it is not surprising that neither alone could provide a firm basis for employers and workers to find each other trustworthy. Some balance needed to be struck between the principles of self-representation and managerial prerogative. The needed balance is justice in a covenantal sense. As will be seen, covenantal justice involves not simply that employers and workers devise a balance of interests, but that they do so in a durable way by recognizing, as morally valuable, the principle most central to the action of each other. The bitter tactics of the nineteenth century can be read most hopefully as the first crude and costly efforts to work out such a balance.

By the first decade of the twentieth century, the conflict between employers and workers was as virulent as ever. Nevertheless, a softening of sorts did occur in the first half of the twentieth century. Both sides adapted their tactics in such a way as to acknowledge implicitly—to some extent—the moral principle of action most important to each other. In this way, they began to forge a shared cause out of the contingencies they presented to each other. This new direction in tactics is taken up in the next chapter, which returns to the historical narrative.

chapter 8

From 1898 through the 1920s: Trade Agreements and Welfare Capitalism

This chapter picks up the historical narrative from chapter 6 by describing a split in managerial tactics which developed during the first three decades of the twentieth century. The most promising development was a short and unexpected honeymoon in labor relations, which enabled employers to modify their tactics in a covenantally more promising direction. Some consented to the union strategy of negotiating a trade agreement; such agreements committed both sides to respect the principle of action most important to the other. Unfortunately, the honeymoon lasted only a few years, and many employers simply carried over and refined the more coercive nineteenth-century tactics, while unionists responded in kind. The number of strikes increased by leaps and bounds, and management tried to suppress unions with legal harassment, public-relations campaigns such as the open-shop movement and the American Plan, and political manipulation. But during the 1920s and 1930s, a considerable number of employers began to experiment with new and more conciliatory tactics to stave off the collective organization of their workforces.

The Trade Agreement

By the end of the nineteenth century, power was beginning to shift towards workers and their unions. Between 1898 and 1904, union membership swelled from half a million to more than two million.[1] The move towards more covenantally viable tactics began against the backdrop of this rising labor power, in what John Commons and his colleagues term the "honeymoon" of general prosperity from 1898 to 1904.[2] The short respite from open struggle was of immense covenantal value, for it permitted unions to embed "trade agreements" into the mainstream of U.S. industrial relations. Trade agreements are bilateral contracts hammered out between employers and workers, specifying the rules under which workers will work and the wages they will be paid. This kind of unionism was pressed by the American Federation of Labor (AFL).

While earlier unions of the "idealistic" tendency had endorsed the use of third-party arbitration to settle disputes, the trade unions insisted upon direct negotiations between themselves and employers.[3] From 1897 through the early 1930s, the percentage of unionized workers affiliated with the AFL rose from 61 to almost 85 percent.[4] From a covenantal perspective, bilateral negotiations are valuable because they enable each party to bind itself as a means of inducing the other to cooperate. Employers could forestall labor agitation by committing themselves to fixed rates of pay; workers could secure such rates by committing themselves to meet the work standards set by their employers. This kind of moral and legal leverage was far superior to the raw coercive tactics more common to the nineteenth century. In effect, it generated a pragmatic accommodation between the two principles employers and workers had been warring over because it served to channel and contain the scope of conflict. The trade agreement committed workers to accept the right of employers to manage their enterprises—within the parameters of negotiations where workers represented their own interests. Negotiations stabilized the expectations of employers and skilled workers around an objective standard: the contract which was ratified by, and binding upon, both parties. For Commons, writing in 1921, "The ideal of the trade agreement was the main achievement of the nineties. It led the way from an industrial system which alternately was either despotism or anarchy to a constitutional form of government in industry."[5]

Of course, this pragmatic accommodation between the two principles did not reach the demanding standards of a covenant. First, the agreements were hardly voluntary in the full sense of the word, since they usually were hammered out under the threat of a strike (by workers) or of a lockout (by employers). Such contracts clearly fell quite short of a covenant as traditionally understood, where two parties pledge a mutual fidelity which transcends their shifting fortunes. Second, the agreements included only members of narrowly drawn trades. They reflected the bias of the early twentieth-century American Federation of Labor against persons of color and women, as well as against the increasing numbers of unskilled, often immigrant, Caucasian male workers.[6] Here trade-unionism fell short of the idealistic strand of unionism. The Knights of Labor in the 1880s, the International Workers of the World ("Wobblies") during the 1900s and 1910s, and the Congress of Industrial Organizations during the 1930s carried the flickering nineteenth-century torch for full self-representation. They were committed to the ideal of including all workers, in explicit contrast to the exclusive policies of the AFL.

Spiraling Resistance and Counterresistance

The numerical strength of the labor movement stagnated for several years, then surged again. In 1910, 10 percent of U.S. (nonagricultural) workers belonged to unions; by 1920, almost 20 percent did.[7] As the U.S. entered World War I, workers engaged in a frenzy of strikes, boosting membership in the AFL from 2 million in 1916 to 3.2 million in 1919.[8] Strikes during the World War I years routinely involved at least half a million workers—and in 1919 alone, almost 4.5 million, or about one-quarter of all industrial workers at the time.[9] By comparison, strikes in the 1880s and 1890s usually involved 100,000 to 300,000 workers per year, and even in the great strike year of 1894, just over half a million.[10] Moreover, workers were demanding self-representation in more pointed and aggressive terms. According to labor historian David Montgomery, a large percentage of the strikes which took place during the great surges of 1901–4 and 1916–20 were "control" strikes, as opposed to strikes simply for higher wages. Workers were two to three times more likely than in the 1880s to demand that management recognize their unions, fire unpopular foremen, or share power regarding the enforcement of work rules, layoffs, or discharges.[11] Indeed, by 1920 workers were developing a desire to run their own particular industries. As one socialist challenged a convention of clothing workers: "It is now our responsibility to establish order in the industry in the place of the chaos created by the employers when they had things their own way."[12]

Nevertheless, the drive to unionize workers stalled during the 1920s. Between 1920 and 1933, the number of unionized workers dropped from 5 million to 2.9 million, while the percentage of unionized workers fell from the 20 percent of 1920 back to 10 percent by 1930.[13] Surely much of this retreat had to do with the energetic counterresistance of employers. The post–World War I economic boom effectively had crowned businessmen with uncritical public adulation. Buoyed by such support, the employers deployed contradictory tactics. On the one hand, they continued to crush unions with the tactics described in the previous chapter. The coercive measures of the nineteenth century were renewed in virulent new forms. In addition to the American Plan of the 1920s, employers engaged in espionage during the 1930s and a welter of aggressive tactics to drive out unions during succeeding decades. These tactics, of course, imply an implacable rejection of worker self-representation in favor of complete managerial control. On the other hand, they sought to understand, pacify, and co-opt their workers. The latter tactics, which occupy the balance of this chapter, include: paternalistic "welfare capitalism," management-controlled "company unions," and "scientific" cooperation with labor unions. These new tactics committed employers, however timidly or ambiguously, to some acknowledgment of worker demands for more effective power and control. The value of these three tactics is that they acknowledged the principle of worker self-representation in some degree.

Company Unions and "Welfare Capitalism"

During the first quarter of the twentieth century, according to historian Stuart Brandes, employers sought to dampen the successes of unions by persuading workers that unions were unnecessary. Two paternalistic tactics are most relevant to this study. First, employers established "company unions" in order to permit workers some voice regarding issues in the workplace.[14] The first known experiment in employer-sponsored "self-government" for workers began in 1905, when the Wm. Filene Department Store of Boston organized its workers into a representative government complete with two houses and a presidential cabinet.[15] A wider precedent was set in World War I, when employers were encouraged to set up joint management-labor committees to smooth the operation of their plants. More than a hundred companies established such "employee representation plans" or "company unions."[16] These committees were authorized to seek redress for worker grievances from management, or from an arbitrator in cases of deadlocked conflict.[17] The idea of employee self-representation survived the war. By 1922, 725 plans were in effect. By 1934, 750 plans covered 2.6 million workers.[18]

Company unions were one element of "welfare capitalism," a broad strategy which extended to even more workers. The basic aim of employers was to institute a degree of care for their workers in order to undercut the material lures offered by union organizers. The early emphasis was upon housing, as hundreds of employers built "company towns" during the nineteenth century.[19] By the beginning of the twentieth century, employers were expanding into virtually every corner of their workers' lives: health care, education, recreation, family culture, pensions, even religion.[20] By 1926, at the height of the movement, half of the 1,500 largest U.S. companies had comprehensive programs. Four million workers were touched by some program or other. "Workers lived in company houses, were treated by company doctors, attended company schools, played on company teams, purchased company stock, and were represented by company unions."[21]

Employers promoted these two tactics primarily as good business strategy. The aims were clear, according to Brandes: company management sought to secure the good will of the public as protection against antitrust prosecution; to discourage unions; and to produce clean, intelligent, industrious, and loyal workers.[22] Given these motives, it is not surprising that the two tactics involved gestures that were self-obligating, but to a very limited extent. On the one hand, the employee representation plans implied that workers had some legitimate claim to participate in the governance of their workplaces, and the welfare plans implied that workers had some legitimate claim upon management for support beyond a bare wage contract. Surely some executives were moved by humanitarian or religious fervor to take care of their extended "families" of workers.[23] Seen in this light, the plans could be interpreted as gestures which obligated the benevolent employers to affirm and improve the well-being of workers.

On the other hand, the welfare programs were in fact not negotiated by their recipients and indeed were revocable by the sole wish of employers. The problem with the plans is that they blunted the capacity of workers to represent their own interests. "By regarding himself as a father to his employees and acting accordingly, an employer unavoidably relegated them to an inferior, childlike position."[24] Indeed, the largest welfare programs were instituted by the trusts which were engaged in the most truculent efforts to suppress unions in their plants, such as U.S. Steel and International Harvester.[25] Brandes observes that the plans for company unions were received by workers with apathy at best and venomous hatred at worst. The apathy was due to the substitution of paternalism for self-representation.[26]

The Rockefeller Plan

The rise and fall of the famed "Rockefeller Plan" illustrates the material benefits but unsatisfying representation afforded by such paternalistic tactics. More than a decade of increasingly bitter struggle in the coalfields of Colorado had resulted in the infamous 1913 "Ludlow massacre," where thirteen women and children were found smothered in a cave while trying to escape machine-gun fire from troops called in to contain union organizing. Miners throughout Colorado responded with violence, and efforts by President Woodrow Wilson to mediate simply failed.[27] In 1915, John D. Rockefeller, Jr., dispatched William MacKenzie King (later a prime minister of Canada) to institute the tactics of enlightened paternalism at Rockefeller's Colorado Fuel and Iron Company: to improve living conditions while keeping the workers from joining a union. The company established clinics, clubhouses, and bathhouses at its mining camps, and had workers elect representatives to a joint committee with management for resolving disputes. Half the workers initially voted for the plan. For more than ten years it generated reforms: the workday was shortened to eight hours, housing was improved, and grievances were answered—and the company avoided having to negotiate with any outside union. But workers became increasingly apathetic about the plan, in part because it failed to raise their wages above industry averages. A new round of strikes in 1927 caused the plan to fold after only twelve years. Miners rallied to a new "Colorado Industrial Plan" which recognized the United Mine Workers union as their bargaining agent.[28]

The Rockefeller Plan serves as a microcosm of the benign counterresistance which hundreds of employers used during the 1920s. Company unions and welfare plans were used primarily to keep out unions initiated by workers, and were effective for several years.[29] But the protection they afforded employers did not last, in no small measure due to the self-deception and hypocrisy that the welfare movement encouraged in powerful executives. Reinhold Niebuhr, for example, during the mid-1920s excoriated the humanitarian pretensions of Henry Ford, who claimed to raise wages and shorten workweeks of Ford autoworkers while effectively doing the opposite.[30] According to Brandes, the "welfare capitalism" movement as a whole was waning by the late 1920s, due to opposition by workers, and the Great Depression finished it off.[31] Employers expanded their use of company unions during the early 1930s, but such plans were declared illegal in 1935 by the Supreme Court for obstructing the right of workers to choose their own representation.[32]

"Scientific Cooperation"

A third tactic, here labeled "scientific cooperation," has greater covenantal value because it embodied the principle of self-representation in purer form. During the 1920s, unions and garment factories in Cleveland, Chicago, and elsewhere set up management-worker committees to establish production methods and standards. The most famous cooperative effort was that undertaken by skilled locomotive repair workers of the Baltimore & Ohio Railroad. These initiatives were promising from a covenantal perspective for two reasons. On the one hand, they offered an intendedly objective basis for cooperation. The joint arrangements centered upon shared standards for worker performance, reflecting the "Progressive" fever for efficiency which was sweeping the U.S. During the 1910s, the engineer Frederick W. Taylor won wide public notice with his proposal that work be reorganized scientifically in order to maximize production, and his ideas revolutionized U.S. industry.

On the other hand, "scientific cooperation" was undertaken on the assumption that the cooperation of workers was to be enlisted through their own organizations. These employers chose to recognize their unions as partners in achieving greater efficiency in the workplace.[33] It was not surprising then that some unions became enthusiastic about the idea, despite their early reservations about Taylor's ideas for reorganizing work. After World War I, the AFL formally endorsed Taylor's system for "scientific management" and attempted to cultivate an alliance with the engineers who were carrying out Taylor's program. According to one 1928 observer, "the most impressive change in the American labor movement since the War consists in the new emphasis on production. The old rough-and-ready trade unionism battled over the division of the product, whereas the new, suave, discreet unionism talks the language of the efficiency engineer and busies itself about ways and means of increasing output."[34]

Like the Rockefeller Plan, the experiments in "scientific cooperation" did not last. The reasons had to do primarily with external economic circumstances rather than the internal reservations of workers about any paternalism. The experiments had been sparked, in large part, as a tactic by already marginal Northern plants for competition against nonunionized shops in the South, and they folded as demand for textiles and clothing collapsed during the Great Depression.[35] And even though the programs were organized strictly through the cooperation of unions, they lost the support of the AFL during the 1930s. Nonetheless, the early experiments provided a template for the cooperation now sought by employers at the end of the twentieth century. They were an early manifestation of the principle of employee self-management, a third moral principle operative in the relationship between management and employees, but which did not become widely evident until well after World War II.

The concessions signaled by management were temporary, and folded under the pressure exerted by the Depression. In truth, neither side surrendered very much for very long. Nonetheless, the honeymoon of 1898–1904 and the paternalistic tactics which crested in the 1920s suggested a tentative but important break with the nineteenth-century legacy of coercion. These initiatives in cooperation foreshadowed a profound shift in the very nature of the freedom sought by employers and unionized workers, and this shift enhanced the prospect of covenantal relations.

CHAPTER 9

Two Measures of Progress in Covenant-Building

Covenantal analysis begins by seeking to explain "what is going on"; chapter 7 does so by suggesting that the nineteenth-century struggle between employers and workers was rooted in two conflicting moral principles. The next task is to explain why and how this struggle is covenantal. The observed conflict of moral principles needs to be accounted for by a normative theory of what it means to covenant. As suggested in chapter 3, there are two measures by which a relation can be known to be evolving in a covenantal direction. The first essential feature is that both parties move toward a shared "cause," to use H. Richard Niebuhr's term. The second, less prominent in Niebuhr's thought, is that both sides use gestures and tactics which bind the self as a means of shaping the thinking and action of the other. This chapter first explains these two measures, and then applies them. I will argue that the more cooperative strategies and tactics reported in the previous chapter presented both sides with a tentative but viable common cause, freedom in its positive sense, and that this freedom could be obtained through the use of self-obligating gestures by both sides.

A Shared Cause

H. Richard Niebuhr, entranced by the oneness of God, borrowed freely from the social psychology of G. H. Mead and from the philosophy of Josiah Royce to argue that all relations are "triadic."[1] Human agents evaluate the reliability and trustworthiness of each other relative to a "cause." This cause, however noble or ignoble, serves to anchor their confidence in something which is more reliable than the passing preferences of each other. It provides a frame for both parties to interpret and evaluate their relationship to each other. The first essential feature of a covenantal relationship is that the cause be shared by both parties, that responses of trust and loyalty appropriately focus upon a "tertium quid" which both parties to a relationship hold in common.

For Niebuhr, the cause shared by God with God's creatures is "creation." Creation loyalty for Niebuhr meant "loyalty to all [God's] creatures, respect for man, but not only for man; reverence for 'life,' but not only life, loyalty to being, to all that is God, and he is all in all."[2] The covenantal history outlined in the Bible offers no dearth of causes which can be subsumed to the broad cause of creation. The people of Israel were called to commit themselves to God's covenant as the basis for their social relationships, while Jesus commended the believers of the New Testament to value each other as members of the Kingdom of God. The visions of lovingkindness, justice, obedience, and shalom preached by the prophets and Jesus, and the love commended by Paul, all provide reference points that members of the believing community could interpret, respond to, and use to influence the behavior of each other.

Yet the transcendental grandeur of these causes is not easy to express within a relationship defined largely by the pressures of a market system, particularly where employers and workers were pitted against each other in a struggle for control of the wealth generated by their enterprises. Already by the end of the nineteenth century, it was unmistakably clear that business companies were instrumental associations, oriented by the intentions of their participants to generating products for consumers, and profits, wages, opportunities, and continuing employment for managers and workers. Employers and workers faced each other less as members of a community than as factions firmly oriented by their respective interests, needs, and work functions to value each other instrumentally. It therefore might be asked, on the basis of what shared value could both sides find each other trustworthy? What shared value might survive the relentless pressures of the market—and of each other?

Towards an expanded understanding of freedom?

During the nineteenth century, the tactics of both sides expressed mutually contradictory causes: employers wanted the unfettered freedom to define the conditions under which workers labored; workers wanted to be recognized as entitled to represent themselves collectively in determining the conditions under which they worked. Both sides sought to insulate themselves against the interference practiced by each other. As such, the tactics of both sides expressed an exceedingly narrow, "negative," or privative conception of freedom: as nothing more than immunity against interference. But during the first decades of the twentieth century, a profound shift occurred which brought both sides closer to a shared cause. The very nature of the freedom sought by employers and workers began to change in a covenantally more viable direction.

As the small enterprises of the nineteenth century suddenly and rapidly turned into the large business corporations of the twentieth, the negative or privative conception of freedom, as nothing more than immunity from influence, appeared incomplete if not obsolete. Businesses were becoming functionally integrated machines, where management and employees were increasingly dependent upon the capacity and willingness of each other to carry out their particular tasks. They needed more than noninterference from each other; they needed freedom in the positive sense of a capacity to reach their respective goals. Rather than simply prevent interference by each other, they needed to be able to shape the thinking and the action of those with whom their actions were tightly interconnected. In short, they needed to enlist the willing cooperation of each other as a means of securing their own interests, not just to do no more than frustrate the troublesome agency of each other.[3]

For two parties bound together in functional interdependence, the freedom of each party to achieve what it wants resides in being able to draw upon the willing collaboration of the other. The collaboration has to be willing because employees and management always retain considerable power to frustrate each other's intentions, no matter how strictly the rules of their engagement are drawn. Of course, freedom in the narrower sense, as simply immunity from interference, will always be needed wherever employers and workers are bound together in tightly interdependent systems of action. But in such organizations, this negative or privative view of freedom is simply not enough to explain how each party gets what it wants, and to explain what shared vision holds the two parties together.

The contrast between the narrower and broader conceptions of freedom surely is overdrawn or exaggerated; employers and workers always have needed some degree of cooperation from each other. Nevertheless, the enlarged idea of freedom was much more evident in the tactics reported in chapter 8 than in the cruder tactics described in chapter 6. The spurt of trade agreements signed during the "honeymoon" of 1898–1904 and the tactics of welfare capitalism in the 1910s and 1920s implied, however ambiguously, that employers and workers were seeking in some measure to enlist, rather than to frustrate, the agency of each other. These tactics brought both sides closer to the shared cause of empowering each other through cooperation, while moving them away from the mutually contradictory tactics of body-checking each other through sheer coercion and intimidation. The shift in tactics signaled that freedom had to be worked out within the relationship—by building some common ground rather than by suppressing the interests and initiatives of each other.

The freedom appropriate to functional interdependence?

Between the 1890s and the 1920s, Catholic and Protestant voices for a more Christian order in labor relations vigorously commended the idea of cooperation to management and workers. Their appeals have a wishful quality because they did not recognize how the increasingly functional interdependence between the two sides not only mandated but was bringing about the transformation of traditional hostilities. In his landmark 1891 encyclical *Rerum Novarum,* Pope Leo XIII analyzed the struggle as occurring between relatively fixed classes, "capital" and "labor."[4] While this analysis helped to focus attention upon one of the two main moral principles in the struggle—property rights—it failed to explain how and why the evolving structure of organizations increased the vulnerability of management and workers to each other, and thus rendered cooperation of some sort a practical necessity. Leo XIII asserted the interdependence of capital and labor as a moral imperative derived from a society of classes with mutual obligations, rather than observing it as a fact of life derived from the functional interdependencies created by large corporations. The lacuna in his thinking is not surprising, given the early date of the encyclical.

Early Protestant thought also endorsed cooperation, with only a slightly firmer grasp of the relevant organizational dynamics. In 1907 and 1912, Walter Rauschenbusch called for cooperation organized through publicly owned enterprises.[5] He saw cooperation principally as a moral antidote to the competition institutionalized in capitalism, acknowledging only briefly that "business is abandoning competition because it is inefficient, and larger and more powerful forms of association and teamwork are being worked out."[6] Still, in Protestant as well as Roman Catholic analyses it was not to become clear for decades how much the changing organizational shape of industry itself imposed upon management and workers the imperative of seeking accommodation with each other's wishes.

The strength of these early analyses lies more in their emphasis upon the triadic character of freedom. Both Leo XIII and Rauschenbusch argued powerfully, in very different ways, that unfettered economic freedom—in the negative sense of immunity from interference—is destructive if not ordered to the common good. This caution applies equally to the enlarged sense of freedom which management and workers began to realize at the beginning of the twentieth century. The willing collaboration sought by both sides has an element of intrinsic value (which will be explored in chapter 16), but it cannot be divorced from its value for the wider society. The power unleashed by genuine cooperation becomes destructive to the extent that such collaboration serves to harm rather than to help the "companions," as Niebuhr terms them, who environ the business enterprise—the communities, consumers, suppliers, and others whose well-being forms part of the common good.

At this point one might ask how the freedom to cooperate, so qualified, actually sustained as a shared cause. How do management and workers go about recruiting the willing collaboration of each other? How can they defuse the resistance and counterresistance they might present to each other? Here the history narrated in chapter 8 raises a second basic feature of covenantal relations to view.

Self-Obligating Gestures

During the "honeymoon" of 1898–1904, workers used trade agreements as an important means to elicit the cooperation, however partial and grudging, of management. On into the 1920s and 1930s, employers established company unions and welfare programs to secure, on their own terms, the cooperation of workers. What all these tactics had in common is that they expressed what might be termed "self-obligating" or "self-binding" gestures. Through trade agreements, management consented to recognize the interests most important to workers, while workers bound themselves to honor the prerogatives claimed by management. By establishing company unions, management implicitly acknowledged, however inadequately and temporarily, that it had some obligation to listen to its workers. Similarly, in adopting welfare programs, management bound itself to acknowledge, however tentatively, that the well-being of workers had some value beyond the sheer utility of their labor. Through these characteristically twentieth-century tactics, both sides sought to shape the behavior of the opponent indirectly by first binding themselves to fulfill commitments or promises of some sort. In contrast, the tactics of the nineteenth century aimed at binding the opponent directly.

From a covenantal point of view, tactics or gestures which bind the self are superior to those which seek to bind the other directly. Self-binding is the essential first move in covenant-making. After all, God's efforts to bind the people to true faith began with God's own assurances of fidelity. The classic biblical covenants were initiated by God's solemn promises, and sustained by the conviction that these divine promises would be fulfilled. H. Richard Niebuhr, in explaining how far the community of faith extends in loyalty to creation, explains the appropriate response as one of taking on obligation.

> Where through the restoration of trust all the conditions have been established for fidelity, there still fidelity is called for as an act of personal self-binding, of commitment. . . . The restoration of trust is in this fashion a most vigorous challenge to the will to believe, to the will to be faithful to the universal cause and to all our companions in it, whether we feel like it or not, in sickness, health, prosperity, adversity. It is the challenge to be faithful in all relations to all companions since God makes them his cause in all their relations.[7]

A basic distinction needs to be drawn between covenantal and non-covenantal uses of "self-binding," however. After all, a person might engage in punctilious self-binding behavior for the most nefarious ends. All economic actors, including manipulative employers and dishonest workers, can avail themselves of social scripts to extend promises and raise expectations about their behavior as a means of eliciting particular responses of trust from their victims. So used, gestures of self-binding work to destroy covenantal relations. The difference between genuine and deceptive self-binding turns upon what Robin Lovin calls "recognition": whether the two parties affirm, through their self-binding actions, that the principles acted upon by their antagonists express moral claims.[8]

Towards a moral equilibrium

Between 1894 and the 1920s, management and workers effectively obligated themselves to acknowledge and respect the moral principle most central to the action of each other. On the one side, the workers who organized themselves into unions were signing contracts which effectively bound them to respect the managerial prerogative claimed by their employers. On the other, the employers who established company unions moved towards respecting the right of self-representation claimed by their workers; those who embraced "scientific cooperation" did so even more decisively. It may not be too much of an exaggeration to suggest that management and workers were beginning to shade industrial relations with a tinge of covenantal love: they were binding themselves to care, however minimally, for the moral principle that was of importance to their respective opponents. Similarly, they were working towards justice as they attempted to work out an equilibrium between the principles of action central to each.

Of course, it is easy to overestimate the covenantal value of the company unions, welfare programs, and scientific cooperation. The concessions by management fell far short of the reckless, disinterested, and self-sacrificial love commended early in the twentieth century by idealists such as the young Reinhold Niebuhr. First, the aims of both sides were primarily self-interested. Even the most generous employers intended to enhance the survival and flourishing of their enterprises, while even the most cooperative workers negotiated trade agreements with the aim of improving their own economic positions. Second, their self-binding was frankly instrumental, and not necessarily oriented towards justice. It is likely that both sides chose to recognize the moral principle central to the action of each other less out of respect for the intrinsic worth of each other than in order to induce their antagonists to reciprocate. The reason workers were willing to sign trade agreements which recognized the prerogatives claimed by management is that they wanted to encourage management to acknowledge and respect their own right of representation. Similarly, the reason why employers organized company unions and welfare plans was to acknowledge and even internalize the principle of managerial prerogative as a guide for their actions. Nevertheless, this slender start provided an edge along which more significant gestures might be made. The essential point is that both sides began to deploy strategies and tactics which bound them to respect a moral principle important to the other party.

Mutual recognition

The pathway along which covenantal relations might grow is suggested by social ethicist Robin Lovin's explanation of how the covenantal polity of the Puritans differed from the classic social contract articulated by John Locke and embodied in founding U.S. documents. Members of a covenant society are enwebbed in relations of moral obligation; they identify themselves as members of a covenant by their willingness to take the claims made by each other seriously as moral arguments which compel attention. According to Lovin, covenant partners become equal when they are recognized as "independent centers of judgment" whose claims are met "out of regard for the justice of the claim and not from fear or coercion."[9] The social contract, in contrast, preserves individuals against interference in their pursuit of private goods. But it leaves them in a vast echoing moral solitude, where claims for justice are understood to be nothing more than interest claims, demands which must be accommodated to preserve social harmony by reducing threats to the well-being of others, but which have no deeper moral hold upon these other members of the society.

This distinction between social contract and covenant points to the growing edge of covenantal relations within business organizations. Obviously, self-interest, fear, and coercion played an important role in persuading management in the 1890s to consent to trade agreements, and in persuading millions of workers during the 1920s to accept company unions and paternalistic handouts. These motives never can be suspended in economic relations, so permeated by the forces of the market. Where management and workers obligated themselves to recognize the principles of representation and managerial prerogative on prudential grounds, simply in order to fend off the power of each other, love was present only in a minimal form. But their relations could grow more covenantal when and if the device of self-binding became filled with the dawning intentions of both sides to concede some degree of moral legitimacy—more than just prudential necessity—to the basic principles of action claimed by each other. It was this possibility which caught the imagination of Christian idealists in the early twentieth century, when they recommended that employers and workers cooperate. A few enlightened employers made firm steps towards the ideal when they bound themselves to honor the need of workers for a decent standard of living and to permit them to represent their interests and help determine the conditions under which they worked. Most of their efforts were quashed by the Great Depression and were not revived, but they exemplified the best which paternalistic relations could offer.

Conclusion

During the early twentieth century, management and workers discovered a potent device in the idea of self-obligation. Many employers experimented with tactics through which they bound themselves implicitly or contractually to respect the material needs of workers, and even to acknowledge the right to self-representation claimed by workers. The company unions, welfare programs, and scientific cooperation exemplified a self-binding which was tentative and flawed but which enabled employers to signal to workers that they acknowledged the moral principle of self-representation. Workers, for their part, also began signing trade agreements that committed them to honor the principle of managerial prerogative. These tactics moved both sides towards the expanded notion of freedom outlined in the first half of this chapter. In essence, each side could achieve the freedom it desired—that of achieving its goals—only by confirming and respecting the moral principle central to the action of the other. Simply isolating themselves from the influence of each other was no longer (if it ever was) a viable tactic. The century-long struggle had demonstrated with unmistakable clarity that both sides had the power to frustrate each other's aims in the tightly linked world of functionally integrated actions, and these capacities were increasing. The route to satisfying their respective economic interests lay in securing the cooperation of each other.

A covenantal ethic enjoins management and employees to express lovingkindness and justice in the tactics they apply to each other. This chapter has drawn from the early twentieth-century history of labor relations a minimal but vital content to such love: the idea that both sides respect the moral principle central to each other's actions. Similarly, they ought to aim at a kind of justice defined as an equilibrium between these principles. To go further is difficult; just how difficult is illustrated by the thinking of Reinhold Niebuhr, who more than any other figure has shaped how ethicists conceive of the struggle among collective economic actors. The difficulty he had in prescribing love is taken up in the next chapter.

PART 3

The Contractual Basis of Covenanting

CHAPTER 10

Reinhold Niebuhr and the Difficulty of Prescribing Covenantal Love in Industrial Settings

What shape can covenantal love take in the resistance and counter-resistance practiced by management and employees against each other? It has been strikingly difficult for ethicists to explain how love ought to be manifested in impersonal institutional spheres without moving quickly to recommend a justice of balanced interests enforced by legitimate coercion. There exists no widely shared conception of how individuals, let alone management or employees as collectivities, might put covenantal love and fidelity into practice through self-obligating tactics.

This difficulty is due, in no small measure, to the way in which Reinhold Niebuhr construed the problem of collective struggle between management and workers. He observed the strife of the 1920s and 1930s with the deepening conviction that capital and labor were social classes engaged in fundamental conflict over the distribution of wealth. His early response was to press upon the wealthy classes a high moral ideal—Christian love. But by 1930 he abandoned this prescription. Instead, he bequeathed to Christian political economy in the U.S. a powerful and enduring prescription for "realism"—a vision of management and employees as self-interested, contending economic agents whose struggle should be bent toward justice by the countervailing power of each other and the state. This model remains a powerful tool for explaining and appraising the clash between collectivities. As Niebuhr argued so forcefully, collectivities never can achieve the sensitivity and self-sacrifice of individuals. Yet such realism caused Niebuhr to overlook the ways in which management and employees can and do bind themselves in such a way as to moderate the clash of collective "egotisms," as he put it. This chapter explores this blind spot in Niebuhr's thinking in order to suggest that a covenantal ethic can be realistic without tarring the contractual relations between management and workers as nothing but an accommodation to the power of self-interest.

The Early Niebuhr on Heroic Self-Sacrifice

In 1920, Niebuhr entered the debate about the "industrial crisis" on high prophetic ground, by proposing self-binding gestures of the most radical degree. He recommended that the church advise its wealthy members—including, presumably, owners and management—to sacrifice "many privileges and rights" so that the "democratization of industry" and the "socialization of property" might be achieved.[1]

> If the church is true to its gospel it will appeal not to the prudent self-interest but to the unselfish instincts of the holding classes and will emphasize that there can be no social salvation without sacrifice, without a love that is willing to sacrifice not merely surpluses of wealth but the very economic power by which inequitable surpluses are created.[2]

This radical prescription was not implausible during the 1920s, the heyday of welfare capitalism. Examples of extraordinary moral energy by Christian or humanitarian employers were widely known. For example, one dramatic gesture hastened the collapse of the Rockefeller Plan described in the previous chapter. In 1928, the heiress Josephine Roche liquidated her fortune and used the proceeds to gain control of the second largest mining company in Colorado. Then she invited the United Mine Workers to organize the workers, and this gave the union a first firm foothold in the state. It was this union that miners of the Colorado Fuel and Iron Company eagerly joined, causing the collapse of the Rockefeller Plan.[3]

Niebuhr could have developed his call for sharing wealth by citing such moral heroes. While there is no evidence he was aware of Josephine Roche, there is strong evidence that he must have known of other successful and laudable experiments through the efforts of his mentor and friend Sherwood Eddy. Eddy took Niebuhr along on study tours of Europe during the mid-1920s.[4] In a 1927 book, Eddy celebrated the efforts of four British and American employers who created robustly successful enterprises by either sharing their wealth with workers or by sacrificing their absolute right to manage in favor of more cooperative schemes of management.[5] In 1916, for example, Arthur Nash of Cincinnati bought a small, struggling garment sweatshop, raised the wages and shared stock dividends with workers, and the company ballooned from 29 to 6,000 workers within ten years. Nash so vehemently opposed the open shop and American Plan movements by employers that he invited the Amalgamated Clothing Workers of America to organize his factories and collaborate in management, as an experiment in "scientific cooperation."[6]

Niebuhr mentioned Nash and another of Eddy's heroes when reviewing a published symposium of speeches by business leaders.[7] But he evidently chose not to celebrate such robust incarnations of Christian love by owners or managers in his own writings. Presumably they still relied too much upon the principle of managerial prerogative—which he otherwise saw abused as the "autocracy" exercised by Henry Ford and other tyrannical employers. Instead, Niebuhr tilted sharply toward the principle of worker self-representation. From 1920 on, he consistently demanded that workers be given—or take—a voice in running their companies. For example, when in 1920 he encouraged the wealthy to give up their privileges, he argued that it would not do simply to encourage "individual business men to adopt a more benevolent attitude toward their workingmen." "Democracy in industry must be guaranteed by something better than the capricious benevolences of individual employers."[8] He already had rejected the early liberal idea that the church ought to serve as a "moral umpire" between employers and workers, in favor of a more partisan advocacy of justice. He joined Sherwood Eddy's "Federation for a Christian Social Order," and began championing the interests of workers.[9] By 1926, he was challenging Henry Ford to exercise his immense, if already declining, power responsibly by conceding some control over the workplace to workers.[10] And by the 1930s, he argued that the right to hold private property had lost its social function altogether, and that the ownership of productive industrial property therefore ought to be socialized.[11]

Niebuhr's Turn to "Realism" in Labor Relations

Much has been made of Niebuhr's transition from a moral idealism to a political realism. During the 1920s, he celebrated the latent social potency of love; during the 1930s, he acknowledged the inevitability and necessity of struggle among interest groups, where the principle of worker self-representation had to be beefed up to counter managerial "autocracy." Christian love, as an ideal to which historical actors might bind themselves, slipped to the background in Niebuhr's occasional articles about labor relations. By 1933 he was sneering at idealistic liberals who, like himself thirteen years earlier, thought that property-owning elites might be educated to yield up their privileges. Instead, Niebuhr envisioned "a strong political labor movement, expressing itself in socialist terms," engaged in "dislodging" the "dominant groups" of capitalism.[12] Even after the 1930s, he interpreted the continuing struggle between management and labor strictly through the "realism" of power politics. In a fascinating 1953 exchange with Quaker economist Kenneth Boulding, who argued that market forces alone would suffice to destroy concentrations of employer power, Niebuhr firmly defended large labor unions and the use of coercive state power to achieve and defend justice. "Justice in a technical society requires that the centralization of power inherent in the industrial process be matched by collective social power."[13] It should be noted that Niebuhr devoted only a tiny fraction of his life's output to this issue; indeed, his interest in the question seems to have peaked in 1927. But from the few articles he published subsequently, it is clear that he failed to hold management and workers to the idealism he voiced so vigorously in the 1920s.

This transition from idealism to realism no doubt had much to do with the moral value of worker self-representation. But it also appears to have been driven by his increasingly pessimistic estimate of moral capacities of both management and employees. Observing the gritty strife between the Detroit automakers and their workers during the 1920s, he saw both sides enmired in a moral mediocrity which apparently rendered the ideal of self-obligating neighbor-love far beyond reach. On the one side, Niebuhr repeatedly attacked the self-deluding "humanitarianism" of Henry Ford, who abandoned his workers to underemployment, unemployment, and poverty as sales of the Model T floundered during the mid-1920s.[14] On the other side, Niebuhr sounded a warning about young workers who were being lulled by "material comforts" into frittering their creative energies away in "sensual excess" rather than engaging in a "rebellious heroism."[15] And he expressed a bemused contempt for the established trade unions, which were too complacent to struggle for any justice extending beyond their narrow self-interest.[16] Perhaps it was the growing power of labor unions in the 1930s that reminded Niebuhr that any group organized around a collective interest tends to demand more than its share and to sink to the lowest common denominator of self-centeredness. Perhaps his idealism was silenced by the power of collective egotisms which he witnessed during the 1920s and 1930s. Whatever the reason, he no longer felt able to call upon management or workers to bind themselves to anything more immediate than the pursuit of their own interest, narrowly conceived.

The Curable Error of Niebuhr's Realism

There is prophetic bite in Niebuhr's turn to realism regarding the "labor question." He steadfastly defended the right of workers to represent their interests collectively against the managerial interests which always have been ranged so powerfully against workplace democracy. He recognized that the much vaunted "freedom" of the marketplace reinforced existing inequalities of power, and so endorsed the use of state power to force recalcitrant management to yield up despotic control. Yet despite the power of these insights, Niebuhr's realism also expressed a significant liability. It was simply blind to the ways in which love might be expressed in industrial settings. The problem is that his emphasis upon the coercive power of interest groups and the state tended to obscure the role and importance of self-binding as a device through which management and employees already were inducing each other to cooperate through the negotiation and informal enforcement of contracts. From the 1930s at least through the 1960s, this "collective bargaining" proved the principal means both parties used to shape the expectations and behavior of each other. What was needed was for Niebuhr to explain what exactly management and employees ought to bind themselves to, as a condition for negotiating covenantally viable contracts. Put more puckishly, what was needed was for Niebuhr to prescribe industrial-strength love.

Niebuhr's systematic ethical treatises provide resources for prescribing an understanding of Christian love keyed to industrial conflict. Both *An Interpretation of Christian Ethics* (1935) and the second volume of the *The Nature and Destiny of Man* (1943) make ample room for love in explaining how divine grace operates in history. In the first, Niebuhr defined love as "the obligation of affirming the life and interests of the neighbour as much as those of the self"; in the second, he defined it more stringently as "agape," a disinterested and self-sacrificing love for neighbor.[17] Surely the contest between the moral principles of employee self-representation and managerial prerogative provides an explicit content to this sense of "obligation" commended by Niebuhr. The management and employees of his day could "affirm the life and interests of the neighbor as of the self" most obviously by binding themselves to respect the moral principle most central to the action of each other. Indeed, the two-century-long struggle between management and workers can be read as an extended campaign by each side to force the other to recognize its central moral principle.

Here Niebuhr's own uncompromising allegiance to the principle of worker representation needs to be seen as a moral blind spot as well as a prophetic truth. He was right to insist that management recognize the "democracy" sought by workers, but he failed to consider the obverse side of the coin: what degree of respect employees owed to the right of managerial prerogative. Of course, the Niebuhr of the 1920s and 1930s likely would have scorned the idea that workers ought to concede any moral legitimacy to the mantle of authority claimed so pretentiously by the Henry Fords who inflicted such arbitrary suffering upon their employees. Yet by not paying attention to the claims of both sides, Niebuhr was not likely to see any potential for love to find expression through the concessions each side might make to the other. Because he so single-mindedly endorsed democracy for workers, he was unable to appreciate how both management and employees were beginning to bind themselves as a means of inducing each other to cooperate rather than simply rely upon the coercive power of the state.

Contracts and industrial-strength love

What was needed was for Niebuhr to identify some effective device through which management and employees might make the self-binding gestures needed to conciliate their differences, and then for him to commend this device to both sides as a vehicle for expressing Christian love. The best candidate for such a device was the trade agreement, or labor contract, negotiated by management and employees through collective bargaining. As will be seen in the next chapter, the great strikes and the Wagner Act of the 1930s established collective bargaining as the basis of the relationship between management and employees. These contracts provided the principal vehicle for management and employees to negotiate practical compromises between the principles of managerial prerogative and worker representation. Management negotiated and signed contracts which obligated it to recognize unions, to respect the right of employees to represent themselves. The same contracts obligated employees to respect the right of management to operate their enterprises as they saw fit.

Of course, the contracts succeeded largely because they were backed by the power of the state. Niebuhr's emphasis upon coercion as a tool of justice was and remains important. Yet these contracts also provided an opening wedge for both sides to shape the action and thinking of each other while holding coercion in abeyance. Through contracts, parties bind themselves as a means of inducing each other to cooperate. It is this feature of contracts that provides an opening for the ideal of Christian love. Niebuhr from his high prophetic vantage point saw the freedom conferred through contracts to be corrosive of social relations.[18] This coin has another side, however. Contracts are constructed of commitments which both sides make as a means of demonstrating their reliability to each other. Precisely drawn stipulations are nourished by the ongoing gestures made by each side to demonstrate their good faith and uphold the contract. The basic device of self-binding provides a growing edge for relations between management and employees, a growing edge for the covenantal values of lovingkindness, justice, and wholeness. Contractual relations always offer each side the opportunity to engage in self-sacrificial behavior which will elicit and reinforce the trust of the other side.

Resources within Niebuhr's Realism

Niebuhr's later systematic accounts of how divine grace operates in history can support a generous but demanding love ethic in the modern business corporation, even if Niebuhr did not exploit the implications of his own thinking. In *An Interpretation of Christian Ethics* and *The Nature and Destiny of Man,* Niebuhr envisaged love as an integral part of historical processes and celebrated its potency. On the one side, he argued that the search for justice is the engine of love. The proximate achievements of justice open up an ever-expanding wedge of expectations, luring social actors onward to greater achievements in justice and "brotherhood." The "rules of justice" serve the cause of brotherhood insofar as they "extend the sense of obligation towards the other."[19] On the other side, the unbounded transcendent aspirations of love serve to expand conceptions of what justice is. Love serves to invigorate and enlarge the range of social relations by enlarging ideas of what treatment is due to previously exploited members. Niebuhr's own polemics incarnated such love as when, for example, he insisted that Henry Ford elevate his estimate of workers as disposable resources. Of course, the more extravagant demands of love may appear unjustifiable when seen from "within" the narrow claims and counterclaims of historical actors, but for Niebuhr love remained "a resource for infinite developments towards a more perfect brotherhood in history," that is, an "uncoerced and perfect mutuality."[20]

The covenantal norms of justice, lovingkindness, and wholeness offer a potent vision of harmonious social relations. This vision serves both to endorse and to relativize any given level of historical achievement in labor relations, as is very easy to do with the modest accomplishments of the early twentieth-century management and workers. But it also helps account for the halting movement towards mutual recognition by both sides, a movement which unfortunately appeared insignificant from within Niebuhr's conflictual view of social relations. As management and employees began to bind themselves to contracts collectively negotiated, they opened up the possibility that the recognition afforded to each other might deepen over time into a more extended acknowledgment of rights and obligations. As Niebuhr himself argues, there are no predetermined limits to how far a "sense of obligation" might be extended.[21]

The self-obligating gestures that management and employees extend to each other in the making of contracts are obviously risky. They establish a kind of predictability which unscrupulous antagonists easily might take advantage of. Moreover, such gestures may be misplaced or shortsighted when they extend farther than an uneasy history of suspicion warrants. Niebuhr was only too aware of the vulnerability of workers and therefore insisted upon the coercive power of the state to back their just demands. Yet as Niebuhr himself argues in *The Nature and Destiny of Man,* risky gestures which may not be reciprocated are needed to sustain the mutuality of social relations at every step against the distorted, partial, self-serving interpretations enforced by recalcitrant contractual partners. Such risky love is conveyed through the everyday gestures expressed by ordinary people in the continuous work of signaling their intent not to transgress the limits of the relations to which they have bound themselves.

Conclusion

Reinhold Niebuhr's occasional writings about labor issues are tinged by a realist pessimism. Unpersuaded that owners and managers might voluntarily obligate themselves to recognize the collective power of employees, he championed the principle of worker self-representation as an appropriate counterweight to managerial "autocracy" of the kind exercised by Henry Ford. But he underestimated the potential of devices such as collective bargaining and contracts to serve as vehicles for expressing industrial-strength love, a means through which both sides might recognize the moral principles basic to the action of each other.

By the 1930s, the mechanism of contracts negotiated bilaterally by management and employees was offering an edge along which increasingly covenantal relations might grow. The next chapter catalogues the tactics through which such collective bargaining was established during the 1930s and 1940s—and the subsequent tactics of both sides which have served to undermine it.

CHAPTER 11

The 1930s through the 1950s: From Hard Confrontations to Hard Bargaining

For almost a half-century, from the mid-1930s to 1980, a truce obtained between management and employees in the U.S. The truce often was violated, and in some industries never even was instituted. Yet it channeled much of the conflictual energies of management and employees into negotiating and sustaining contractual relations with each other. The signal event which initiated this era was congressional passage of the Wagner Act in 1935, a law which gave employees significant legal protections against the antiunion tactics of management. Empowered by the Wagner Act, unions organized fully one-third of U.S. workers in the private sector by the mid-1950s.

It would be an exaggeration to suggest that the historic conflict between management and employees was tamed by the procedural fairness of collective bargaining mandated by the Wagner Act. To be sure, the expanding U.S. economy between the late 1940s and the 1970s permitted as much stability as there is ever likely to be in the relations of employees and management. While the system of collective bargaining was largely successful in providing a basis for cooperation, it was challenged and undermined by both sides. This chapter outlines some of the coercive tactics used by management and employees during the years of transition and during the era of collective bargaining. These tactics demonstrate both the value and the fragility of contractual relations and raise the question of what, if any, place coercion has in constructing covenantal relations, an issue taken up thematically in the next chapter.

1930s: Illegal Tactics by Both Sides

The Depression which began in 1929 shattered public support for business and reduced the struggle between management and employees to the elemental terms of the late nineteenth century. In 1933, a first wave of unrest swept the steel, automobile, and other industries, according to labor partisan Irving Bernstein, whose lengthy and celebratory narrative provides the principal resource for the following discussion.[1] Workers united in striking and organizing; management responded with coercive measures of its own. The significant victories were won by workers. For example, three of the most notable prolonged, bloody, and successful strikes served to install collective bargaining in Toledo, Ohio, end the era of the open shop in Minneapolis, and give longshoremen the legal right to control hiring in San Francisco.[2]

In contrast to the previous century, management lost ground on the legal front as well. President Franklin D. Roosevelt's 1933 National Industrial Recovery Act (NIRA) had permitted employers as well as workers to organize collectively, to set up associations and company unions. But the NIRA soon was struck down by the Supreme Court. The 1935 Wagner Act, the successor to NIRA, denied legal protection to collective associations of employers, offering it only to employees and their unions. After a two-year firestorm of legal challenges by management, the Wagner Act became effective and served to redefine the terrain of conflict between management and employees. The Act mandated that management and employees resolve their conflicts through collective bargaining, that is, through negotiations between representatives of the company in the person of its management, and employees in the person of their unions. The Act forbade management from interfering with the efforts of employees to organize unions, whether by harassing, discharging, blacklisting, or refusing to negotiate with them. At one stroke, the Act rendered illegal or moot many of the intimidating, manipulative, and simply coercive tactics used by management to break strikes and suppress unions.

The Wagner Act backed the principle of representation with the power of federal law enforcement. Not surprisingly, the power of that enforcement was challenged by the illegal tactics of management, while the property rights of management were violated by employees. On the one side, management stonewalled efforts by employees to institute collective bargaining. The tactic most notorious among labor historians was the "Mohawk Valley formula," devised by James R. Rand of the Remington Rand Corporation of New York in response to a 1936 strike against six company factories. The formula was a dramatic script for a public relations campaign to defeat a union by appealing to public fear, or, in Irving Bernstein's phrase, "the mobilization of local community sentiment and power against the strike."[3] It included the following sequence of steps: disseminating propaganda against the strikers; mobilizing the community against anticipated violence by appealing to "law and order"; staging a mass meeting to rally public support; assembling law-enforcement officials to intimidate the strikers; inducing loyal employees to stage a reopening of the plant; dramatizing the reopening with police protection and a flag-raising; and disseminating propaganda to the effect that the plant was now open, operated by those employees who believe in the sacred "right to work." The formula assaulted the employees' right of self-representation powerfully, if indirectly, by whipping up public fear, often fear of communism. According to Bernstein, the formula was used most effectively by Bethlehem Steel in 1937. And even though it was judged illegal by the National Labor Relations Board in the same year, it was further used by management in Iowa and Philadelphia in 1938.[4] Indeed, elements of the formula were used as recently as 1981 to defeat the efforts of nurses at a Vermont hospital to organize a union.[5]

Workers, for their part, also refined their tactics by going outside the law. In essence, they attacked the principle of managerial prerogative at its core by refusing to honor management's property rights. The most egregious example occurred in Flint, Michigan, late in 1936. Striking General Motors employees occupied key automotive manufacturing plants. When a month of negotiations failed to dislodge them, the General Motors management obtained a court injunction—which the strikers simply refused to obey. Michigan Governor Frank Murphy, a devout Catholic committed to the humanism of Jacques Maritain, refused to send in troops. In effect, the employees held General Motors and the state of Michigan hostage to the threat of a bloodbath, and won. Moreover, they used this leverage to press for a more ambitious aim: the "exclusive representation" which General Motors was loathe to concede. Within weeks, General Motors acknowledged the United Auto Workers as the sole union authorized to represent the employees.[6]

A related tactic was less risky for workers and just as effective. During a 1933 strike at the Hormel Company in Austin, Minnesota, employees pioneered the "sit-down" strike. They remained at their workstations but simply refused to operate their machines. The tactic spread rapidly. Labor journalist Kim Moody credits the tactics of the sit-down for causing union membership nationwide to double, from 3.7 million to 8.3 million by 1938.[7] Through such strikes, employees dared management to remove them by force. Not surprisingly, sit-down strikes were outlawed by the Supreme Court in 1939.[8]

The Covenantal Value of Coercion

From a covenantal point of view, such tactics by management and workers obviously represent the antithesis of self-obligating gestures—gestures which serve to inspire confidence by acknowledging the claims of one's antagonist. The strikes in support of unions often involved enormous sacrifices and heroic actions by workers and their families. Yet the sacrifices were not gestures which could serve to obligate management, for they defied rather than acknowledged the principle most important to employers: that of managerial prerogative anchored in property rights exercised on behalf of company stockholders.

Given that era of bare-knuckled conflict, however, it might be asked what would have constituted a reasonable confidence-building gesture or, more pointedly, whether one party is obliged to offer self-binding gestures when the other is unlikely to reciprocate. On the side of management, a sterling example was provided by the surprise 1937 decision by Myron Taylor, head of United States Steel, to recognize the principle of worker self-representation in spirit and letter. In what became known as the "Myron Taylor formula for industrial peace," he wrote:

> The Company recognizes the right of its employees to bargain collectively through representatives freely chosen by them without dictation, coercion or intimidation in any form or from any source. It will negotiate and contract with the representatives of any group of its employees so chosen. . . .

This gracious gesture was so unusual for its time that historian Irving Bernstein devotes four pages to wondering what might have prompted it.[9]

On the side of workers, such unilateral disarmament was not in evidence, nor perhaps feasible as a tactic. The vulnerability of workers appears to have been the chief fact of moral significance. In the late 1930s, argues contemporary labor scholar Rick Fantasia, employees seeking to organize unions faced not only the prospect of being displaced by "scabs" or replacement workers hired to operate the plant while strikers demonstrated outside; they also faced a network of spies hired to single out union organizers for punishment or discharge. In 1938, a Senate hearing was told that management was spending $80 million per year for espionage services. A union account of the era asserted that employers had hired 237 detective agencies to infiltrate their plants with the staggering total of 100,000 spies.[10] One journalist at the time argued that the odds simply were stacked badly against workers:

> [Workers] had their eyes opened wide. They saw that the only thing that counted was what they did for themselves. Even [the Wagner Act] was of no importance unless they made its terms and promises valid by their own enforced demands. The "system" would find a way to cheat and circumvent. . . . Nothing short of greater power and force, concentrated, organized and led, can possibly break this ancient rule of privilege, intrenched [sic], rich, able.[11]

Against the rough tactics of management, sit-down strikes had covenantal value in that they enabled employees to solve at least three problems without resorting to violence. The sit-down strike enabled strikers to insulate their leaders against spies, to deny replacement workers access to factory machinery, and to discourage violent assaults by troops—all while damaging the income, but not the property, of employers. As such, it implied a minimal acknowledgment of the property rights, if not the managerial prerogative, of employers.

Management-Worker Relations Become Contractual

World War II imposed a brief moratorium on the conflict which had raged so freely during the 1930s. Under pressure to maintain war production, management agreed to suspend its tactics for keeping unions out. Unions were granted access to organize plants, where they quickly became entrenched—unlike in World War I, where the cooperation of workers was channeled only through company unions and faded after the Armistice. By the end of World War II, it was clear that unions could neither be ignored nor easily ousted from their industrial plants. In 1946, the largest spasm of strikes in U.S.

history induced management to abandon rather than renew the antiunion tactics that had proven effective before the war.[12] Instead, it resolved to accept the "collective bargaining" mandated by the Wagner Act as the basic device for regulating its relationship with employees already unionized, and dug in for hard bargaining.

The most aggressive policy was developed at the General Electric Company. In the late 1940s, marketing expert Lemuel R. Boulware initiated a campaign to undercut the appeal of unions through the techniques of advertising and mass persuasion. Dubbed "Boulwarism," the tactic involved saturating employees and their communities with propaganda impugning the sincerity or usefulness of unions to their members; expressing interest in employees and responding assiduously to their questions about unions; indoctrinating every executive and worker with twelve hours of instruction in "How Our Business System Operates"—and then taking a hard line by presenting the union with nonnegotiable wage offers.[13] Yet despite such hard tactics, the principle of representation triumphed. By 1958, 15 million workers, or fully 38 percent of the workforce in the private sector, were unionized, including two-thirds of blue-collar workers.[14]

The tactics of workers once unionized shifted to negotiating trade agreements, often under the threat of a strike. By 1956, 125,000 agreements were in force.[15] These contracts were enforced by employees using a "grievance" procedure. Grievances are formal claims that the management-union contract has been violated. These claims could be filed by the union, with four to six levels of appeal through the company hierarchy, culminating with judgments rendered by arbitrators, professionals trained for the work of labor negotiation.[16] During the 1950s, more than 100,000 grievances reached this final step annually.[17] The arbitrators rapidly established a body of law which held management and employees accountable to the norms of impartial, nondiscriminatory reasonableness.

The Covenantal Advantages of Collective Contracting

In principle, the idea of bilateral bargaining and neutral adjudication has much covenantal value in establishing a firm basis for regulating the convergence or collision of interests of management and employees. The federally mandated framework for negotiation organized adversarial discussions around points of agreement as well as of difference. It bound management and employees to commit themselves to respect the principles of self-representation and managerial prerogative, respectively. As such, collective bargaining gave both sides a stable channel for eliciting predictable and reliable behavior from each other. Business scholar James Kuhn, writing in 1961, praised the system: "A system of 'laws' replaces the arbitrary decisions of individuals, and an orderly appeal to reason replaces the disruptive use of force and coercion in disputes."[18] A massive, management-oriented study of collective bargaining published in 1958 by eminent labor scholars Sumner H. Slichter, James J. Healy, and E. Robert Livernash asserted that this "rule of law" greatly improved upon traditional managerial methods for promoting and disciplining employees.[19]

Given the tarnished history of conflict between management and employees, a system of steps intended to protect fairness of procedure appears indispensable to covenantal relations. It is hard to imagine how the rights of employees, particularly the right of self-representation, could be articulated and preserved without a judicial process of the sort which has been found sound and necessary over centuries of Western legal development.

From the point of view of management, collective bargaining was hardly a neutral judicial procedure; its advent reflected a decisive shift of power towards bureaucracies of adjudication where unions enjoyed considerable influence, and so presented a challenge to the principle of managerial prerogative. "American managements must conduct their operations within an elaborate framework of rules and policies imposed by collective agreements and trade unions."[20] To be sure, in decisions handed down by arbitrators (the final step in the grievance procedure), management in the 1950s legally retained the "unrestricted" or "absolute" right to manage in matters not covered by union contract. These included the legal right to hire, lay off, or reassign employees; to change job standards, work schedules, and to require overtime; to determine what is produced, where, when, and how fast; and to make rules to maximize efficiency.[21] Nevertheless, already by 1958 unions had gained considerable power to shape decisions about: which employees would be laid off (via seniority); how long the work week would be; who would be promoted; how work would be scheduled and assigned; and when subcontractors would be used.[22] And of course workers were winning steady increases in wages and benefits all the while.[23] In effect, unionized workers began to achieve a considerable degree of control over the conditions of their work, at the expense of managerial prerogative.

Nonetheless the efforts by workers to institute collective bargaining appear to have conformed more closely to the covenantal model than did the evasive tactics of management. After all, the aim of collective bargaining was, and remains, to draw management into sharing the power to administer relations of mutual obligation, while the aim of management, certainly as illustrated by "Boulwarism" at General Electric, the "Mohawk Valley Formula" at Remington Rand, and other such strategies was to retain unilateral control over workplace relations.

Further, there is a deep resonance between the contractual form sought by unions and the covenantal form presented in the Bible. Both devices share the same basic relational form, in that both rely in the first instance upon the self-binding of both parties. Like a covenant, a contract comes into being as one party sets boundaries upon its behavior as a means of eliciting the commitments it desires from the other party. Workers agree to abide by the rules stipulated by management as a condition for receiving pay; management agrees to abide by contractual conditions as a means of securing the compliance of employees. In short, both contracts and covenants are founded upon promises, promises which are used to draw the other into the relationship. Both affirm, in principle, that the appropriate means to elicit the self-binding of others is to bind oneself, specifically, to the nature of the sanctions one will undergo if failing to perform the specified stipulations.

The Covenantal Liabilities of Collective Contracting

Because it is fundamentally similar to a covenant, a contract depends for its viability upon the quality of will of management and employees. This viability turns in part on external factors, to be sure, but to a large extent upon the readiness of management and employees to accept the rewards and sanctions they formally have agreed to, to internalize that willingness as a commitment which they can rely upon in each other. The mere existence of a contract does not mean it will not be violated, and being hedged about with sanctions does not guarantee that a contract will elicit the compliance of both sides. The U.S. economy between the late 1940s and the 1970s permitted as much stability as there is ever likely to be in the relations of employees and management. Even so, the system of collective bargaining, while largely successful in providing a basis for cooperation, was challenged and undermined by both sides.

As collective bargaining developed into a legal framework for resolving disputes, the system began displaying covenantal liabilities. First, it enabled unions to impose arbitrary demands upon management, such as "make-work" rules which drove up the cost of doing business and fueled managerial cynicism about unions.[24] From management's point of view, collective bargaining imposed costs measurable in terms of time and decreased flexibility. Second, collective bargaining fostered a bureaucratic approach to resolving conflict, which proved to be a mixed blessing. Fairness was leached from the grievance process as the lumbering machinery bogged down management and employees in time-consuming processes of adjudication. And as rule upon rule was instituted in order to assure fair procedures, even well-meaning unions and management were tripped up by the complexity of their relations. They coped with each new problem by making a new contractual rule, which resulted in lengthy, rigid, endlessly detailed contracts that smothered spontaneous problem-solving on the shop floor. Such legalism moved management and employees away from, rather than towards, the internalized sharing of values which is essential to covenantal relations.

Fractional bargaining and wildcat strikes

Third, collective bargaining generated a new locus of conflict: between employees and their unions. During the 1940s and 1950s, employees began to chafe under the bureaucratic weight of what derisively has been termed "business unionism." Business unionism resulted from the tendency of union officials to centralize power in hierarchies of their own making, where they concerned themselves only with negotiating contracts rather than with broadening their representation (to include other workers) or deepening it (to foster genuine democracy).

This intramural conflict had deep roots. The American Federation of Labor from its start in the 1880s incarnated the principle of representation to only a very narrow breadth. It represented only skilled workers of particular trades, a fact of signal importance since the AFL by the mid-1930s represented almost 85 percent of unionized workers.[25] The AFL effectively excluded not only millions of unskilled workers but its constituent unions discouraged white female and African-American workers of both sexes from joining or organizing unions.[26] In 1935, several large unions broke away from the AFL to form the Congress of Industrial Organizations, which sought to organize all unskilled workers on a democratic basis. But unions of the CIO, while more free of bias, still succumbed to the bureaucratic tendencies of "business unionism," effectively disenfranchising member workers from influencing union policies.[27] Contract negotiations tended to pit large industries against large unions, or large local unions against large corporations, encouraging the development of autocratic union leadership and squeezing out democratic initiatives from the shop floor. Bargaining which was massively collective offered workers little individual voice.

As rifts opened up between the union officials and their members, workers engaged in what James Kuhn terms "fractional" bargaining. Fractional bargaining includes all those tactics applied by employees, individually or in groups, aimed at exerting control in a manner not sanctioned or intended by their contracts. A large range of tactics was available to employees dissatisfied with their contracts with management, or with their union representatives.[28] At the least confrontational end of the scale, employees might catch the attention of management by flooding the system with nuisance grievances, or insisting upon a strict and literal interpretation of contract rules. Such tactics, used with or without the blessing of the union, technically remained within the confines of the contract. More deviously, employees might organize "slowdowns," in which they decreased production covertly for no reason discoverable to management.[29] The slowdown long has been recognized as the classic tactic of individual and group resistance. The incidence of slowdowns is difficult to count, but some sociologists, fascinated by the tactic, periodically report that it is alive and well.[30] Such nonconfrontational tactics could be used to force foremen and supervisors to engage in negotiations with workgroups, or even to cultivate covert alliances with them, in conflict with the wishes of more senior managers and union officials.

At the other end of the scale, employees could use more confrontational tactics, in particular the "wildcat" strike. Wildcats are strikes called by employees in violation of contracts they have signed with management. The tactic was common during World War II; almost 5,000 such strikes occurred during 1944 alone, according to Moody.[31] While less frequent during the 1950s, the number of wildcats increased during the decade of social upheaval, from 1,000 per year in 1960 to 2,000 in 1969.[32] The 1960s and 1970s were punctuated by the struggles of dissident steelworkers, coalminers, and others to regain control of their unions from corrupt leaders.

These struggles suggest that some kinds of fractional bargaining could have some covenantal value, by providing a kind of representation which is discouraged by collective bargaining. The 1930s model of collective bargaining was designed to bring together large unions and management in large industries; its machinery made no room for dealing with internal corruption by instituting a level of organization intermediate between workers and local unions dominated by centralized national unions. One level of needed representation is that of the workgroup, whose significance for shaping tactics has been grasped far more thoroughly in recent years by management than by unions committed exclusively to the collective bargaining system. No tactics for enlisting whole workgroups appear to have been adopted widely by unions as management began to devise workgroup-centered tactics of their own during the 1980s.

Conclusion

During the 1930s, unions struggled desperately to bring management to the bargaining table and to hammer out advantageous contracts; management struggled just as hard to avoid collective bargaining and minimize its concessions. A truce was achieved during the boom years following World War II, resulting in a "social contract" which provided employees with unprecedented income and security.[33] This strategy was administered by large corporate, union, and government bureaucracies, which processed and adjudicated the claims of management and employees against each other. But while the conflict was attenuated, it hardly came to an end. There were continuing struggles about the stipulations of the contractual agreements, about grievances, and about the increasing power of large bureaucracies. The social contract first was challenged by dissatisfied employees in the 1960s and 1970s, and then, as will be seen in chapter 13, it was dissolved unilaterally by aggressive management during the 1980s and 1990s.

During the middle and later decades of the twentieth century, the device of a contract gained a central role in mediating the conflict between the principles of managerial prerogative and employee self-representation. Pragmatic accommodations of justice were administered through the procedures of collective bargaining. But these decades of truce suggest that contracts cannot suffice to contain the contingencies that management and employees present to each other. The fractional bargaining of the 1940s onward, whether

management and employees, rather than superimposing judgments from a historically privileged standpoint.

Boulding argued that the larger interests of society and even of individual workers were best served if the impersonal forces of the market were relied upon to regulate the contractual relations between management and employees. The market would discipline the expectations and tactics of both sides. It would winnow out even those powerful and well-established economic actors who fail to attract others into mutually beneficial contractual relations. Appealing directly to his Quaker abhorrence of coercion, Boulding recommended that unions as well as management rely upon their ability to attract, rather than coerce, each other.[2] The largely unspoken assumption behind Boulding's argument is that the device of the contract, backed by law and by the internal commitment of the parties to abide by negotiated stipulations, would serve to keep order as well as move all parties towards more just relations.

Niebuhr countered that the market alone could not serve to bring about justice, due to certain dynamic trends in organized economic development. The unprecedented growth of large corporations in the U.S. had generated great and enduring inequalities of power. The centralized power of management placed employees at a disadvantage which employees needed to overcome by organizing their own collective power.[3]

> The simple fact is that a technical civilization produces large-scale organizations . . . because every interest of life, including the economic interest, tends toward collective expression in any event. But the development of the modern machine also makes collectivization of power in industrial management a technical necessity and the subsequent organizations of labor power a necessity of justice.[4]

For Niebuhr, the bargaining advantage of more powerful parties—management—should be met by collective pressure exerted through unions, allied with the power of the state to enforce their claims of justice.

The disagreement between Boulding and Niebuhr turned in large part upon their differing assessments of coercion. Boulding regarded the use of force as an intrinsic evil, one which ought to be minimized in the conflict between management and employees: "I regard the lessening of coercion as one of the most fundamental long-run objectives of human organization and one of the most profound moral tests by which any social movement is to be judged."[5] For Niebuhr, the centrifugal forces of collective human selfishness presented a greater threat to human well-being. For Niebuhr, coercion had a twofold value; it served as an instrumentality not only for achieving fairness in relations of unequal power but also to hold together economic arrangements which otherwise would fragment into anarchy.[6] "A tension of competing interests may quickly degenerate into an anarchy of competing interests. That is why a community must avail itself of coercion to establish a minimal order."[7]

These answers—market discipline vs. countervailing political power—represent two traditional poles between which economists and theologians move when arguing for or against the use of coercive political power as a means of establishing justice between management and employees. Of the two, Niebuhr's realism was much more closely attuned to the struggles by labor during the 1930s and 1940s. Union organizers were all too aware of the power of management to thwart their aims, and heartily would have endorsed Niebuhr's claim that centralized managerial power has to be met with collective labor power. The coercive tactics applied by workers may have been necessary.

Yet Niebuhr failed to grasp Boulding's claim that economic relations call for a different kind of pressure than sheer coercion. In effect, Niebuhr missed half the story: the fact that contractual relations are sustained in the first instance by an "internalized" coercion which operates very differently than the "external" coercion which was the focus of their discussion. Coercion is external when it is practiced by one party against another. Coercion is internalized when absorbed voluntarily as a constraint upon one's own action. It may seem odd to term such freely chosen self-binding as coercion. The paradox quickly evaporates when management and employees are understood to be creatures endowed with will. When will meets will—especially within a self divided by contrary impulses, to comply with commitments already agreed to requires suppressing the impulse to resist.[8] Internalized restraint is the most important species of self-binding in the contracts between management and employees. As such, it is this internalized restraint—not the absence of coercion, let alone external coercion—which brings the growing edge of love discussed in chapter 9 into contractual relations.

External Coercion: Indispensable, but of Limited Effectiveness

Niebuhr rightly insisted that external coercion is indispensable to achieving justice and securing order.[9] The crude tactics by workers of the nineteenth and early twentieth centuries generated the pressure that led to the institution of the procedural rules and arbitration forced upon recalcitrant management by the Wagner Act. Moreover, external coercion was needed not only to institute collective bargaining but to ensure that the resulting trade agreements were carried out. Without the threat of external coercion, it is hardly likely that contracts once negotiated would have sufficed to bind management and employees effectively together. The contracts management and employees signed were heavily laced with threats of external coercion—and appropriately so. After all, contracts are legal devices which invest the parties with the power of punishing each other for nonperformance. Such legal provisions are needed to enable the parties to protect themselves against the anarchy which results from the collision of collective forces.

But external coercion is at best of limited usefulness for introducing a covenantal quality into management-employee relations. From a covenantal point of view, which attends closely to how the wills of antagonists contend with each other, external coercion is liable to set off a spiral of mutually reinforcing resistance and counterresistance. Such a spiral can be seen both before and after collective bargaining became the norm for regulating industrial relations. The heavy-handed tactics of management during the 1930s roused workers to fight, not to surrender. Similarly, the forceful tactics of workers during the same era hardly served to contain the opposition of management. The passage of the Wagner Act in 1935 inspired management to develop a series of evasive tactics during subsequent decades. These included the Mohawk Valley Plan of the 1930s, the antiunion tactics sanctioned by the Taft-Hartley Act in the 1940s, and perhaps most important, a subtle but effective antiunion campaign which began in the 1960s and has continued through the 1990s. In short, the interplay of coercive tactics illustrates a potentially limitless spiral. Many managers responded, and continue to respond, to mandated collective bargaining by seeking to rid themselves of their unions. Just as important, many employees resorted to fractional bargaining to redefine their contracts, and undoubtedly many continue to "negotiate" unilaterally how much and what quality of labor (the so-called "effort bargain") they will furnish to management.

The tactics of external coercion may be necessary, but they inspire responses of resistance, which prompt counterresistance, and on into a spiral of tit for tat. As such, external coercion undermines the aim of covenant-building, which is to engender within management and employees the will to cooperate.[10] The larger strategy of God in building covenants is to move antagonistic partners towards internalizing the values of lovingkindness and justice, rather than relying upon external agencies to enforce these values. The aim is to convert the wills of each, so that the demands of justice presented under threat of sanction will be internalized as norms which operate powerfully in the absence of such sanctions.

Internalized Restraint: The Genius of Contracts

To a Reinhold Niebuhr disillusioned by the moral mediocrity of management and workers he witnessed in Detroit, such a covenantal vision might appear naively idealistic. After all, during the 1920s, both Henry Ford and the established craft unions of the AFL proved themselves incapable of internalizing and acting out a norm of justice which transcended their interests, narrowly drawn. Yet during the 1930s and 1940s, collective bargaining was an important if crude step, for management and employees began to trade external coercion for internalized restraint. It is this trend which needs to be strengthened in order to encourage the development of more covenantal relations.

Collective bargaining is intended to produce a binding contract. The genius of the contract as a form of relationship is that it requires internal self-binding as well as external coercion. In "internalized restraint," two parties bind themselves to accept the use of coercion against themselves should they fail to perform the stipulations of the contract. They effectively concur in advance to the sanctions that will be applied against them in retaliation for their nonperformance. The coerciveness of the sanctions becomes infused with consent. In effect, the external deterrent becomes an internalized discipline, as both parties seek to comply with the contract as a means of warding off the sanctions they have agreed to. In signing contracts, both sides effectively offer themselves up as hostages to each other.

Of course, this explanation applies most fully to the ideal contract, executed without fraud or duress. Probably no trade agreements are drawn up in a complete vacuum of pressure applied against the signing parties. Nevertheless, to the extent that it is operative, internalized restraint is an ingenious device. Restated in theological terms, the mutually agreed upon sanctions which constitute a contract effectively blend the coercive, external power of law with the internal, voluntaristic character of the Gospel to generate a kind of relationship which cannot quite properly be subsumed by either. And the device of internalized restraint was the most widely practiced tactic used by management and employees during the heyday of collective bargaining. It established a considerable dike against Niebuhr's twin evils of anarchy and collective selfishness. It proved a potent tool for both management and employees to bring the other into their respective orbits of influence, despite the erosive force of fractional bargaining by employees and evasion by management.

In their 1953 debate, Kenneth Boulding saw more clearly than did Reinhold Niebuhr the potential for contracts to regulate the relations of management and employees. Boulding argued that the least coercive market system was one in which large numbers of small producers were linked by contracts, even if he did not explore the specific manner in which contracts serve to reduce the need for external coercion in economic life. In contrast, Niebuhr evinced little enthusiasm for contractual relations. He voiced what has become the common complaint of Christian ethicists against contractually defined social relations: contracts are devices for enforcing limited commitments which undermine the communal nature of social life for the sake of individualistic gain.[11]

Later ethicists have rendered the same verdict. Ten years ago, Joseph Allen spelled out the moral shortcomings of the contractual form of relationship in detail. A contract lacks the distinguishing features of a covenant because it is closely bargained rather than freely offered; it lasts for a limited time; it is contingent upon the performance of stipulated actions by both parties; and finally, it assumes that the value of the contracting parties to each other is reductively instrumental. For Allen, a relationship is grounded in God's covenant when it aims at the mutual entrustment of selves who discern and honor the intrinsic worth of each other, and attend to each other's needs, rather than restrict themselves to the mutual satisfaction of interests.[12]

This criticism surely is valid; Allen's ideal vision vividly and correctly illustrates how far labor contracts fall short of full covenantal relations. But it should not serve to obscure the specific kind of self-binding which is integral to both contracts and covenants.

Internalized Restraint in Biblical Narratives

As seen in biblical narratives, internalized restraint is integral to the making of those covenants which require ratification by human covenant partners. In such bilateral covenants, the biblical template for the idea of internalized restraint is evident where the people pledge their fidelity, and specifically where they "witness against themselves." They effectively commit themselves to accepting punishment should they fail to fulfill the stipulations of the covenant offered by God. The idea of internalized restraint is hardly limited to the covenants between God and Israel. The Old Testament includes several stories of individuals punished for failing to keep solemn promises. See, for example, how Solomon rid himself of Shimei, a rival, by holding him to the letter of a promise (1 Kings 2:36–46).

A clear example of such internalized restraint is reported at the end of the conquest, as the aging Joshua dissuades the Israelites from entering lightly into the divine covenant by warning them of the consequences for their nonperformance. Says Joshua,

> "If you forsake the LORD and serve foreign gods, then he will turn and do you harm, and consume you, after having done you good." And the people said to Joshua, "No, we will serve the LORD!" Then Joshua said to the people, "You are witnesses against yourselves that you have chosen the LORD, to serve him." And they said, "We are witnesses."[13]

The editors of Exodus and Deuteronomy are particularly careful to record the rituals by which the people obligate themselves to obey the covenantal law upon pain of retaliatory punishment. In Exodus, as in the book of Joshua, the people voice their consent at least three times, as a means of indicating how serious and irrevocable their commitment is.[14] In Deuteronomy, a more intense form of such self-binding is recorded in one ritual, where the people shout "Amen!" to each stipulation of the law presented as a curse upon nonperformers. "'Cursed be anyone who deprives the alien, the orphan, and the widow of justice.' All the people shall say, 'Amen!'"[15]

The commitments recorded in Deuteronomy returned to haunt the people in times of tribulation.[16] But the theme of internalized restraint is picked up principally in the prophetic materials of the Old and New Testaments. Amos, Jeremiah, and Isaiah explain invasions and other woes as the punishment which the people should have understood would be visited upon them. Jesus adopts just such a prophetic stance when measuring the scribes and Pharisees against covenantal requirements of justice and mercy which they should be aware of, and finds them wanting.[17]

The rhetorical device of prophetic denunciation does not exhaust the tactical uses to which the idea of internalized restraint is put in the Bible. The parables of the Old and New Testaments apply this idea as a kind of jujitsu to challenge and overturn the self-righteousness of self-deceived listeners. The prophet Nathan brings to King David the fictitious case of a stolen lamb in order to elicit a kingly verdict of guilty. When Nathan reveals that the real case concerns David's murder of Uriah and adultery with Bathsheba, David finds himself condemned by the verdict he rendered regarding the stolen lamb.[18] Similarly, Jesus tells the parables of the two sons and of the ungrateful tenants in the vineyard as a means of breaking through the smug certitude of the chief priests and Pharisees regarding their own righteousness.[19]

Covenantal theorists mine biblical accounts of covenant-building for evidence principally of God's gracious lovingkindness and tireless justice as a model for human action.[20] Yet when attempting to discern the first stirrings of covenantal mutuality in the relations between management and employees, useful resources also are to be found simply by analyzing the formal structure of the relationship. As illustrated by the agreements to which the prophets and Jesus appeal, bilateral covenants consist of a specific kind of self-binding. The parties obligate themselves to channel their behavior in certain directions, at the risk even of willingly accepting punishment should they fail to perform. It is this willingness which provides contracting partners the basic assurance of their mutual reliability, and as such, provides a thin edge of acknowledged responsibility along which justice and lovingkindness might grow.

To be sure, the device of self-binding also serves to inspire legalism. In the Gospels, Jesus reserves his most bitter attacks for the Pharisees and scribes who attend to specific conditions of righteousness at the expense of broader conceptions of justice and mercy.[21] But the most stubborn enemy of covenantal love is also its closest kin. After all, Jesus' most significant and sustained conversation occurred with the Pharisees. Their rigid contractual understandings of God's special covenant with Israel had to be broken open by prophetic indictments, parables, and acts of miraculous healing, but it was that commitment to internalized restraint which brought them within the orbit of covenantal thinking in the first place. The Apostle Paul similarly had to shatter the sectarian, works-centered piety of his fellow Jews. But it was their legalistic misunderstandings that provided a common currency of ideas which he could exploit to explain the transcendent graciousness of God in extending the covenant beyond the original contracting parties.

In short, the biblical model of building covenants through internalized restraint provides a new way to understand contractual relations between management and employees. The internalized restraint mandated by collective bargaining and labor contracts needs to be seen as the template for asserting and enlarging the commitments by both parties to each other, rather than as a legalistic obstacle to the kind of justice and lovingkindness which are the hallmarks of covenantal relations fully flowered. Indeed, it is difficult to imagine how the broad ideals of justice and righteousness ethicists have called for might be institutionalized in the absence of contracts between management and employees.

Conclusion

Since there are two kinds of coercion, the initial question needs to be rephrased. What kind of coercion moves management and employees along the pathway of internalizing the norms appropriate to a covenantal relationship? Here a categorical preference can be asserted. Internalized restraint always is superior to external coercion. The power of a contract to bind parties to compliance has to be renewed by the commitment of each to abide by the agreed-upon schedule of performances, rewards, and sanctions. It is better that the parties bind themselves to acknowledge the claims of each other than that they be forced. But a covenantal ethic asks more, for the will to bind oneself to accept sanctions cannot be assumed, nor is it self-sustaining. Rather it must be cultivated and nourished. Therefore, the tactics of employees are to be evaluated according to whether they are seeking to move management towards absorbing covenantal values as effective guidelines for their action. Similarly, the tactics of management are to be seen as covenantally viable to the extent that they genuinely seek to foster within employees the will to cooperate.

From this perspective, the tactics of workers from the 1930s through the 1950s must be seen as tragic, however necessary they might have been to enforce and establish collective bargaining. Employees may have had no alternative than to exert external coercion in the form of strikes and, later, through fractional bargaining, but the liabilities are clear. Far from causing management to internalize values of justice and lovingkindness, such tactics encouraged a potent and enduring counterresistance. Of course, the coercive tactics of management during the nineteenth and early twentieth centuries only encouraged the spiral.

The next chapter returns to the historical narrative, to take up the managerial counterresistance which was renewed between the 1960s and the present. If labor history fitted into a comfortable evolutionary schema, the rest of this narrative could outline the ways that management and employees internalized restraint against themselves as a step towards constructing covenantal relations. But any such illusions have been shattered by the drastic transformation in labor relations that occurred during the 1980s and 1990s. As the next chapter will show, this transformation began already in the 1950s, when management began to arrest, then reverse, the great tide of collective bargaining. In effect, management displaced workers as the principal actors in the great ongoing drama of struggle to control who defines the conditions of work.

CHAPTER 13

The 1960s through the 1990s: Coercive Countertactics by Management

To this point, workers and unions have seemed to be the principal protagonists in the covenantal drama. Throughout the nineteenth century they were taking the initiative, struggling to establish their vision of an objective foundation—a negotiated trade agreement—against harsh, unremitting, and brutally consistent counter-resistance by employers. Employers, in contrast, adopted primarily defensive and preemptive tactics. They sought to incapacitate the collective agency of workers, and so to undercut any basis upon which workers might relate to employers as equal in power. Moreover, in an important sense the workers won. The frequent spasms of strikes during the 1930s and 1940s served to institutionalize the trade agreement through the bureaucratic apparatus of collective bargaining. This apparatus served to negotiate pragmatic compromises between the principles of representation and managerial prerogative. At the level of official contacts between unions and management, procedural fairness became the firmly enforced norm for negotiating and adjudicating differences, and the results have been of significant benefit in covenantal terms.[1]

But at least half the story must lie elsewhere, for as the twentieth century closes, the system for adjudicating conflict is faltering. The unions which depended upon collective bargaining have slipped drastically in their membership during the 1970s and 1980s. While the causes of such decline are complex, the reasons surely have to do with the tactics used by management. Workers achieved their victory basically through the use of one coercive idea, which might be termed the withdrawal of effort, that they applied and elaborated in walkouts, sitdowns, slowdowns, boycotts, and other ingenious variants. The obvious managerial response was to exert countercoercion through threat and punishment: to lock out striking workers, to tighten discipline, and to resist the pressure exerted by workgroups and individuals who withheld their effort.

Management continues to apply such tactics, but especially since World War II they have deployed a broader variety of strategies and tactics. Some of the ideas are new; some hearken back to earlier eras. All appear aimed at containing, if not eliminating, the power unions achieved through collective bargaining, or at preventing unions from gaining a foothold among unorganized workers. Overall, these management initiatives appear to have been far more innovative and adaptive since the 1970s than those of employees. Of course, there is no independent covenantal value to sheer variety or ingenuity in strategy and tactics, but the fact of such diversity opens up the possibility that some initiatives might be more viable than others for cultivating covenantal relations.

In general, strategies and tactics have more covenantal potential as they seek to foster genuine cooperation rather than reinforce coercion. What is so bewildering about contemporary managerial initiatives is that they evince both extremes—even within the same firms. It is not uncommon for a corporate management to invoke the language of values, to call for loyalty and cooperation, while playing hardball with unions and laying off employees. What connects both extremes is the reassertion of managerial prerogative—a triumphal resurgence of the will by management, the will to achieve the "flexibility" needed to reshape work relationships as it sees fit.[2] Still the ambiguity remains. Many managers have instituted efforts to decentralize their operations, to give more effective power to employees regrouped into self-managing teams. Many have made bold efforts to construct, from the ground up, a policy of eliciting the cooperation of their employees, and these initiatives also deserve a close look.

For Christian ethicists, this deep ambiguity in strategy suggests that two kinds of peril are to be avoided in charting out a "realist" covenantal interpretation of current trends. On the one side are the ethical managerialists, who call for values and cooperation while ignoring the more coercive strategies and tactics used by management; on the other are the prophetic critics, who focus solely on the more destructive effects of management tactics and discount the possibilities for genuine cooperation. In order to paint a more balanced picture, this chapter describes the coercive strategies and tactics that are of little covenantal promise, while chapter 14 explores more promising initiatives for achieving cooperation. Given the recent profusion of managerial initiatives, these two chapters can be only suggestive rather than conclusive.[3]

Evading the Law

Chapter 9 argued that relations become more covenantal as management and employees bind themselves to not abuse whatever margin of power they possess to frustrate or exploit each other. One bulwark for mediating the self-representation of employees and the prerogatives of management is the law which established and regulates collective bargaining. This law works by virtue of what in the preceding chapter is termed "internalized restraint," where management and employees accept the use of sanctions against themselves for violations of the law. Where this commitment to inernalized restraint is lacking, many employers have viewed federal law negatively, as an external hindrance, or opportunistically, as a resource for efforts to avoid or eliminate labor unions.

For years, management found the 1935 Wagner Act a burden, in that it established detailed procedures protecting employees in their efforts to organize themselves into unions and negotiate collective contracts. Management sometimes responded by seeking simply to evade, obstruct, or stonewall the mandated procedures. During the 1970s, for example, the most notorious symbol of Southern inhospitality to labor was the North Carolina-based J. P. Stevens Company, at the time the world's second largest producer of textiles. The Stevens management simply fired union organizers as it discovered them—almost 300—in direct violation of the Wagner Act. (This hardball tactic was of rapidly growing nationwide significance. In 1957, fewer than 1,000 workers were judged by the National Labor Relations Board to have been discharged illegally. In 1975, more than 7,000 were, and by 1980 the number had risen to over 10,000.)[4] It took Stevens cottonworkers four decades to unionize just one plant. And when they succeeded, in the early 1970s, the Stevens management resorted to the hardest of bargaining tactics, by refusing to commit itself to widely used procedures for working with unions such as third-party arbitration of disputes.[5]

Just within the law, management also has devised ingenious ways to use the letter of the Wagner Act to violate its spirit, in particular by using the detailed procedures and requirements of the Wagner-mandated voting process to delay elections. It has sought the help of more than a thousand legal and consulting firms that specialize in the legally delicate work of discouraging and preventing workers from voting for new or existing unions.[6] A manual produced by one such consultant distinguishes in casuistic detail what management may and may not do in its campaigns. It explains how to veil threats, how to delay the elections, how to gather intelligence about worker attitudes from supervisors, without transgressing the bounds set by the Act.[7]

Exploiting the Law

Management lacking a commitment to collective bargaining found a more directly useful resource in the 1947 Taft-Hartley Act. This amendment of the Wagner Act virtually was drafted by the National Association of Manufacturers, according to one congressman at the time. It has assisted management in two ways.[8] First, it prohibits unions from using some of the more coercive tactics which they found most effective in the past. It bans secondary boycotts, which discourage or block business with the company's suppliers or customers, and sympathy strikes, where one union strikes to support another. It outlaws closed shops, or plants where only union members can be hired (although it does permit union shops, where new workers can be required to join the union). It allows union officials to be penalized heavily for failing to break wildcat strikes. In essence, the act "rendered illegal those forms of solidarity that had previously proven themselves effective," according to labor scholar Rick Fantasia.[9] From the perspective of employers, of course, these "forms of solidarity" trespassed upon the property rights and prerogatives vested in management.

Second, the Taft-Hartley Act also grants useful permissions to management. Perhaps the most useful is the provision which permits the hiring of replacement workers ("scabs," to union members). It allows replacement workers hired during strikes to vote in elections certifying or decertifying a union. Employers are legally barred by the Wagner Act from pressuring workers regarding their collective representation, but they can use replacement workers to dilute the voting strength of striking workers. More ominously, perhaps, the Taft-Hartley Act also permits employers to retain the new hires as permanent replacements for strikers. In 1980, the Reagan administration signaled its support for this aggressive use of the Taft-Hartley Act by firing striking air traffic controllers and giving their jobs to hired replacements. A decade later, a coalition of religious leaders protested precisely this legal permission.[10] Their protest was part of a long campaign by labor to repeal the Taft-Hartley Act, a campaign which has not succeeded despite the nominal support of the Democratic administration elected in 1992.

These law-related strategies and tactics are considerably more sophisticated than the crude stonewalling practiced a decade earlier by J. P. Stevens. And they appear to have yielded considerable gains for management. During the early 1980s, according to one count, almost a thousand unions were challenged each year, and only 30 percent survived the decertifying elections.[11] Overall, the percentage of unionized industrial workers dropped precipitously from 32 percent in 1970 to 20 percent in 1984, to less than 16 percent in 1993.[12]

Despite their effective sophistication, these tactics for evading or exploiting the law express the antithesis of covenanting, in that they still emphasize "external" over "internal" coercion. Employers have used the Wagner and Taft-Hartley Acts as a resource for denying the self-representation sought by employees, rather than as a means to induce each other to cooperate, as through the contracts of collective bargaining. As such, these tactics reflect a continuation of the coercive manner in which law was used in the nineteenth century. As one journalist put it, "Today's employers have turned against labor the whole edifice of federal laws originally designed to foster collective bargaining and union activism."[13]

A Return to Organizing

Of course, management has not stood alone in applying coercive tactics. Unions have deployed coercive countertactics, even if with less success. The number of work stoppages held steady from the 1940s through the late 1970s at 3,000 to 6,000 per year, with peaks occurring in the mid-1940s, early 1950s, late 1960s and 1970s.[14] But by 1992, the annual number of strikes fell to its lowest level in forty-five years.[15]

Now the number of strikes appears to be climbing again as some unions begin aggressive efforts to organize. Some activists hope for a return to the militant 1930s, but the signals are unclear. On the one hand, there is evidence of increasing confrontation, although with little evidence of violence or destruction of property. The AFL-CIO, which still represents the vast majority of unionized workers, has pledged to invest heavily in organizing drives, after having let this strategy lapse for a decade or more. The movement is attracting young, highly educated organizers, as well as seasoned "salts" who seek to infiltrate nonunion construction sites.[16] The share of the construction market which was controlled by unions has fallen from 75% to 25% since the early 1970s, and the unions hope to win a portion back. Some unions, such as the Service Employees International Union, use pressure tactics. The covenantal viability of confrontational tactics is limited, however necessary the tactics might appear to be. What counts is whether such campaigns move in the direction of the "internalized restraint" of commitments. At least the aim of confrontation by employees is to negotiate a binding contract, while the aim of management has been to impose its will without the mediating step of negotiation.

On the other hand, it appears that the strike, labor's central tactic of external coercion, is less useful now than in the 1930s. Unions are experimenting, trying boycotts and town meetings in order to gain the attention and support of consumers in an updated and often ingenious version of nineteenth-century tactics. For example, AT&T workers used electronic means to solicit pledges from consumers to boycott AT&T services; 70,000 signed up, which the union estimated would have cost AT&T $3–5 million per week.[17] The covenantal value of such tactics is twofold. First, while coercive, they rely more upon threats and deterrence than upon actual punishment. Second, they avoid disrupting the process of production. In this way, they demonstrate a commitment by employees to a central interest of management: to keep the operations of companies going. The question is whether unions can develop a broad and potent enough array of such tactics to match the wealth of strategies and tactics management is using to deny them collective self-representation.

At the same time that unions are stepping up efforts to organize employees, labor as a whole has encountered defeat in another strategy. For years, the AFL-CIO had devoted much effort to shaping the legal contours of the relationship between management and employees. It pressed Congress to institute a national policy of full employment, require corporations to provide advance notice of plant closings, and establish a ban on hiring permanent replacement workers. This campaign reflected the nineteenth-century drives by labor to have social legislation enacted. But the effort has failed in large part, despite the fact that Congress was dominated by Democratic majorities during the 1970s and 1980s. The major success so far has been a law mandating family and medical leaves.[18] This agenda was pursued "at the expense of grass-roots work," according to one analysis.[19] The AFL-CIO's new direction echoes the turn by unions in the nineteenth century away from shaping the larger political system and towards negotiating trade agreements. The increased organizing marks a return to what might be termed the "core competence" of unions and may be more viable, to the extent that it succeeds, from a covenantal perspective.

Eliminating, or Threatening to Eliminate Jobs

During the past forty years, the most direct maneuver of management has had nothing to do with labor law: management simply has separated its operations from what it sees as troublesome unions or employees. This strategy has been carried out through two distinct sets of tactics: relocating or shutting down individual plants and "downsizing" or "reengineering" whole firms.

During the boom years of the 1960s, expanding companies chose to open new plants where unions were scarce—in the "sunbelt" states of the South and West or in rural areas of the Midwest untainted by a history of unionism. As labor scholars Thomas A. Kochan, Harry C. Katz and Robert B. McKersie point out, "One of the best guarantees for keeping a plant unorganized was to locate it in a southern state. It was not the right-to-work legislation found in most of these states per se that made a difference, but rather the area's generally antiunion social and political climate as well as lower labor costs that made the location attractive."[20] They also began to move their operations beyond U. S. borders, to developing nations. Already between 1966 and 1973, more than a million jobs moved overseas, prompting loud cries during the early 1980s about the "deindustrialization" of America.[21] Closely allied with the tactic to move away is the threat to do so. The globalization of trade during the 1980s and 1990s rendered such threats quite credible, particularly in small firms which employed impoverished workers to operate simple technologies which could be easily packed up and moved to other countries. Between 1977 and 1992 no fewer than seven efforts were made to organize 200 minimum-wage workers at a baby-products plant in Monroe, Louisiana. The owner beat back these efforts in part by threatening to move the plant overseas.[22]

Far more extensive than these tactics has been a burgeoning trend among large corporations simply to eliminate, rather than move or export, high-paying jobs. "Downsizing" is the policy of deliberately cutting staff. Corporations often reduce their workforces in order to ward off, or to pay for, the purchase of their companies in "leveraged buy-outs"—deals financed by offerings of bonds or by the anticipated sale of company assets. In the decade between 1982 and 1993, the 500 largest manufacturers in the U.S. cut almost 4 million positions. (The entire private-sector workforce includes some 90 million jobs.)[23] To an increasing extent, these full-time employees are replaced by "contingent" workers—individuals hired for part-time work, at much lower rates of pay and without benefits. In 1982, early in this trend, virtually all the employees of the BankAmerica Corporation—a major bank in California—were full-time. A decade later, management was vigorously converting 80 percent of the positions to part-time work.[24]

In the most recent trend, dubbed "reengineering," corporate management has rethought, from scratch, the processes by which it generates products or services. Such fundamental reorganizing has enabled companies to dispense with many functions.[25] More than 600,000 jobs were eliminated in 1993 alone.[26] And reengineering now is sweeping from the long-shrinking manufacturing sector to the vast service sector, which accounts for three-quarters of the jobs in the private sector. AT&T has eliminated 100,000 jobs since the mid-1980s, or one-quarter of its payroll.[27] The picture is complicated by the fact that the service sector is at the same time the major engine for creating jobs; the 500 largest service-sector companies created 1.2 million new positions between 1986 and 1991. Yet overall, the prospect is for millions of more jobs to be eliminated.[28]

A Covenantal Evaluation of "Discipline"

This churning of jobs reflects the "creative destruction" which many economists and other observers regard as a vital factor in renewing the U.S. economy. There has been a robust economic revival after the stagnation of the 1970s. But such a judgment values productivity, managerial prerogative, and overall utility—indispensable elements in the moral foundation upon which market systems stand—to the exclusion of other perspectives and considerations. From the vantage point of employees, the destruction of jobs might better be termed "discipline," in that it has generated a climate of anxiety in which unionized employees have little leverage in resisting concessions demanded by management regarding wages, benefits, and job security. The concession-bargaining and layoffs of the 1980s and 1990s appear to be fulfilling Karl Marx's vision of a vast army of the unemployed and contingently employed, the sheer numbers of which serve to intimidate employees into accepting lower wages and less security in their work.

From a covenantal point of view, there is nothing inherently wrong with discipline, despite the distasteful and even sinister name. By "discipline" I mean the efforts by one party to reduce, unilaterally, the expectations held by the other. Both God and God's people are engaged in shaping, even transforming, the expectations which each side brings to its relationship with the other. Expectations are not sacrosanct and immune to influence, for they are based neither on perfect knowledge nor perfectly oriented desires. Expectations need to be negotiated, for it is in the clash of opposing expectations that realistic and appropriate aspirations become manifest.

Downsizing and reengineering can have some margin of covenantal value in preserving the economic viability of corporations. The actual evidence is less compelling. Management likes to argue that massive layoffs are needed to position companies to compete effectively in the lean 1990s. Employees might grudgingly see the need for layoffs, but the downward adjustment of their expectations needs to take place upon the platform of a truly shared aim: fostering the survival of their company and of jobs. One disturbing irony is that management appears not to have gained much from massive cutting, either in terms of higher profits or reduced costs.[29]

The basic problem with downsizing and reengineering is that employees hardly can have a shared interest with management in seeing these strategies succeed. "Millions of American workers are embarking on a journey of insecurity," as one *Wall Street Journal* reporter puts it.[30] The problem extends beyond simple job security. Employee loyalty is an important lubricant of production in many enterprises. Not only the victims but also the survivors of massive layoffs suffer psychological wounds, as they wonder whether the ax will strike them next.[31] Downsizing and reengineering sap the loyalty of the survivors. Once embittered, they shrug off not only a sense of responsibility for their companies but inhibitions against taking revenge. Observers have noted that employees can sabotage their companies as their workloads soar and their prospects for job security sink.[32]

These problems have created a new cottage industry of managers and consultants who take on the seemingly hopeless task of regenerating the loyalty of employees even as jobs continue to be cut.[33] At least one such consultant views the loss of a job as an opportunity for an employee to cut ties of codependency with a paternalistic organization and take responsibility for his or her own empowerment and autonomy.[34] From a covenantal point of view, this prescription is hardly adequate. The tactics of disciplining the expectations of those who remain becomes legitimate only to the extent that the sacrifices demanded are genuinely shared, that is, backstopped with correlative sacrifices by management. The canon of simple tit-for-tat fairness—less a revealed biblical value than a widespread norm—serves to reveal whether management is engaging in genuine gestures of self-binding. During the 1980s, what was so offensive about the enormous salary increases awarded to executives was that they were achieved at the expense of employees laid off. Even mergers and downsizings resulted in the termination of redundant executives, the "golden parachutes," or generous severance packages, they received testified to the unwillingness or inability of management to answer forced sacrifice with voluntary sacrifice. (In one remarkable exception, the CEO of a large real-estate firm capped off several years of downsizing his corporation by eliminating his own position as well.)[35] The case for fairness is further tarnished when layoffs are pressed as profits rise. For example, Sears, Roebuck, the giant retailer, in 1993 eliminated 50,000 jobs, or 14 percent of its merchandising division's positions, even as its sales revenues were rising more than 10 percent.[36]

Perhaps the only major evidence of fairness in pain is the fact that downsizing and reengineering have hit middle management at least as hard as employees lower down in the organizational hierarchy. Such cuts suggest that tactics of downsizing and reengineering truly may be aimed more at eliminating inefficiency than at thwarting the principle of collective self-representation by employees. The remaining problem is that, however fairly these tactics for eliminating employees might be spread through the organization, they represent the blatant, harsh, and astonishingly successful resurgence of the principle of managerial prerogative, and as such, promise a resurgence of coercive tactics by employees in order to reestablish the shattered equilibrium between managerial prerogative and employee self-representation.

Conclusion

This chapter has examined two kinds of strategies management has used to stymie the efforts of employees to organize their own collective self-representation. In the one, management has evaded or exploited the law to frustrate the aims of the Wagner Act; in the other, management simply has eliminated or moved jobs away from unions. The major problem with these strategies, and the myriad tactics used to carry them out, is that they have split the shared interests of both sides as defined by the collective bargaining system, and they express the very contradiction of the self-binding gestures which serve to establish a mutual trust.

Simple trust, as the confidence which two parties repose in each other, is not the limit of what a covenantal ethic requires. There needs to be a growing edge of justice as fairness, of mutual regard denominated in firm commitments, both of which appear to be lacking in the confusing flux of the market system. Management is hardly to blame for the pressures enforced by competition, but the aggressive strategies it has pursued can be faulted for expressing the unbridled assertion of managerial prerogative, particularly when administered disproportionately to employees. This will-to-power is visible particularly where management has sought, often successfully, to crush the self-representation sought by employees. It is difficult to see much covenantal value in the strategies and tactics described in this chapter.

From a covenantal perspective, the rapid decline in the negotiating power of workers raises problems just as acute as their rapid increase in that power during the heyday of collective bargaining. Management has sought to replace contracts negotiated collectively in favor of individual contracts presented to workers in personnel offices. Given the intransigence evidenced by management, the countermeasures taken by employees likely will involve the use of external coercion. Such coercion may be a tactical necessity, in the name of broader social justice, but are no more covenantally viable than the reassertion of managerial prerogative. Just as the militancy of the 1930s lifted a generation of manufacturing workers into the middle class, it appears that another surge of militancy is needed to lift the poorly paid and often contingent workers in the service industries into a similar prosperity.[37]

This large judgment should not be seen as an uncritical endorsement of labor militancy in every business enterprise. However necessary coercive tactics may be for broader social welfare, they offer too limited a moral horizon for a covenantal ethic. The aim of a covenantal ethic is that management and employees develop viable common aims, and that they shape the thinking and action of each other by binding themselves to particular commitments. This internal restraint constitutes the pathway along which the covenantal values of justice and lovingkindness find expression within business enterprises. The next three chapters take up the most recent initiatives in management strategy, which move along this more promising pathway.

PART 4

Costly Cooperation

CHAPTER 14

From the 1970s through the 1990s: Recruiting the Active Cooperation of Employees

If the resurgence of coercive tactics reported in chapter 13 told the whole story, the prospects for covenantal relations between management and employees would be as dim in 1997 as they were a century earlier, in 1897. Fortunately there has been a second direction in managerial strategy. This direction has been incarnated in the wide diffusion of programs aimed at gaining the willing and eager cooperation of employees. As at least one expert in industrial relations points out, seeking cooperation is hardly a new strategy.[1] Management has wooed employees before, most notably during the peak of the corporate welfare movement, in the 1920s. What does appear to be new are wholesale efforts to delegate to employees significant freedom and responsibility for their work. These programs have been labeled variously "participation," "quality circles," "quality of work life," "employee involvement," and more recently, "self-managed teams." They differ somewhat in the degree of delegation they offer. This chapter represents this variety by reviewing three well-known experiments: employee involvement at General Foods; quality circles at Ethicon, a unit of Johnson & Johnson; and self-managed teams at the Saturn division of General Motors.

The idea of management delegating freedom and responsibility to employees expresses covenantal value—or does it? The participation programs have attracted both effulgent praise and sharp criticism. Read most hopefully, they offer management and employees a pragmatic shared aim and a way of escaping the impasse between the principles of managerial prerogative and employee self-representation. Read most cynically, participation programs are seen as undermining the collective self-representation of employees through a problematic blend of empowerment with subtle tactics of control and, as such, amount to nothing more than the latest and most sophisticated triumph of managerial prerogative.[2] This chapter will give play to both sides in this debate. Since evidence easily can be found to support both, the accent here will be once again upon the potential of these strategies, rather than simply the evidence of the present.

The contemporary managerial drive to elicit the cooperation of employees is in full swing, and so it is difficult to offer more than a tentative covenantal evaluation of participation programs. The management initiatives appear to mark an important breakthrough. In effect, management has established a new principle—what might be termed employee self-management—as a normative anchor of the relationship. The principle of self-management is of great covenantal value. It repeats the trajectory of the biblical history towards what might be termed the moral self-management by the people of God. The value of cooperation and self-management are explored at length in chapter 15. But it appears that the principle of self-management has been of ambiguous value to employees.

There are three problems. First, there is the possibility that management might offer employees self-management as a ploy to undercut their self-representation through unions. The two principles point towards different kinds of employee interests and, as such, can be pitted against each other. Self-management has to do with fostering the capacities of employees to design and govern their own work, while self-representation historically has had to do with protecting wages and the security of employment. This first problem is illustrated vividly by the Ethicon case taken up below, and is always a threat where management presents employees with uncontrollable contingency.

Second, even a management with the best of intentions is subject to the tyranny of market pressures. The General Foods and Saturn cases illustrate how such pressures—for greater output or greater efficiency—can undermine if not wreck experiments in cooperation.

Third, running like a thread through programs of participation is the problem of what might be termed entropy. Efforts at self-management tend to last only a few years, and for good reason. Genuine self-management requires enormous amounts of energy and foresight from employees—and a corresponding appetite for risk and uncertainty by management.

Workplace Democracy vs. "Worker Dissatisfaction"

The current wave of solicited and programmed cooperation appears to have started in the early 1970s, as a reflection within industry of the ferment in the broader society during the 1960s. Labor activists and some scholars dreamed that the American ideal of democratic self-rule might be extended into the workplace, which was regarded as an enormous bastion of autocracy in American public life.[3] This sentiment spawned a number of ambitious early experiments, such as those at International Group Plans in Washington, D.C., and Harman International Industries in Bolivar, Tennessee.[4] As with early efforts in the corporate welfare movement, these projects were driven by the vision and indulgence of benevolent owners. They also were assisted sometimes with federal funding, and so did not necessarily represent the real-world value that management would place upon the strategy of encouraging employee participation.

The movement spread into industry, but less as a campaign for workplace democracy than as a strategy to dampen worker unrest. The management of larger corporations framed the problem in personal rather than in political terms. They were concerned about increasing "worker dissatisfaction," as signalled by wildcat strikes, absenteeism, sloppy work, and low productivity. Nevertheless, this apolitical formulation of the problem still kept the focus upon strategies and tactics which would enlist, rather than coerce, the energies of employees. The widespread attention to worker dissatisfaction during the 1970s helpfully pointed management in the direction of delegating to employees some significant degree of autonomy for arranging their work and being responsible for their output.

General Foods at Topeka

Such programs in principle appear to be a covenantally viable way of addressing the durable problem: the contingency employees and management present to each other as willed beings capable of cooperation as well as domination and resistance. But economic pressures can erode the mutual confidence necessary for such programs to succeed. One famous early experiment illustrates how management can ruin an experiment by not protecting it against extreme economic pressure. The General Foods Corporation wanted to escape the union at its troubled Kankakee, Illinois, pet-food plant.[5] The General Foods management in 1971 built a new plant in Topeka, Kansas, starting from scratch with a nonunion workforce—a popular strategy, but problematic for a covenantal ethic.

Despite these ambiguous beginnings, the effort proved laudatory. Seventy employees were selected carefully, trained for four months, and given wide latitude to control the conditions of their work. They essentially ran the factory; they had a significant say in hiring new workers, they disciplined each other, and they were paid according to the skills they learned. This model effort, insulated from the traditional hierarchy of the General Foods Corporation, successfully engaged the cooperation of employees. But by 1976, the experiment was in decline. Corporate headquarters demanded that the plant increase its production. According to one sympathetic observer, the autonomy of employees was undercut. The pressure to produce more generated a more competitive spirit within the plant, while encouraging a retreat from self-run teams to the use of foremen.[6] While the plant continued to operate, the experiment in cooperation was terminated as management reinstituted traditional hierarchical relations.

Quality circles at Ethicon

A second kind of deep-seated problem can tarnish the potential for cooperation: management might use a program of cooperation to manipulate or directly pressure employees into rejecting the kind of collective self-representation offered by unions. One study suggests that "quality circle" (QC) programs are particularly susceptible to this kind of abuse. The idea of a QC was introduced from Japanese industry into U.S. industry in 1974, and caught on in a large way during the early 1980s, as U.S. management grasped for new techniques to meet the competitive threat from Asia.[7] Quality circles are small groups of workers organized by management to meet regularly to discuss and resolve production problems. As such, they fit the hierarchical but group-centered ethos of the large Japanese corporation. They are oriented somewhat more towards increasing productivity than enhancing the self-management of workers.

Independent researchers have found it difficult to study the viability of quality circles from the inside—with one exception which outlines in alarming detail the kind of abuse QC programs are susceptible to. In the early 1980s, the Ethicon unit of the Johnson & Johnson company, a huge medical-products manufacturer with an enviable reputation for ethical conduct, established a new plant near Albuquerque, New Mexico. The Ethicon management organized employees into workgroups staffed by trained "facilitators," who effectively were in charge of the groups. These social psychologists were given the charge to extirpate any prounion sentiment. One of them, Guillermo Grenier, quickly became disillusioned, and documented at length how management subverted the QC ideal of free and open consultation in order to render employees powerless and incapable of joining together in solidarity to form a union.[8] The facilitators used group processes during meetings in order to intimidate individual employees, to discourage them from developing the confidence to organize themselves. The Ethicon management also institutionalized fear as a means of control by sharing with employees the power to punish. When used within the manipulated groups, that power became an awesome tool of intimidation.[9] Such peer pressure proved a major resource for enforcing managerial will, particularly since management refused to commit itself to written standards and the rule of law, the standard instruments of the internalized coercion necessary for covenantal relations. Some observers have criticized the poor fit between stereotypically individualistic American workers and the more organic ethos assumed by the quality circle and related Japanese techniques. Yet the covenantal liabilities of Ethicon's approach appeared to have little to do with cultural differences. In covenantal terms, the Ethicon management refused to bind itself to respect the true self-representation of employees. Instead, it set up and enforced a manipulative apparatus of closely controlled participation.

The Ethicon program rode a domestic crest of interest in quality circles. By 1982, at least 200 and perhaps as many as 750 U.S. firms had organized their workers regularly to discuss issues in production.[10] The Westinghouse Corporation alone had 2,000 circles involving 20,000 employees by 1984.[11] By the early 1990s, some $150 billion had been spent by management to train employees in Japanese management techniques of all kinds, including QCs.[12] It is easy to extrapolate an Orwellian nightmare from these large numbers. But exactly how many managers used QCs to control their employees with such manipulation is hard to determine. By the early 1990s management was abandoning the concept of QCs.[13] The demise of the concept may have had to do with the resistance of middle managers to defer to suggestions by employees, and a more general unwillingness of management to delegate real decision-making power.[14] According to some observers, QC programs tended to fade into inanity as employees at weekly meetings ran out of significant problems to discuss. The limited advisory role given to employees bogged the workgroups down in trivial discussions.

Two Ambiguous Trends in Management Strategy

Even if the kind of abuse Grenier observed was not broadly representative, it reflected two larger trends which are likely to extend well beyond the decade-long popularity of quality circles. The two trends reflect both a threat and an opportunity from a covenantal perspective. The first is a fundamental reorientation of management attitudes towards unions, as explained by industrial-relations experts Thomas Kochan, Harry Katz, and Robert McKersie. The era of collective bargaining beginning in the 1930s encouraged management to set up a "human relations" function, charged with devising ways to work with, rather than against, unions. Human relations officers developed expertise in negotiating peaceful, predictable settlements, as mandated by the Wagner Act. Through such officers, management could demonstrate its commitment to the rule of law, in contrast to the kind of tactics described in the previous chapter. During the 1980s, however, these officers were eclipsed in power and influence by "human resource" officers and specialists charged with designing work systems that intentionally undercut the appeal of unions to employees, as at Ethicon.[15]

In a second and complementary trend, management has shifted its unit of control from employees as atomic individuals to whole workgroups. In a sense, this trend is hardly new. "Group processes" have been a staple area of research in the field of industrial psychology for decades. Already in the 1930s, researchers discovered that U.S. workers like to work in groups, and recommended that management harness group sentiment as a tool for reducing resistance to management and for increasing production. What is new is that management has developed increasingly refined techniques for controlling employees. The Ethicon program, with its trained "facilitators" assigned to every group, illustrates the abuses to which expert knowledge of group processes can be put.

Just as important, management has discovered in the long run that workgroups can do more than control the motivation and behavior of their component individuals. In group settings, the capacities of individuals to take initiative and responsibility for their work can be developed. So increasingly during the past twenty years, management has delegated autonomy and responsibility to workgroups as a means of eliciting their cooperation. Workgroups and teams have come to be seen not only as the most "natural" units of human association in notoriously impersonal large organizations, but also as the most potentially productive in organizations, as purposefully constructed and densely interdependent networks of work.

Best known have been the "quality of work life" (QWL) programs which were especially popular during the 1970s and 1980s. QWL programs aimed to make work more attractive by giving employees some significant degree of control over the conditions of their work on the shop floor.[16] Now during the 1990s, management speaks of setting up self-managed teams, where the exchange of managerial prerogative for greater productivity is more explicit. Management commits itself to delegate considerable decision-making power to groups of half a dozen or a dozen employees whose jobs are closely interlinked. The idea evidently has proven wildly popular. By 1992, according to the *Wall Street Journal,* one-fifth of U.S. companies had set up self-managed teams, involving 7 to 9 percent of all U.S. workers; industry promoters claim an even higher rate of participation.[17]

The amount of power effectively delegated varies widely, of course. In the same industry study, the surveyed companies revealed that teams take responsibility for setting work schedules and performance targets in two-thirds of the teams surveyed, for purchasing equipment and dealing with suppliers in one-half of the teams, and to a lesser extent, for hiring, firing, budgeting, and performance appraisals in fewer than a third of the teams.[18] Some visible success stories include AT&T, the Harley-Davidson Company, the automobile industry, and some firms in the steel industry.[19]

The Emergent Principle of Employee Self-Management

Since the 1970s and 1980s, involvement programs have refined the means by which groups of employees take charge of their work. These efforts have cracked open the door, by intention or not, to the "workplace democracy" sought by early activists. Managers who have delegated significant power to employees effectively affirm what might be termed the moral principle of employee "self-management": the claim that employees ought to have some significant influence over how their work and workplaces are arranged in the pursuit of managerial goals. This principle is hardly new. Already in the nineteenth century, employees set up craft-based unions to control the work process of factories and steel mills. Those guilds were crushed by management by the beginning of the twentieth century, and employees retrenched in the principle of employee self-representation, whose limited scope had to do with the protection of material interests. Now, once again there is an impulse towards the democratic reorganization of work, by delegating authority and responsibility to workgroups, but this time the impulse comes from management more than employees.

Indeed, some labor scholars and activists find self-managed teams a dire threat to both genuine self-management and, perhaps more important, to the principle of self-representation. Mike Parker, a unionist and freelance expert on cooperation programs, argued that management and employee interests do not coincide in promoting cooperation. He aimed his 1985 comments at QWL programs, but likely would make similar arguments about the more ambitious management initiatives to establish self-managed teams. According to Parker, management has four ulterior aims. It uses such programs to gain access to one of the most potent resources of power held by employees, detailed knowledge of the work process; to neutralize the resistance of employees to automated technology that destroys jobs; to make work hours and assignments more flexible, so as to reduce labor costs; and to soften up employees for contract concessions, so as to undermine unions more easily.[20]

There is evidence for these claims. Elsewhere, for example, Parker has reported how the Fremont, California, management of the well-regarded "NUMMI" joint venture between General Motors and Toyota habitually pushes the automobile assembly line to the point that it breaks down, in order to drive employee teams to gain knowledge which then is used to speed up the line even more.[21] Next, many company managers indeed did institute quality circles in part as a means to reconcile employees to increasing automation, although, it should be noted, they are now abandoning automation because such machinery proved less adaptable to changing production lines than were human workers.[22] Further, it has been an undisguised goal of participation programs for management to wedge open union-controlled rigidity in work hours and assignments, so that management might deploy workforces with more flexibility. And finally, it is hardly a secret that management hopes that employees will absorb a managerial perspective as they become more responsible for their own production; that they will see their own contributions in the context of the overall productivity and profitability of the company. Of course, the sharing of knowledge, flexibility, and management's perspective also is essential to a cooperative relationship.

It still needs to be asked: is it harmful for employees to consent to developing a managerial perspective, and if so, why? From opponents of cooperation, the answer is clear: only unions are genuinely concerned with preserving the jobs of their members, and so self-representation is vital for preserving the material well-being of employees. Management appeals to the cooperative instincts of employees in order to redirect their loyalty to small workgroups. Pressed to internalize managerial values, workers are urged to encourage their peers to do the same. In so doing, they forge a group identity which attenuates and displaces their ties with the union.[23] Such a narrow focus of loyalty is risky, for management will not provide the same security that unions strive for.

Self-representation vs. self-management

Framed within a covenantal perspective, the basic issue is whether the sudden blossoming of self-managed teams represents nothing more than a dangerous reassertion of managerial prerogative, or whether employees share some substantial interest or goal which warrants endorsing and even embracing the efforts of management to gain their cooperation. Labor activists warn that employees are wise to recognize that their interests may overlap with those of management but that both sets do not and will not converge.[24]

The suspicion which these skeptics bring to cooperative programs may be hard to fathom until it is understood that employees have two distinct kinds of interests, and that the pathway toward developing more covenantal relations requires keeping them separate, as unions have insisted. Employees historically have sought to represent themselves collectively at the negotiating table in order to secure their jobs, higher wages, and other "material" interests. Initiatives to enrich those jobs or to develop managerial capacities to be responsible for the shape of work suggest that workers have a second set of interests that are important as an antidote to "worker dissatisfaction" and even to the survival of their companies, but that these are not the bread-and-butter interests unions traditionally defend for their members. What arouses the suspicion of labor activists, and undoubtedly many union members, is the possibility that management might entice employees to see self-management through groups as an alternative to the collectively bargained self-representation of the employees as a whole. The Ethicon experiment illustrates precisely this problem, in that management used quality circles to dampen the ardor of employees for organizing a union. Labor activists warn that any benefits conceded by management are fragile if not supported by a unity which employees have developed among themselves. Employees are naive to trust inducements which can be revoked as easily as they were offered by management.

But there are other voices from the front besides those who oppose cooperation with management. Not surprisingly, the labor movement itself appears split over the value of managerial initiatives to gain the cooperation of employees. Within the automobile industry, long the bellwether of management-union relations in the United States, some leaders of the United Autoworkers have engaged their union in support of risky experiments for reorganizing work into a self-managing team approach. Other unions, such as the Communications Workers of America and the Steelworkers, have also embraced cooperation, welcoming the management strategy of delegating effective decision-making power to employees. In effect, these unions accept the paradoxical argument made by management: that both sides have a shared interest in increasing productivity and introducing new technology because that is the most viable way to save jobs. The argument is paradoxical in that increased efficiency and new technology historically has rendered workers redundant, costing them their jobs. But by improving the financial health of the company, such gains can serve to expand production elsewhere within it.

The split between opponents and advocates of cooperation likely runs right through the heads and hearts of many employees. On the one hand, they would like to gain more effective control of their work and work relations, but on the other hand they mistrust the sincerity or durability of managerial intentions. There appears to be no magic key for resolving these conflicting sentiments. Given the contingency that management always will present to employees—and employees to management—both sides always will have grounds to mistrust each other. The philosopher Immanuel Kant asserted that nothing is so inaccessible to empirical verification as a goodwill. Given this irreducible contingency, both sides must continue to interpret and respond to the intentions of each other, as these intentions are given expression in tactics and strategies.

Covenantal Guidelines

From a covenantal perspective, there is much to commend in managerial efforts to enlist employee enthusiasm as a crucial edge in improving productivity. But there are important guidelines or, more properly, limits, which must be observed. To inspire the confidence of each other, both sides need to engage in gestures which commit them visibly to a common goal. Their intentions are measured best—if indirectly—by the tactics they use. As explained in chapter 7, both sides need to restrict themselves to applying tactics and gestures which express respect for the principles of action most important to the other party. In practical terms, this suggests that management should seek to elicit cooperation by appealing to the budding principle of self-direction while not threatening the principle of collective self-representation. Employees, for their part, need to respond by not resisting the prerogative of management to carry forward the business. In the endless flux of market relations, an equilibrium needs to be worked out and continually adjusted. Both sides need to make gestures which clearly signal boundaries they will not cross in the defense of their respective principles of action. From a covenantal perspective, management needs to set limits upon its exercise of managerial prerogative by defining—and respecting—zones of autonomous action by employees. Employees need to reject the use of obstructive tactics which directly threaten managerial goals.

The Saturn experiment

Nowhere have both sides attempted to achieve this equilibrium on a more ambitious scale than at the Saturn plant of General Motors in Spring Hill, Tennessee, and nowhere has this equilibrium foundered more painfully than at the midwestern plants of the Caterpillar Corporation. The balance of this chapter reviews the Saturn experiment, which has highlighted on a colossal scale the potential and some basic problems of cooperation. Discussion of the Caterpillar case is reserved for the next chapter.[25] The Saturn case is important for several reasons. First, it not only has succeeded financially, it has preserved an equilibrium among the three principles of managerial prerogative, employee self-representation, and employee self-management. Both management and union appear to have acted in good faith, and so the strategies and tactics they used should illustrate the covenantally viable solution outlined above. Second, the Saturn venture illustrates how difficult it is to sustain cooperation when both parties, driven by the best of intentions, collide with unforgiving pressures imposed by the market. Third, the Saturn venture projects another, perhaps more durable problem onto a vast screen: how to sustain cooperation against seemingly natural forces of entropy?

By the early 1980s, the top management of General Motors was looking enviously at the efficiency and low costs Japanese management had achieved through cooperation with their workers.[26] GM already had ten years of experience with cooperative experiments with the United Autoworkers, beginning in a Tarrytown, New York, plant. But Saturn was planned, at the urging of the UAW, to involve employees as full partners. It began in 1982, when GM invited fifty-five members of the union to join forty-four managers to design a plant for building a new small car.[27] The group recommended a completely separate subsidiary, complete with its own union agreement, to build a new car from scratch, and GM's senior management concurred in what was to be an investment of $5 billion. Ground was broken in 1986. Three thousand employees were chosen initially from among tens of thousands of recently laid-off GM workers. As in the Topeka experiment, management invested hundreds of hours training each carefully selected employee in the techniques of self-management. The plant workforce was organized in 150 rigorously trained and integrated teams of 6 to 15 members each.[28] They were directed to exercise goal-centered leadership, decision-making by consensus, and to link accountability with actual responsibility.[29]

According to one sympathetic observer, "The sense of freedom and learning at Saturn in 1989 was unprecedented for GM and significant for American industry. The training was linked to risk and rewards, to the presumption that long-conditioned union workers could rise to the occasion, could not only absorb a flow of new information but integrate it into their character and act with heightened awareness and understanding. Of course, the training also had to improve productivity and lower costs, making Saturn lean and competitive."[30]

Soon after the plant began producing cars in 1990, the experiment became strained from both sides, for reasons which apparently had much to do with finite human capacities and little to do with bad faith. By 1991, the team concept still had not gelled.[31] The teams were uncomfortable with conflict; consensus decision-making was proving too slow; and newly hired workers, less committed to the Saturn vision, wanted a clearly defined authority telling them what to do.[32] On the other side, support by GM headquarters for this experimental teamsmanship also eroded. The Saturn division lost $1.7 billion in its first two years of production, while GM as a whole lost over $30 billion.[33] But GM's need for Saturn increased. The car had become a hit, and as such was the key to improving the corporation's sagging bottom line. GM headquarters demanded that the cost of producing the car be slashed, pressuring the teams for creative and risky solutions at the same time that the teams were being pressured to yield effective decision-making power to management.[34] By mid-1993, the partnership between labor and management was seriously stressed. Saturn was no longer seen as the initiative which would transform the adversarial relations between GM and the UAW.[35] But neither would it founder; the division turned a modest profit, for the first time, and the market for Saturns seemed assured.

A covenantal evaluation

When measured against the three problems outlined at the beginning of this chapter, the Saturn experiment looks covenantally viable, even as it illustrates how these problems cannot be resolved exhaustively or with finality. First, both union and management founded their cooperation upon a careful equilibrium among the three principles of managerial prerogative and the self-representation and self-management of employees. This successful triangulation, no doubt, was due to the fact that both union and management participated in devising it, unlike the failed General Foods experiment at Topeka, Kansas, ten years earlier. In essence, the jointly ratified strategy was to inculcate employees with managerial values and then grant them significant autonomy, while not undermining their principle of collective self-representation. The Saturn management did not attempt to present the self-managing team as an alternative or improvement upon the union, which negotiated their collective interest in wages and job security. Employees, for their part, left their tactics of resistance at the door, working with rather than against the imperative to be more efficient. There is great covenantal value to this strategy, as originally conceived, and as both sides have tried to sustain it. Of course, it should be noted that the sheer strength of the UAW gave the General Motors management a strong incentive to work with, rather than against, the union. Unlike General Foods in the 1970s, General Motors in the 1980s did not have the luxury of starting a new plant with "unorganized" workers. To what extent the equilibrium achieved here could be replicated outside industries already heavily unionized is unclear. Furthermore, the Saturn experiment had an enormous pool of talent—thousands of laid-off General Motors workers—to pick from. Finally, it must be conceded that the experiment is hardly inclusive, given that non-UAW residents of the Spring Hill area were excluded from applying for jobs at the plant.

Second, the Saturn experiment has been financially successful, although at some risk to the covenantal quality of relations. The Topeka experiment in employee self-management failed in large part because the General Foods management forced a drive for productivity upon the plant. The Saturn experiment similarly was threatened by 1993 as the pressure for productivity encouraged management to back away from having the plant governed by self-directing teams. The market can make such temptations all but irresistible. Nevertheless, management must bind itself to the promise that solutions to the woes of competition will not be imposed arbitrarily by management, but sought cooperatively. Management must find concrete ways to demonstrate that more production and more efficient production are truly shared goals. One crassly material but effective way which Saturn management used to bind employee welfare to the success of the plant was to make 20 percent of employee wages contingent upon the profitability of the plant.

The market's impersonal demand for efficiency in production makes the work of creating and sustaining covenantal relations more difficult. If this work required only equilibrating the intentions and goals of management and employees—balancing the moral principles central to the action of each—it would be difficult enough. But the relationship of management and employees is "triadic," not "dyadic," to borrow the language of H. Richard Niebuhr. Both sides must devise initiatives in response to the intentions of each other not simply as isolated individuals but as economic actors answerable to "common third" elements, such as market pressures. The past two decades have demonstrated the power of the market to move management in potentially covenantal directions, as the well-intentioned efforts of management during the 1970s to ease "worker dissatisfaction" were redirected and stepped up during the 1980s to achieve greater productivity. The goal of worker satisfaction, which always has been instrumental to productive efficiency, has become even more intensively so. At the same time, economic pressure, especially that exerted by increasing market demand, strongly encourages management to scuttle the principle of employee self-management for restored managerial control.

Third, the management and employees of the Saturn plant appear to have struggled with considerable success against the "entropy" of self-management. As the Saturn plant went into production, the teams were sorely tempted to short-circuit the time-consuming procedures of self-management and reestablish direct managerial control through standard hierarchical relations. The carefully reinforced new relations between management and the union began tilting back toward tradition. Apparently the temptation appears to have been resisted, although the commitment to the Saturn way of doing things has been diluted by the hiring of new employees who lack the vision of self-management forged in the early years.

This entropy appears hardly unique to the Saturn plant, or perhaps even to economically stressed experiments in cooperation. One review of QWL programs during the 1970s concluded that most atrophied or were abandoned within a few years.[36] It appears that the a policy of cooperation simply may not be as comfortable to management and employees as more hierarchical and adversarial relations. Cooperation requires an ever-renewed effort to build bridges and broaden perspectives, to communicate intentions carefully, to inspire and motivate eager collaboration across large networks of action. It requires single-minded faith and effort, engaging heart as well as head around the durable problems of sustaining mutual trust and loyalty.

Conclusion

Almost a century ago, Walter Rauschenbusch asserted that meaningful cooperation in the workplace required an end to capitalist control of economic enterprises.[37] He did not anticipate the day when management would invest billions of dollars into retooling factories around self-managing teams, embedding the idea of cooperation into the very physical layout of the workplace. This chapter offers no more than a sketch of how tortuous and incremental the recent progress has been. During the past two decades, management has pursued a multitude of tactics, all of which center more or less imperfectly around a core idea: there is more to be gained in enlisting the enthusiasm and brains of workers in the management cause than in continuing traditionally adversarial relations.

From a covenantal perspective, the strategy of delegating authority and responsibility to workers appears to have the most covenantal appeal of any recent strategy by employers—as an ideal. It seeks to acknowledge the principle of self-management by permitting workers to take on responsibility for their own work. Not surprisingly, the actual strategies and tactics used by management have been of ambiguous value, when measured against two covenantal requirements: that management articulates a truly shared interest or goal with employees, and then stands behind that shared vision with the kind of self-binding gestures that are worthy of employee confidence. Rightly or wrongly, labor advocates remain suspicious. They see a strong historical parallel between current managerial overtures and the cooperation management sought in the 1920s, and argue that the best antidote to the seductive poison of cooperation is massive resistance.[38]

Employee skepticism seems appropriate as a benchmark against which the sincerity of management ought to be measured. Employees have grounds for mistrust when management promotes self-management as an alternative to the self-representation employees traditionally have sought through unions. Such was the strategy at Ethicon, where management used "quality circles" to intimidate employees into voting against having a union. Obviously much rides on whether management makes significant and durable gestures which commit it to delegating genuine authority and responsibility to employees. Where cooperation succeeds, as at the monumental Saturn project, management is careful not to manipulate employees into sacrificing the principle of self-representation for gains in self-management.[39] A covenantal ethic endorses this wall of separation between these two complementary moral principles of employee action.

Even where well-intentioned management woos the cooperation of employees in good faith, the most laudable experiments are easily stressed and crushed by at least three factors: the harsh demands of the market for productive efficiency, unanticipated changes in managerial policy, and the ebbing enthusiasm or entropy of either side. Both management and employees may have a genuine interest in increased productivity or efficiency; that, after all, is the instrumental justification for cooperation. But competitive pressures stress the time-consuming and intensive processes of self-management, tempting both management and employees to return to the more familiar hierarchical and adversarial ways. Or management may change, abandoning previous commitments. Or a cooperative mode simply may be too demanding in the carefully plotted coordination and decentralized decision-making it requires. A covenantal ethic has no ready remedy for these problems; rather, its work is to make the ideal of cooperation important enough that the effort and sacrifices required of management and employees will seem worthwhile.

The sheer difficulty of initiating and sustaining cooperation leads logically to the question: why bother? Of what value is cooperation, and of the employee self-management which supports genuine cooperation? Do the managerial initiatives reviewed in this chapter have any significance, apart from their instrumental use in generating greater productivity and profits? These must be serious questions for a covenantal ethic which prizes the historically long search for common ground between management and employees, and commends gestures of rigorous self-binding to both sides. The next chapter outlines the nature of cooperation, to prepare the ground for answering these questions.

CHAPTER 15

The Nature and Costs of Cooperation

This chapter is an excursus intended to sharpen the question posed at the end of the last chapter: what is the nature of cooperation? Here I will develop a theoretical perspective more akin to the field of organization theory rather than, as elsewhere in this book, the history of management-employee relations. Yet before understanding what covenantal value cooperation has, it is important to know what cooperation actually involves in the functioning of business corporations as densely interconnected networks of human action. Only then can we proceed meaningfully to the main question: why cooperate? In Western Christianity, the past one hundred years of Roman Catholic papal encyclicals on work have devoted sustained attention to this question, and this teaching needs to be developed even further. From a covenantal perspective, the principal point to be stressed in this chapter is that efforts to initiate and sustain cooperation are costly to both management and employees. The path to appreciating what I term the "intrinsic" value of cooperation as an expression of covenantal relations lies through appreciating this costliness.

What Is Cooperation?

The idea of cooperation most commonly implies a quality of will: a readiness to work harmoniously with others. Now, it is tempting to couch the idea of cooperation in terms of personal feeling. As such, it is a psychological term, referring to the attitudes and motivations of participants. And indeed, the vocabulary of personal psychology and the affections, long familiar in the field of Christian ethics, surely is relevant to the construction of cooperation, especially as well-meaning management and employees struggle against a long legacy of antagonism and betrayals. But it is not sufficient for management and employees to care for each other as individuals; if it were, the long story of management-labor relations could have been shortened into a single recipe for generating and reciprocating good intentions. Cooperation involves more than the feelings which management and employees bring to their work together. Feelings and intentions, attitudes and motivations are not the primordial stuff which binds networks of organized action together.

Management and employees also encounter each other as factors of production. The fundamental requirement is for a *coordinated effort* oriented to some identifiable productive aim or aims. What is of particular interest to a covenantal ethic is how the needed coordination gets accomplished—how management and employees cope with the contingencies they present to each other. As illustrated by the past ten chapters, there appear to be three principal alternatives: conflict, compliance, and somewhere between these two, cooperation. It might help to locate these alternatives along a continuum, ranging from more to less coercive. The complete spectrum of alternatives for coordinating human actions ranges in one direction (towards coercion) beyond conflict to outright servitude at one end, where there is no choice of participation. In the other direction (towards voluntariness) it ranges beyond compliance to the ephemeral association of free spirits, where there is no coordination. Of course, both servitude and disorganization are out of bounds in the discussion of how management and employees construct covenantally viable relations. Cooperation is a mode of coordinating activity and so is the antithesis of disorganization. It requires the meaningful consent of management and employees, free choice, and as such is the antithesis of servitude.

Cooperation is not compliance

Perhaps the most common alternative to cooperation during the past two hundred years has been "compliance," where employees simply choose to obey, willingly or grudgingly, the direction exercised by management through the corporate chain of command. Compliance is such a familiar way of coordinating action in business enterprises that it has not been discussed explicitly in this study. To put the matter crudely, management offers wages to employees in order to buy their acceptance of managerial authority. Usually this exchange has proven a viable way to stitch together whole corporations.[1] According to traditional pyramids of authority, executives outline goals and strategies, managers develop plans, and supervisors transmit orders and exercise discipline. Despite a widespread distaste for hierarchical authority, this alternative often appeals to employees, for it relieves them of the laborious work of arranging their work, coordinating it with that of others, and being responsible for its success—jobs that are reserved for managers and supervisors. The whole structure of collective bargaining erected from the 1930s on formalized this division of labor between managerial decision-making and employee obedience. Even in so enlightened an experiment in cooperation as the Saturn project, employees have been sorely tempted to let management be management, taking over authority and responsibility for the work carried out by employees.

This "compliance" expresses the idea of cooperation only in a weak sense: the willingness of employees to abdicate their own judgment and accept managerial direction. Cooperation in the strong sense used here involves more than such simple surrender. It requires the active engagement of employees as well as management in coordinating their efforts around common aims. In essence, cooperation is the *coordination of self-guided efforts, as sustained by the mutual entrustment of contingent wills.* It involves both sides giving up some significant measure of coercive power over each other, and, instead, relying upon each other to exercise initiative in the "right" direction. From the side of management, it occurs when employees are entrusted with significant power in the direction of their own work; this is the ideal expressed in the principle of self-management, and incarnated, however imperfectly, in the management initiatives described in the previous chapter. From the side of employees, cooperation occurs when they choose to exercise initiative and responsibility, rather than to offer nothing more than simple compliance with directions given. Cooperation, in short, is the synergy which results when the delegation of meaningful managerial power is answered by the meaningful self-management of employees.

Cooperation is not conflict

The second alternative to cooperation is "conflict." In conflict, management and employees struggle for control of their relationship and of the productive process. In U.S. industry, this struggle has taken place primarily on shop floors, where employees and unions have resisted the efficient coordination and tight rules sought by management. Interestingly enough, a condition of conflict need not be any more alien to cooperation than the passive compliance outlined above. Employees who have taken up an antagonistic posture towards management have engaged their wills in the struggle to control their own work; the problem for management then is how to recruit and channel that energy, while the problem for employees is how to enlist the active collaboration of management. The struggle can yield to cooperation when both sides find a plausible common aim in boosting their productive efficiency, and employees are permitted and enabled to manage their own work. As will be seen in the next chapter, such a transformation occurred during the mid-1980s at the Illinois plants of the Caterpillar Corporation. Such transformation can occur when employers and employees disentangle the value of productive efficiency, an aim which they can share, from the tyrannical exercise of managerial prerogative or employee obstructionism, which they cannot. Successful programs in cooperation, like that at Saturn, keep the second from poisoning the first.

One further set of distinctions is needed to delineate the specific character of cooperation in business enterprises. According to industrial relations experts Kochan, Katz, and McKersie, cooperation can occur at any of three levels of the relationship between management and employees.[2] First and most simply, employees and management can address basic workplace issues, such as the relations between supervisors and employees, or problems in production. Such was the focus of quality circles. Second, they can reform the organization of work, by setting up teams or changing the manner in which employees are paid, as in the Saturn project. Third, they can address questions pertaining to overall management strategy, such as job security, union influence in managerial decision-making, and sharing of company profits. The third choice clearly represents the greatest infringement upon traditional managerial prerogatives, and was just the kind of participation which the UAW employees asked for at Caterpillar and which the management found to be so troubling. Nevertheless, all three represent growing edges for a covenantal relationship between management and employees.

Given the sheer variety of business, it appears unlikely that there could be a single formula for building covenantal relations across the American landscape of more than a million enterprises. It is more likely that all three modes of coordinating human action have a role in developing an equilibrium among the principles of managerial prerogative, employee self-representation, and employee self-management. The pragmatic balance among basic moral principles of action is necessary for a covenantal quality of relationship, as argued in chapter 7. But cooperation appears to have more covenantal value in that it addresses the basic problem of human relations in business settings at its biblical root. The basic problem is: how, given the demands of tightly interlinked systems of action, are human agents to cope with the unquenchable contingency each presents to the other? The guideline abstracted in chapter 4 from the long history of biblical covenant-building calls for recruiting that contingency rather than suppressing it through conflict or surrendering it through obedience.

The value of cooperation in Roman Catholic social teaching

Of all Western religious traditions, none has paid more sustained and detailed attention to the relations between management and employees than the hundred-year-old Roman Catholic tradition of addressing papal encyclicals to the world of work. One of the most noteworthy developments in this rich vein of thought has been the steadily ripening conviction that management and employees ought to enlarge their capacities to cooperate actively with each other. In 1891, Leo XIII asked only that owners and workers give each other what natural justice required: honest labor for fair wages.[3] Forty years later, Pius XI retained Leo's interest in wage justice but moved away from the static social analysis which undergirded it by emphasizing the functional rather than class distinctions between management and employees.[4] He qualified what here has been termed the principle of managerial prerogative.[5] This was an essential step towards an endorsement of the self-management of employees. Thirty years later, in 1961, John XXIII explicitly called both sides to a partnership, where workers might "have a say in , and may make a contribution toward, the efficient running and development of the enterprise."[6] After another twenty years, John Paul II in 1981 developed the evocative metaphor of a shared "workbench," depicting the work process as an arena of fulfillment in which employees have a legitimate claim to meaningful participation and joint ownership.[7] Most recently, on the one hundredth anniversary of *Rerum Novarum,* John Paul II confirmed this direction: "This teaching also recognizes the legitimacy of workers' efforts to obtain full respect for their dignity and to gain broader areas of participation in the life of industrial enterprises so that, while cooperating with others and under the direction of others, they can in a certain sense 'work for themselves' through the exercise of their intelligence and freedom."[8]

So developed, Catholic social teaching provides a rich image of human fulfillment as an answer to the question of why cooperation is good: through partnerships with management, employees ideally can achieve some meaningful control over their work, elevating the quality of their labor and reinforcing their dignity. This answer has the ring of covenantal truth, for experience has demonstrated that programs of cooperation can be a means for employees to achieve an inestimably greater dignity in work than that provided by mindless repetitive work on the manufacturing or informational assembly line.[9] Nevertheless, this ideal vision oversimplifies the dynamics of cooperation. It leaves the impression that cooperation can be achieved if only management relaxes its demand for control and shares power with workers. John Paul II, for example, devotes a long section of *Laborem Exercens* to hedging in the principle of managerial prerogative by attacking the "priority" of capital over labor, the "economist" fallacy, and the pretensions of management to absolute control.[10] The ideal of cooperation receives much less attention. It appears to be invoked simply as the obvious and unproblematic alternative to the conflict of labor and capital. According to papal teaching, it seems to be a state of harmony towards which management and employees spontaneously should gravitate, in the absence of compelling reasons not to.[11]

It might help if the more recent papal encyclicals subjected the ideal of cooperation to the same critical scrutiny to which they subject the principles of property rights and managerial prerogative. The uncritical endorsement of cooperation reveals the abstract distance of papal teaching from the competitive realities of organizational life. Business enterprises are the creations of human artifice and will, whatever patina of "naturalness" they may take on over decades of their existence. Cooperation between management and employees is hardly the obvious direction to move in. What is needed is to silhouette the value of cooperation in its full height—and depth—and so provide a powerful rebuttal against what John Paul II calls the "economistic" thinking which values the joint labor of management and employees in reductively financial terms.

The Costs Imposed by Cooperation

From the theoretical perspective opened up by a covenantal ethic, "active" cooperation imposes three kinds of serious cost upon management and employees. First, a commitment to cooperation requires both parties to give up some measure of coercive power, and so to reduce the array of means by which they can shape the thinking and action of each other. On the one side, management has to give up control in order to elicit genuine cooperation. In delegating significant autonomy to employees, it exposes itself to the contingencies presented by employees: the potential for inattention, incompetence, laziness, rebellion, or even sabotage. Management which gives up the traditional resource of hierarchical power must appeal to the sense and goodwill of employees, or resort to covert and manipulative tactics which risk eroding the cooperative spirit it is trying to instill. On the other hand, those employees desirous of cooperating expose themselves to the contingencies represented by management when they give up some significant portion of their power to resist. As noted by labor activists, the most potent sources of coercive leverage that employees possess while on the job derive from rigid workrules, job definitions, and schedules. A union which cooperates in setting up work teams effectively abandons these important forms of insurance against managerial pressure. Moreover, as explained in the previous chapter, employees cooperating in teams may attenuate the solidarity bred by the collective resistance of earlier decades. This becomes a particular danger if a cooperative management gives way to a more hard-nosed regime which chooses to renege on the earlier promises, as happened at Caterpillar. In short, the risk of cooperative gestures and tactics is that both sides will deprive themselves of the residual contingency they need to safeguard themselves against betrayal by the other.

Second, even where management and employees wholeheartedly want to collaborate and readily concede the power needed by each other, their cooperation requires enormous effort. In dry terms more familiar to behavioral sciences than to theology, a partnership in cooperation imposes upon all sides heavy "informational" costs. They have to invest more energy and thought into coordinating their efforts and consulting with each other anticipating the problems they need to resolve.

Third, a state of cooperation does not relieve management and employees of the necessity of shaping the thinking and action of each other; it simply relocates the existing struggle of wills onto new terrain. In tightly interlinked systems of action, neither side can afford to walk away from the often complicated and onerous work of influencing the perceptions and behavior of each other. To initiate and sustain cooperation, both sides must make gestures and tactics which communicate their trustworthiness to each other, but without simply abdicating their wills to the control of each other. Cooperation moves both sides from the terrain of war to the terrain of politics, where the deployment of influence tactics becomes all the more demanding and difficult as both sides renounce the use of coercion. Committed to sustaining cooperation, both sides must cultivate and retain the support of each other through ongoing gestures. A difficult balance must be struck between affirmations of trustworthiness and bids for change.

The difficulty of sustaining such a higher order of coordination is illustrated by the experience of one seasoned facilitator of labor-management cooperation. He saw a recurrent pattern during a decade of well-intentioned experiments in a large midwestern city. Some economic crisis—stiffening competition or evaporating markets—would convince management and employees that they had a common interest in abandoning conflict and indifference for a more active partnership. Both sides would make constructive initiatives but soon hit a plateau where repeated efforts by management to secure even more cooperation elicited no responses from employees or unions. Management then would draw back, frustrated that their initiatives were not paying off, and the partnership would wither into a hollow, formal shell of cooperation.[12]

Conclusion

The problems of achieving and sustaining cooperation in business enterprises are formidable because of their organizational location within densely interconnected systems of human action. Business enterprises impose more intense demands than do other forms of human association where individual parties are not so dependent upon the performances of each other. Churches, for example, involve a hardworking core of volunteers and clergy in interdependent networks of action, and leave the remaining members wide latitude as to how intensely to participate. University faculty may have little need to coordinate their work with other departments. It may suffice to nourish cooperation mainly by mutual demonstrations of goodwill and competence.

Cooperation can be secured with relatively little effort where only affirmative feelings have to be cultivated. But when casually supportive parties fall into situations where they depend upon the work of each other, and so become vulnerable to each other, the costs of achieving and sustaining cooperation become serious. This costliness raises a difficult question which a covenantal ethic may not skirt: why bother striving for cooperation? Why can't a covenantal ethic simply endorse the command-obedience model for coordinating human effort in business enterprises? Or why not settle for conflict? As Reinhold Niebuhr realized, conflict is a potent means for achieving rough justice between collective groups such as big management and big unions. Why ask management and employees to engage their minds and hearts in active cooperation? Clearly, the value of costly cooperation ought not be assumed, but must be argued for. This task is taken up in the next chapter.

CHAPTER 16

What Is the Good of Cooperation?

Cooperation is now in vogue. At least since Thomas J. Peters and Robert H. Waterman, Jr.'s, *In Search of Excellence* was a runaway best-seller in 1982, legions of business consultants have been preaching, with the fervor of revivalists, the benefits of "empowering" employees to achieve higher levels of cooperation with management. Consultants and managers are entranced by the "win-win" value of willing cooperation, viewing it as a happily converging interest of management and employees. Others are more skeptical, and their skepticism is reinforced by a long historical view. After all, if cooperation were the obvious, unexceptionable, inarguable, and most economic solution to the problem of how to coordinate human action within dense networks of interdependence, it would have become the "normal" solution decades ago. The proverbial "market" would have forced cooperation upon management and employees alike. The fact that it hasn't, and that experiments in cooperation even fail, testifies to a more complex phenomenon.

If the business history of the past two hundred years is a reliable guide, the current frenzy of enthusiasm for cooperation and employee self-management will subside. It will erode under the accumulated pressure of a thousand disappointments and betrayals; it will be stifled by increasing competitive pressures and squelched by the rising militance of employees responding to coercive managerial tactics. Yet this near inevitability does not warrant a retreat from cooperation as a covenantal ideal. A covenantal ethic has all the more reason to seize the moment and articulate a durable foundation for cooperation by spelling out what might be termed the "deep" value of cooperation which underlies its sheer economic utility.

The basic claim elaborated in this chapter is that the enduring value of cooperation is a function of its costliness. Efforts to elicit cooperation are good because they mirror, however distantly, the nature of God's struggle with God's very human people. Such initiatives serve to uplift and intensify relationships defined by coercion or compliance. From a covenantal perspective, cooperation is a moral achievement, more than nature's own arrangement. It is created through struggle, not through spontaneous, effortless transactions of reciprocal interest. Cooperation, as defined in the previous chapter, is the coordination of self-managed effort as sustained by the mutual entrustment of contingent wills. To generate and sustain such willing coordination involves struggling against centripetal and entropic pressures of many kinds, but principally—according to a covenantal ethic—those generated by managerial and employee fears of the irascible human contingency in each other. The value of cooperation turns not only upon how great a profit it returns but, in a deeper and more important sense, upon what it does to those who participate. As such, cooperation has an intrinsic theological value altogether different than the mutual economic utility that draws management and employees together.

This chapter will illustrate the "deeper" covenantal value of cooperation not with another success story but with the story of a failure: the rise and fall of cooperation at the Caterpillar Corporation during the 1980s and 1990s. This tale poignantly sketches how great is the loss, in covenantal terms, when a successful partnership is deliberately destroyed. A caveat is in order. Not all instances of collaboration between management and employees are economically viable, nor even covenantally valuable; their mutuality needs to be regulated with reference to broader aims and values, as Aristotle long ago noted about genuine friendship. Nevertheless, the implications are stark: as far as the mandate of management and employees to build covenantal relations is concerned, it is hard to imagine a worse sin than to destroy the cooperation both sides have labored to bring about as an antidote to decades of antagonism.

The Destruction of Cooperation at Caterpillar

Perhaps the most bruising recent failure of managerial strategy to sustain cooperation occurred during the early 1990s, at the Illinois manufacturing plants of the Caterpillar Corporation, a worldwide producer of construction equipment. For decades, the relations between Caterpillar management and its principal union, the United Autoworkers (UAW), had been deeply antagonistic. The depth of this antagonism was underlined by more than a half-dozen walkouts since 1955. But especially bitter strikes in 1979 (lasting 80 days) and 1982 (205 days) convinced both sides to inaugurate an experimental program in cooperation.[1]

Begun in 1986, the program gradually won the enthusiastic participation of an increasing number of the 2,200 employees at Caterpillar's plant in Aurora, Illinois. They gained a sense of ownership, and generated ideas which saved the plant $13 million in three years. A spirit of camaraderie began to grow between managers and employees. Then in 1991, a new management team of the company decided to break the power of the UAW to shape the labor contract (which was renegotiated every few years, and was coming up again in 1992). In retaliation, the UAW terminated its cooperation and walked out; the management then locked striking workers out and threatened to replace them with the thousands of eager applicants who quickly queued up for the high-paying jobs. Since 24,000 employees already had been cut from the Caterpillar payrolls since 1979, this threat effectively forced the employees back to work. Plant relations rapidly reverted to the bitter conflict of previous decades.[2] "Caterpillar has a deeply disaffected workforce," wrote a *Business Week* reporter in early 1993.[3] Said one union official, "I will go to my grave with hatred for the company and what it did to people."[4]

Subsequent events have not eased the antagonism. The UAW attempted to have employees stall production by punctiliously following established procedures, but the effort sputtered. In 1994, the UAW went on strike again. This time it protected itself legally against any threat by management to hire permanent replacements.[5] But the Caterpillar management outmaneuvered employees once again by developing a plan to run its plants despite the strike. The union was split, as almost one-third of the 13,400 UAW-affiliated workers crossed the picket lines to work. "We can go on this way as long as we need to," said a Caterpillar president in late 1994.[6] Surely there is blame enough for both management and the UAW to share; as one advocate of cooperation put it during the 1992 standoff, both sides "believe in power, greed and winning at all costs."[7]

In covenantal terms, the struggle pitted two principles most fundamental to the action of each side against each other. When contract talks started in 1992, the new, tough-minded team in top management saw the self-representation of employees as a costly threat to managerial prerogative. Its worry derived from demands which the UAW placed on the bargaining table. The union demanded that management commit itself to remain neutral as the UAW sought to sign up employees not affiliated with the union. While this demand may not have been unreasonable, given the fact that the UAW had become an engine of cooperation, it was rejected out of hand as a serious infringement of managerial prerogative regarding control of some 2,000 nonunion jobs at the company.[8] "How much is it worth to be able to manage your own company?" asked the new CEO of Caterpillar.[9] Management inflamed the conflict by demanding and extracting concessions which effectively broke the solidarity of employees in the present and crippled their self-representation in the future. It provided current employees with job security for only six years (by which time many will have retired), and won the right to hire new workers at half the wages of existing workers. Given these and other major demands, it is surprising that the union was unwilling to insulate the program of cooperation from the struggle of union members for their basic material interests, something necessary for viable covenantal cooperation.[10] Both sides formally canceled their participation in the program.

In essence, the Caterpillar management (with some help from the UAW) deliberately opted for a return to the conflicts of the past. It forced employees back into a defensive posture of renewed conflict, or sullen obedience—the two major alternatives for coordinating activities within a tightly interdependent system. It smashed the "workbench" which John Paul II had called upon management and labor to share. The tragedy of unraveled cooperation became particularly visible in union members like Rich Clausel, an important leader in the program of cooperation. He first helped redesign a dangerous parking lot at the plant. When management paid for its construction, he became an apostle of cooperation, leading workshops to awaken both sides to the harmful consequences of mistrustful attitudes. He also served as a facilitator to manage the fast-sprouting work teams. He worked tirelessly to incarnate a vision of collaborating with management, even to the point of crossing the picket line in late 1992—only to suffer bitter retaliation by the UAW as well as abandonment of support for the program by management. From the union's point of view, such divided loyalty weakened its collective resistance to management.[11]

Now, it would be permissible for management to withdraw from cooperation if the self-management of employees was proving to be economically disastrous; after all, unproductive cooperation has no potential for sustaining covenantal relations when a business corporation is failing financially. Caterpillar management was and remains justifiably worried about sustaining its competitive advantage in the global trade of heavy construction equipment. But this concern seems to have been applied as a club rather than as a tool of persuasion. Employees and management were working successfully toward a shared aim: improving productive efficiency. The UAW estimated that employee involvement boosted the productivity of Caterpillar plants 30 percent, saving as much as $50 million from 1988 to 1991.[12] To management, however, this economy was not as significant as the $80 million expected to be saved during the next three years through the new contractual provisions it forced upon employees in 1992.[13] If these two figures are representative, the difference between them appears less important, morally speaking, than the cooperation that was lost, particularly in light of the fact that labor costs amount to less than 7 percent of Caterpillar's total expenditures.[14]

The Extrinsic Value of Cooperation

Why was it so wrong, from a covenantal perspective, for the Caterpillar management (with some help from the UAW) to destroy six years of carefully nurtured cooperation with employees? The UAW argued that its cooperation with management was good for the corporate bottom line. No doubt many Caterpillar managers agreed, and also felt betrayed when the programmed cooperation was terminated. This "extrinsic" value of cooperation surely is a relevant moral consideration; in business enterprises, strategies and tactics cannot be pursued without regard for their financial sense. But if efforts to unite management and employees in cooperation are valued only for the profits and efficiency they bring, ethicists can mount no objection when such efforts are terminated because some more profitable alternative comes along—as happened at Caterpillar. There is the further problem with measuring the value of cooperation strictly according to the bottom line. Among experiments in cooperation, the Caterpillar case may have been unusual in its claimed profitability. "Participation" programs, as they are termed by academic researchers, usually do not correlate strongly with increased productivity. According to one recent review of the literature, the efforts by management to delegate meaningful power and control to employees tend to yield some measurable economic gains (rarely losses), not spectacular returns.[15]

From a covenantal perspective, the lackluster economic performance of cooperation is not discouraging. To be sure, programs of cooperation have to be economically viable. The market imposes upon business enterprises the discipline of generating a profit, and this discipline effectively controls how ambitiously management may experiment in delegating power. Here the academic studies are encouraging, in suggesting that cooperative ventures are profitable, even if only lukewarmly so. Programs in cooperation need only be profitable, not more profitable than coercion or compliance as alternative modes for coordinating work. The morally significant distinction resides not between management that embraces profitability and management that ignores it. Rather, it resides between management, like Caterpillar's, that measures the value of cooperation strictly according to profitability and management (like Saturn's, presumably) that measures the value of cooperation by other yardsticks as well.

The Intrinsic Value of Cooperation

Cooperation has a second kind of value, an intrinsic value which cannot be reduced to instrumental usefulness, even if it sometimes is outweighed by pressing economic considerations. From a covenantal perspective, what is valuable about "active" cooperation as a mode of coordinating productive activity is its resonance with the divine model of covenant-building. The cooperation which has been modeled by the self-managed teams at Saturn, Caterpillar, Chrysler, and other flagship programs reflects, however imperfectly, the costly manner in which God prods the people to build covenants with each other. The basic similarity is this: just as God chooses to accept, and then recruit, the contingent energies and will of the people for the never-ending work of building up covenantal relations, so management and employees are to enlist rather than suppress the contingent energies of each other. God seeks the cooperation of the people—their active commitment to the work of extending covenantal relations throughout creation. Such cooperation is not an instrument for attaining some extrinsic end, but is itself the end. The work of eliciting and sustaining cooperation aims at a higher quality of relationship between God and God's creatures, but this higher quality of relationship is the means by which the end is reached. In other words, there is no vocation to which cooperation in covenant-building is instrumental; the work of building and sustaining covenantal relations is fulfilled in the authentic effort expended.

Measuring the quality of a relationship is notoriously difficult. The intrinsic value of cooperation shines like quicksilver, reflecting an elusive brilliance. Roman Catholic social thought has coined a term helpful for capturing its value. A "common" good is one which can be experienced by all participants but cannot be divided up and possessed individually. The indivisible aspect of cooperation is its most intriguing, even mysterious, dimension. When wills become aligned in the pursuit of a common aim, by some alchemy a larger whole can be produced which surpasses the previous expectations and anticipations of all parties but cannot be carried away as the exclusive property of any, or even be preserved beyond the synergy of the moment. This common good is a thin, spiritual fire, powerful as a means of motivating collaboration but easily quenched by betrayals or misinterpreted gestures. When the spirit is quenched, it is not easily rekindled.

Cooperation and character

Fortunately the intrinsic value of cooperation can be measured by something more concrete and perhaps durable than such elusive synergy. It adds a specifiable value to the individual characters of those caught up in carrying out and coordinating the myriad tasks of production. In essence, the intrinsic value of cooperation resides in what it does to the managers and employees who seek to recruit the contingent energies of each other.

The idea that cooperation might shape the characters of managers and employees for the good is hardly novel. Recent philosophers admiring of Aristotle's vision of ideal social life have coined the term "social practice" to denote a cooperative activity whose value is to be measured by the "internal goods" it produces. According to Alasdair MacIntyre, "internal goods" include those excellences necessary for carrying out specific practices, and more generally, the virtues of justice (treating others according to their merit or desert), courage (risking harm to oneself), and truthfulness.[16] Of these virtues, perhaps the most relevant is courage for building covenantal relations in networks of tightly coordinated action. No covenant of durable value is achieved without a struggle between the colliding expectations of covenant partners. Moreover, the work of building covenantal relations can generate resistance within each party, as they become aware of the choices involved in choosing to cooperate with their erstwhile antagonists. But it is precisely this costliness which deepens the value of cooperation to participating individuals. Cooperation is valuable precisely because it demands so much more than do the two major alternatives—coercion or compliance—of participating management and employees.

The Three Goods of Cooperation

There are three intrinsic goods of cooperation which correspond to the three burdens outlined at the end of the previous chapter. The first is an awakened sense of responsibility. Management incurs a risk when delegating real power to employees, the risk of becoming vulnerable to the abuse or simply the poor use of that power. Surely many nightmares have been concocted of fears that empowered employees will not exercise adequate diligence, insight, dynamism, and careful attention to the complexities and nuances of organizing work—or respectful of remaining managerial domains of authority. But if power can be a corrupting aphrodisiac, surely programs of industrial cooperation like that at Caterpillar also have shown it to be a potent catalyst of personal responsibility. In the early 1980s, the workforce at Caterpillar's Aurora plant was notorious for absenteeism, indifference, and substance abuse. As the programs in cooperation took hold, the workforce came alive. Management turned teams loose to solve problems, rather than having to continue to impose new ideas upon resistant employees. One team visited Caterpillar dealers, and learned that customers had been complaining about the dull finish of Caterpillar's signature yellow paint on the heavy equipment in showrooms. The employees took the initiative, spending months overhauling the painting process to produce a glossier finish, to the delight of the Caterpillar dealers.[17] Once employees are awakened by the availability of exercising real and significant power, it is not at all clear that the privilege will be abused. The reason is that managerial values—increasing efficiency, reducing costs, attracting and retaining customers, and the like, are hardly the arbitrary whims of management. They are designed into productive processes, and are likely to exert a powerful influence over employees who are given the leverage to enact them of their own will.[18] For example, the president of a small firm in Springfield, Missouri, took the major risk of opening the financial books of the business to employees. He gave up a key source of management power, the power which derives from privileged information. But he was rewarded with a record growth which was fueled by employees who had become fascinated with the numbers and used their inside knowledge to reduce costs of production.[19]

The second intrinsic good is expanded vision, which derives from the often burdensome input of energy and skill that cooperation requires of both employees and management. Of course, the time-honored bureaucratic pattern of transmitting commands downward and securing obedience from compliant employees is much easier. Saturn workers grew fearful and weary of the endless consensus-building and consultations needed to coordinate the work of teams and assembly lines in the absence of direct hierarchical relations. Nevertheless, the effort which management and employees must invest to keep cooperating has a payoff of deep value, far beyond the economic gains it might bring. A policy of cooperation calls management and employees out of their sequestered certainties and narrow loyalties. It puts both sides into the position of having to expand their vision. The "informational" demands of cooperation challenge the intelligence of both sides, forcing them to develop their capacities to hear and absorb perspectives other than their own. Caterpillar managers and workers grew by listening to each other. The unemployed UAW workers taken on at Saturn were stretched beneficially by having to organize themselves as self-managing teams to solve problems. Similarly, the emotional demands of cooperation challenged Caterpillar employees to break up prejudices cemented through years of mutual antagonism. During the era of cooperation, one group of employees invited their foreman to their annual pig roast. "Friendships bloomed between people who had long gone their separate ways," according to the *Wall Street Journal*.[20]

The third and last intrinsic good of cooperation is intensified consultation. It reflects the fact that cooperation deepens, rather than relieves, the burden of mutual influence which a network of interdependent action places upon participants. Having forsworn the use of coercion, management and employees must devise ways of persuading each other. Success in persuasion requires that they first listen to each other, acknowledging the interests, claims, and proposals of each other. But while it means more effort, cooperation also yields great benefits. It has intrinsic value in channeling the energies of both sides in the direction of consultation and consensus-building. A policy of cooperation encourages both sides to knead the principles of managerial prerogative and managerial self-representation into pragmatic compromises. Here can be heard a distant echo of God's strategy to recruit and teach followers, rather than to bribe or suppress these wayward people through rewards, punishments, threats, and promises.

Enlarged freedom

In choosing to cooperate, management and employees enter into a mutual vulnerability which challenges them to develop capacities to work with each other. They now encounter each other as resources of latent insight, ingenuity, experience and skill. In the terms developed in chapter 9, they enlarge their freedom to act. Rather than being constrained to find ever more ingenious and effective ways to resist or suppress the contingencies presented by each other, they are now liberated to benefit from those reservoirs of energy and initiative. What they are trying to achieve, through cooperation, is a mutual dependence of a higher order than mechanical linkages, where bosses dictate or design the content of work and employees respond by complying or resisting. For example, no one employee on the Caterpillar paint line could have done more than dream of retooling the process to produce a glossier finish, given the entrenched antagonism between management and union employees; as the proverb has it, "one hand cannot clap." The unthinkable became possible when employees were authorized and encouraged to visit dealers as emissaries of management.

Of course, this enlarged freedom can be lost, as is particularly visible in the case of Rich Clausel. Like other union members who fully embraced cooperation, he found his loyalties deeply divided during the 1992 contract talks and so penned a manifesto calling both sides to reconsider their errors. Figures like Clausel had grown beyond conflict. They were modeling a pathway which transcended the endemic antagonisms between the two sides. Their partisan instincts to obstruct the other side had been shelved in favor of impulses to seek common ground, to build a consensus and push the common work forward. But when cooperation collapsed, this resource was wasted. Rich Clausel returned to the plant floor as a worker with a defined job on the paint line. The aura of empowerment had vanished. He closed out his enthusiasm for cooperation by throwing away two trash bags full of material on management-employee relations.[21]

Three Qualifications

From a covenantal perspective, it is shocking that a management willingly would destroy the cooperative impulses of its employees, driving them back into a posture of resistance or sullen obedience. Of course, the same indictment applies to unions which choose to undermine a pattern of cooperation patiently nurtured by sincere (as opposed to duplicitous) management. Walter Rauschenbusch criticized capitalist industry for promoting competition and conflict between management and employees, and surely the destruction of cooperation qualifies as a sin according to the Social Gospel.[22] But cooperation is not of the unqualified value Rauschenbusch attached to it, for three reasons.

First, the cooperation which has value in a given organizational setting might work against other social interests. This study has treated the relations of management and employees in isolation from virtually all external considerations. It is quite conceivable that management might solicit the most substantive cooperation of employees while generating products or services which exploit customers and clients, cater to mindless consumerism, ravage local communities, destroy the environment, or contribute to the repression of human rights. A moral inventory of these wider linkages lies beyond the scope of this study, which is concerned strictly with the employee relation. Clearly, the constructive work of establishing covenantal relations requires measuring the intrinsic value of cooperation for all affected parties. Building covenantal relations might require a prior work of reforming or even destroying anticovenantal elements bearing upon the relationship. For example, employees may find it necessary to blow the whistle on destructive business practices, while management may find it necessary to resist discriminatory union practices.

Second, cooperation in itself does not express a full equilibrium among the three principles central to the action of management and employees. Management might argue that if it keeps focused upon an aim truly shared with employees, and eschews the use of coercive tactics, it can protect the self-representation of employees unilaterally. One recurring temptation for management has been to delegate some margin of meaningful power to employees so that they will not be tempted to organize unions. Such engineered cooperation has recurred since the joint labor-management committees of World War I and the "corporate welfare" movement which peaked in the

1920s. Undoubtedly, many managers today hope that programs of genuine cooperation will serve to ward off the unionization of their employees. But the idea of management organizing employees into company unions was deemed illegal by the Wagner Act precisely because such efforts might forestall or supplant the efforts of employees to organize themselves. Employees should not be put in the position of having to choose between managing their work and struggling for their self-representation, as they were at Caterpillar. From a covenantal vantage point, an equilibrium must be achieved not only between managerial prerogative and employee self-management—as cooperative programs attempt to do—but with reference to the principle of employee self-representation. Maintaining this equilibrium means maintaining a balance between the three principles. In 1993, the Dupont Company was ordered to disband worker-management teams because it had organized them, and their jurisdictions overlapped areas covered by collective bargaining.[23]

Third and finally, genuine cooperation may be precluded by the nature of the work employees do. Of course, the potential scope of self-management and cooperation is not fixed. Fifty years ago, the rigidly controlled assembly lines of General Motors offered employees little hope for meaningful labor, but such work has been revolutionized by the decentralized teams of a Saturn plant today. Nevertheless, some tasks are so atomized, mechanized, and dehumanized by the technologies used that they leave little or no scope for employees to be empowered to reorganize and govern their work. "(M)ost work is not intrinsically fulfilling," argues ethicist Stanley Hauerwas.[24] Clerical work in the service sector is rapidly taking on the character of factory work, with the rapid pacing of mind-numbing tasks: processing of insurance claims, for example, or even the making of repetitious telephone calls.

Conclusion

For both management and employees, cooperation imposes serious risks and requires a great expenditure of effort. The question "why cooperate?" will always be appropriate, whether asked by management or unions. Behind this question lies a religious query: in any given business enterprise, is God building covenantal relations through cooperation, through conflict, or through the simple obedience of employees to management? The intrinsic value of cooperation needs to be argued for, in every different setting, because cooperation is costly. A case needs to be made, and making the case will involve calculations of financial as well as other costs.

But financial considerations should not be allowed to preempt the less countable benefits of cooperation. Continuing the program of cooperation at Caterpillar, for example, apparently would have required some financial sacrifice, relative to the gains achieved through the harsh economies management reimposed upon its plants during the early 1990s. From a covenantal perspective, paying the reported differential would have been worthwhile, as management continued to reap the harvest of willing, imaginative collaboration with its employees. Through eyes of faith, management and employees ought to see that the risks they take by entrusting themselves to the contingency presented by each other are mirrored as abundant benefits. Cooperation forces both sides to develop noncoercive and nonmanipulative tactics for shaping the thinking and action of each other, and to open themselves to being influenced by each other. It expands their liberty by enabling them to tap the initiative, skills, and insights of each other, rather than expend continuing energy to suppress the contingencies presented by each other. Cooperation thus has an intrinsic value which of course is no substitute for economic viability, but which can and should temper the tendency of management and employees to value each other in reductively economic terms.

CHAPTER 17

Covenantal Realism and the Future of Cooperation

One striking feature of labor history has been the periodic rising and ebbing of conflict between management and employees during the past two hundred years. If this cyclical pattern is a reliable guide, the conflict between management and employees very likely will intensify during the next decade or two, less as a matter of historical inevitability than because of broad trends. The generation which enjoyed the post–World War II "social contract" hammered out between management and unions during the 1930s and 1940s is passing. Millions of managers have been cut loose from this contract; further millions of younger workers have been excluded from it by the shrinkage of unions and whole industries. Those employers squeezed relentlessly by competition are not likely to restore or extend the generous provisions of the old social contract. As a result, millions of employees, particularly those in the enormous service sector, now suffer the low pay and fragile employment which historically have spawned efforts to organize unions. Given the deep deposit of historical experience and memory, the struggle may intensify in its old form: employees resisting collectively by coalescing in unions and evading, resisting, or undermining managerial control; management offering counterresistance by evading, minimizing, or destroying those unions.[1]

A Symbol to Integrate the Field

Where will God be in this struggle, if and when it intensifies? Interpreters of the faith likely will be pulled strongly in two different directions, as partisans either of management or of employees. Within the field of Christian ethics, the current divisions are likely to remain deep, as ethical managerialists continue to challenge management to meet worthy ideals, while prophetic critics cast doubt upon the moral will or effectiveness of management to do so. Some ethicists may strive for a more neutral ground. This study provides one pathway to that more neutral ground through the strong gravitational field exerted by ethical managerialism. It is aimed at those Christian realists who want to pay fair heed to the perspectives of both management and employees, to the elements of both conflict and cooperation in the employment relation. I have developed here a theory which I hope will afford Christian business ethicists with critical but not antagonistic leverage against the ideology of ethical managerialism.

I have striven for fairness by lifting up what was of covenantal value and criticizing what is of disvalue in the strategies and tactics of both management and employees. On the one side, there has been much to affirm in the astonishing series of efforts by management to elicit the cooperation of employees, from the paternalistic efforts of early industrialists to raise their employees' standard of living, to the scientific cooperation terminated by the Great Depression, to the "social contract" in effect with organized labor after World War II, to bona fide contemporary efforts to engender a cooperative spirit by empowering employees. Similarly, employees turned constructively from revolutionary strategies to trade agreements and collective bargaining, and from more violent to less violent strike tactics and have responded again and again to good-faith efforts by management to replace conflict with cooperation. On the other side, management has displayed a continuing, often virulent, hostility to unions through tactics which have evolved from lockouts, court injunctions, open thuggery, and political efforts such as the open-shop campaign, to extralegal or marginally legal tactics for undermining unionization, to a variety of ways to eliminate or relocate jobs, from outsourcing to downsizing. And employees have employed extralegal or marginally legal tactics of their own, from the violent strikes of a century or a half-century ago, to wildcat strikes and other forms of fractional bargaining. Virtually all the strategies and tactics used by both sides are deeply ambiguous; fairness has required working through these strategies and tactics one by one and offering an assessment which pays due heed to the temper of the times. The inclusive approach I have taken is liable to errors of emphasis. My account is likely to please neither ethical managerialists nor radical critics, but it may appeal to realists as an effort to give the moral claims of both management and employees relatively equal weight.

If the budding field of Christian business ethics is to integrate mutually antagonistic viewpoints into some coherent program of inquiry and reflection, a common basepoint is needed. A religious-minded ethic, as I have sought to develop here, requires a symbol or metaphor which possesses an evocative power that is recognized and shared by all wings of the debate, however much its meaning and application to the world of business might be debated. To date, the symbol most widely shared by mainline Protestant, evangelical Protestant, and (admittedly to a lesser extent) Roman Catholic approaches to business ethics is that of "covenant." With its rich overtones of promise-making and promise-keeping, it might serve as an ecumenical standard for ethical reflection on business enterprises.

The question which needs to be pressed by Christian business ethicists is simple: can business enterprises be covenantal communities, as Stackhouse and McCann have asserted?[2] In what sense and to what extent? To date, "covenant" has been an aspirational term. It has been used to point to the moral quality of mutual obligations which ought to bind business enterprises to their internal and external stakeholders. More is needed, however. For the idea of covenant to have normative power, it must be shown to have a descriptive basis, a plausible organic linkage to what "really" happens in the relationship between management and employees. Otherwise, covenantal thinking will slip into an impotent dichotomy, where a covenant is palpable only where management visibly cares for its employees and other stakeholders but otherwise follows its own harsh business rules. Here I have sought to resist such a dichotomized approach. I have argued that there is a covenantal logic visible in the history of the employment relation in the United States. I develop this logic by narrating and interpreting the succession of strategies and tactics that management and employees have used to enforce their will against each other, or to recruit each other to cooperation. Out of this struggle, durable goods have emerged; these goods express, however tentatively, the lovingkindness and justice mandated by the biblical prophets.

A Biblical Theory of Covenant-Building

My aim here is to develop a theory, a testable explanation of the employment relation. It might be most helpful to begin an exposition of this theory with a vision interpreted from biblical history. The vision is this: God has a project, to create and sustain a people of faith. God works through every kind of human relationship, to bring the whole human commonwealth into covenantal relations of mutual respect, care, and justice. No sphere of human life, not even the most hard-nosed business enterprise, is immune to God's influence or lies beyond God's claim. Indeed, business enterprises exhibit elements basic to God's struggle, elements which are immediately familiar to participants in business enterprises as systems of densely interconnected human action. Management and employees present irreducible contingency to each other, a contingency derived from the fact that they are creatures endowed with will and spirit. Embedded as they are in systems of functionally interdependent action, they are vulnerable to each other. As a result, both sides are engaged in defining the basis upon which each can find the other to be reliable; moreover, they seek to bend the other to fit that mold. The struggle need not be conflictual, although it often has been; it need not even be particularly visible. In the absence of simple surrender, this kind of struggle occurs inevitably where will meets will.

From a covenantal perspective, the contingency of human action has been rendered durable, and effectively ineradicable, by God's sovereign choice to work primarily with and through the hearts and minds of God's people—to enlist more than to suppress those human energies which variously undermine or press forward with the fulfillment of God's project. At issue here is not the great contest of justification which Paul, Augustine, and Martin Luther described as occurring between God's will and rebellious human wills; that contest was resolved, in principle, by the classic Reformation insight that God is the sole agent of human salvation. Rather, this study is concerned with what might be termed the "horizontal" dimension, the relationships among human actors. God works either with our active engagement or against our resistance to bring a covenantal quality to our social relations, to secure our cooperation in infusing all human associations with the love, justice, and wholeness demanded by the prophets. To say anything less is to admit that God has abandoned entire spheres of human life to a void from which God's will is absent—something unimaginable from a covenantal perspective.

But how can we claim knowledge, in faith, of what God is doing to bring about covenantal relations between management and employees? The obvious approach is to measure the struggle between management and employees against biblical norms, by asking whether both sides have manifested lovingkindness, justice, and shalom in the strategies and tactics they have applied to each other. I suspect that such an approach is doomed to frustration, at least to the extent that such norms are simply grafted onto business enterprises. If not grounded in the reality of functionally interdependent human action, covenantal norms are easily subject to co-optation by managerial ideology or to polarization by prophetic discourse into oppositional polemics. A more helpful approach is to explore the history of labor-management relations for the moral parameters which have developed within it, and then develop a normative biblical vision in resonance with those parameters. The specifications of what God means by covenantal love and justice need to be sought within, rather than imposed upon, the particularities of each kind of human relationship.

Two Durable Goods: Justice and Love

Here, then, is the theory which has emerged from the intersection of biblical narrative with the history of management-employee relations. A covenant is a device through which agents—human and divine—cope with durable contingencies by making durable commitments. But what kinds of durable commitments have management and employees made to each other? What are the durable goods in this relationship? This study tracks the emergence of two: the common "cause" of positive freedom through cooperation, and the "internalized restraint" exercised by management and employees who bind themselves to respect the moral principles basic to the action of each other. These two kinds of covenantal goods are indispensable to genuine cooperation, for they provide two means by which management and employees can convert the durable contingencies they present to each other into resources for the benefit of each other, thus incarnating covenantal love. These covenantal goods are durable not in the sense that management and employees have been willing and able to maintain them for decades on end—although some exemplary firms have. Rather, these goods are durable in the sense that they refuse to disappear from the horizon of possibility within a history that has intertwined raw conflict, contractual commitments, and costly cooperation in a rough evolutionary sequence.

Management and employees have moved towards justice as they have worked out a pragmatic equilibrium among three moral principles central to their capacity to be human agents in tightly interconnected systems of action: the autonomy or "prerogative" claimed by management, and the "self-representation" sought by employees, along with the "self-management" of employees of interest to both parties. All three principles appear indispensable to the functioning of employees and management within business enterprises. As a result, covenantal justice in business enterprises appears to be a moving target, an equilibrium which can slip downward in quality, or be raised upward as both sides improve their capacity to honor the principle or principles of action most central to each other.

Achieving covenantal relations has been difficult because, historically, the first two of these three principles often have been polarized into direct conflict. This conflict was no historical accident; strictly speaking, the first two principles cannot be honored in full because they, when pressed to an extreme, are mutually contradictory. During the last quarter of the nineteenth century, managerial prerogative gained ascendancy; during the first half of the twentieth century, the principle of employee self-representation rose and crested. Now managerial prerogative again appears on the rise, even as management pays increasing heed to employee self-management. Chapters 6 through 16 offer an outline and covenantal interpretation of this history. The conflict between managerial prerogative and employee self-representation, so deeply embedded by the end of the nineteenth century, moderated briefly as both sides began to bind themselves to exercise what here has been termed "internalized restraint." They began to manifest the first exceedingly tentative gestures of covenantal love appropriate to business enterprises, by committing themselves not to undermine the agency of each other, upon pain of the contractual sanctions they agreed to through collective bargaining.

However modest, such covenantal love has been difficult to sustain. The conflict between the principles of managerial prerogative and employee self-representation intensified during the 1930s, then was relieved by a half-century of collective bargaining; now it has intensified again in the 1980s and 1990s as management has sought, with considerable success, to discourage the collective self-representation of employees. Employers have developed ever more ingenious ways to thwart the efforts of employees to organize or sustain unions, principally by avoiding committing themselves to collective bargaining.

The covenantal ethic developed here opposes these initiatives by management, whether they are openly coercive or covertly manipulative. At the core of covenant-building, as modeled by God across the long sweep of biblical narrative, lies the elemental requirement that both sides bind themselves not to exploit the weaknesses of each other. This stricture rules out the tyrannical and arbitrary exercise of power by either side. A covenantal ethic modeled upon the "internalized restraint" and tactics of enlistment and teaching practiced by God through Jesus offers a strong presumption against the use of coercion by either side. Here the coercive measures used by employees to organize unions appears somewhat more covenantally viable: the aim of collective bargaining has been to draw management into sharing the power to define relations of mutual obligation, while the aim of management has been to retain unilateral control over workplace relations.[3] Of course, as unions grew and some became corrupt, both management and employees have come to distrust them.

Cooperation as a Common Aim

If the two principles of managerial prerogative and employee self-representation exhaustively defined the relationship between management and employees, both sides might be locked into an unresolvable struggle of perpetually shifting advantage. Yet both sides also are answerable to a third moral principle: the claim that employees ought to be engaged in governing the work process, as well as representing their material interests collectively. This principle of "self-management" operated powerfully in the small workshops of the nineteenth century, then was suppressed by the emergence of large bureaucratic organizations early in the twentieth century. It now is gaining currency again, and can be stated as a second formal condition of covenanting: that both sides join in the pursuit of a common aim. The common aim here is an "active" cooperation which relies upon employees to internalize both freedom and responsibility to direct their own work in pursuit of business goals defined mainly by management. This common aim can be contrasted to both the surrender or compliance traditionally sought by management and to the resistance and conflict traditionally practiced by employees.

Such an ideal of active cooperation is hardly new. For a century, Roman Catholic papal encyclicals have been calling upon management and employees to recognize and honor the essentially collaborative nature of their enterprises. Nor has this ideal emerged in an economic vacuum. The proverbial market "demands" that a business enterprise be economically viable, which requires that the labor of employees and management be ordered to the value of efficiency. Management, always vulnerable to the failure of employees to perform adequately, has begun to realize that its enterprises can operate more productively if they enlist the initiative, intelligence, and energies of employees by delegating meaningful power and responsibility to them. During the past three decades, ample experience in cooperation has been gained by both management and employees. Yet this experience has been ambiguous. Contrary to naive hopes, it is costly and difficult to achieve and sustain cooperation in a system of densely interdependent action. Moreover, managerial strategies and tactics to elicit cooperation have been marred by manipulation and betrayal, as well as crowned with success. The problem is that a policy of cooperation presents both management and employees with risk. In covenantal terms, it intensifies their vulnerability to each other.

Cooperation requires a strong form of industrial love, marked by courage and sheer persistence. Both sides must dare to take substantial risks in their attempts to elicit the cooperation of the other, and they must invest large quantities of energy in sustaining that collaboration. Yet despite the formidable costs, there are payoffs. Cooperation has an extrinsic value in the economic gains (usually modest) which it usually generates. More important from a covenantal perspective, it has intrinsic value in shaping the characters of both sides around valuable skills: skills in listening and persuading; skills in organizing work and deploying resources without resort to coercion; skills in exercising power within networks of moral accountability. Cooperation brings both sides to acknowledge the claim of justice in the sense of recognizing each other as resources of insight, ingenuity, and experience. Such justice enlarges the freedom of both sides to achieve their goals.

Towards a Realistic Business Ethic

The willing, active collaboration of management and employees appears the most commodious expression of covenant-building within networks of densely interdependent action. Yet ideal visions of cooperation, such as that proffered by Walter Rauschenbusch, have blossomed, then faded, in the past, and likely will continue to appear and then disappear in the future. This study closes, then, not with a triumphant evocation of cooperation as the pinnacle of covenant-building, for such a consummation may not be reached or sustained in history, but by anchoring its vision in four realistic requirements for a covenantal quality of relationship between management and employees.

First and most important, a covenantal ethic needs to begin on the ground, as it were, and attend closely to the practical questions all participants bring. Business enterprises focus the attention and interests of both management and employees upon an exceedingly practical problem: how each side can come to rely upon the other in a network of densely interdependent action. On what basis can both parties have confidence in each other? Any practical covenant-building advice must take seriously the vantage points of all sides, rather than impose sentimental ideals which may be void of relevant practical content. The covenantal ethic developed here, being so resolutely interactive, accords much authority to the standpoint of both participants. It assumes that norms are revealed within history and are discovered and clarified through conflict as well as agreement.

Given the respect a covenantal ethic accords to the viewpoints of participants, it is evident that a strategy of cooperation might not be appropriate in all settings. Some obvious reasons were sketched at the end of the previous chapter: the content of work may be so degraded and mindless that it offers no scope for employees to participate in the governance of their activities; management might delegate self-management and seek to elicit cooperation as a ploy to avoid having to recognize and negotiate with representatives of employees; or cooperation might be gained at serious cost to third parties outside the business enterprise.

The second qualification of the ideal is that the path of covenant-building does not lead inexorably upward. To be sure, a progressive view is implied by the organization of this study. It began with a focus upon strategies and tactics of conflict, then moved to contractual relations, and finally took up the potential of cooperation. Overall, there is some evidence of progress, in that the fierce head-to-head battles of the nineteenth century have not been renewed in as openly a violent form. Management and employees have gained sophistication in dealing with each other. Yet according to at least one eminent authority, there has been no essential change in the nature or amount of cooperation sought by management during the past century.[4] And there certainly have been stunning failures in cooperation. My theological conviction is that the potential for building covenants resides in all forms of human association, but that does not imply a naively progressive view of history. There are no irreversible leaps forward, nor are there permanent retreats. A new era of contractual relations must be built, contract by contract. The very costliness of cooperation means that its practice must be learned anew the hard way, by trying and trying again.

Third, a covenantal analysis must not gloss over what the Christian faith terms "sin." It seems likely that the more destructive strategies and tactics deployed by management and employees are compounded by sin. I have avoided the terminology of sin in this study because concrete denunciations of sin retard rather than advance our understanding. Judgments of particular sins generate more heat than light, while more abstract and universal judgments of sinfulness may generate less heat, but equally little light. Moreover, it easily becomes gratuitous for an observer to pass moral judgment upon corporate actors, whether managers or employees, who must make their way amid risks and vulnerabilities to which the observer is not subject. For example, it is unclear what might be gained by judging as "sinful" the motives which drive small-business owners to run their enterprises into the ground rather than bargain with employees.[5] Far more constructive appears to be the incremental approach of evaluating each strategy and tactic for its potential to strengthen, rather than erode, a covenantal quality of relations. The term "covenant-building" points to the task ahead, rather than allocating responsibility for the failures behind. For this reason, I have focused upon actual strategies and tactics of both sides, leaving the interpretation of actual motives to the partisans and historians of both sides.

Fourth and finally, neither management nor employees are free agents, in the classic sense of possessing autonomy to conceive, will, and do. Both sides are subject to finitude, that morally neutral inability which derives from the limited extent of individual human powers. The nature of business enterprises as tightly interlinked task networks both extends and also channels and limits human powers. However individual managers feel about the cooperation they achieve with employees, they are not at liberty to buck policies laid down by unsympathetic senior management. Furthermore, enterprises are tightly linked with other organizations, introducing other pressures which serve both to extend and limit the powers of management and employees.

Given these four constraints upon a covenantal ethic, it may be that genuine cooperation can proceed only as management and employees come to believe, as a matter of faith, that business enterprises simply are cooperative systems by their very nature, as Chester Barnard argued more than half a century ago.[6] This is a core conviction among ethical managerialists, and it always deserves a hearing. Professing Christians on both sides need to believe that God wants them to overcome the substantial barriers of risk and vulnerability which discourage active efforts to seek genuine partnerships with each other. If this study provides the conceptual apparatus for making such managerialist confidence credible, it will have served its purpose.

Notes

Chapter 1

1. Niebuhr 1941, 12–18.

2. Stackhouse and McCann 1991.

3. This consensus is inferred but appears real. Most Christian business ethicists devote only a few pages to the idea of covenant and say little about the employment relation; they seem rather to focus upon the relationship between a corporation and its customers, suppliers, and other elements of its environing society (McCoy 1985, 223–24; May 1995, 696; Siker, Donahue, and Green 1991, 820–23; Reeck 1982, 164–66; Childs 1995, 66–70; Walton 1988, 209–11). The holistic views they articulate about responsibility and mutuality nonetheless seem to carry over, explicitly or implicitly, into the internal relations of the corporation. Not surprisingly, a concern for the dignity of employees is more visible in the few texts which do focus explicitly on the employment relation, and use covenant to introduce biblical conceptions of justice (Sturm 1973; Chewning et al. 1990, 26–32). The pithiest but most expansive invocation of covenant is to be found in DePree 1989, 15, 28, 37–38, 60–61, 90.

4. See Laura Nash, for example, who distinguishes a "covenantal ethic" of "mutually enabling relationships" from an extractive ethic of "self-interest" (1993, chap. 5).

5. Because this study addresses collective struggles, I juxtapose the term "management" with "employees," for whom no term of aggregation is available. The exceptions occur in chapters 6 through 10, where for reasons of historical accuracy I juxtapose the terms "owner" and "employer" with "workers." Large bureaucratic corporations did not become widespread until the early twentieth century, displacing smaller owner-operated firms. And through the first half of the twentieth century, it is perhaps more accurate to speak of "workers" than "employees," given that struggles to unionize occurred mainly in manufacturing industry.

6. Niebuhr 1954, 134 .

7. Ramsey 1950, 2–24, 367–88.

8. Sturm 1973 .

9. Allen 1984, 60–81.

10. Davis 1961; see Stackhouse and McCann 1991, chap. 8 for a startling set of claims about the premodern roots of the modern corporation.

11. Raushenbusch 1912, pt. 3, chaps. 4–7 and pt. 5, chs. 2–7.

12. "Managerial ideologies" generally, according to sociologist Reinhard Bendix in his classic study of authority relations in industry, are "attempts by leaders of enterprises to justify the privilege of voluntary action and association for themselves, while imposing upon all subordinates the duty of obedience and service to the best of their ability" (Bendix 1973, xxii). Such ideologies are "ethical" to the extent that they make moral arguments, appeals to some good served by the control management exerts over employees.

13. Lovin 1995, 41–46, 67–71.

14. MacIntyre 1984, 30, 74; Bellah et al. 1986, 45.

15. See his classic statement (Drucker 1954) and his lengthier 1974 compendium of managerial "tasks, responsibilities and practices." In a nutshell, he views the responsibilities of managers as threefold: sustaining economic performance, generating suitable work for employees, and managing the impacts of the enterprise upon society (Drucker 1974, 40–41). This holistic ideology is embodied institutionally in the Academy of Management, the professional association of management consultants and teachers, and particularly in constituent interest sectors such as the "social issues in management" division.

16. Shriver helpfully has delineated three stages in the evolution of managerialist ideology, and his analysis is reinforced and amplified by two classic sociological studies. First, as pyramids of arbitrary economic power were built by entrepreneurs in the late nineteenth and early twentieth centuries, figures such as John D. Rockefeller, Andrew Carnegie, and Henry Ford gave voice to an early managerial ideology which attributed their power and success to individual striving. Ethical managerialism thus has unpromising roots in a harsh social Darwinism, but even here was encased in a broad utilitarian argument. Frederick Winslow Taylor, father of "scientific management," argued that increasingly technocratic managerial control over the work process would yield great benefits to consumers in terms of more goods at cheaper prices, and higher wages for workers.

This utilitarian argument carried over into what Shriver identifies as the second phase of managerial ideology, but was extended beyond narrowly economic considerations. As businesses grew into large corporations during the early decades of the twentieth century, the arbitrary power of owners gave way to the bureaucratically defined authority of managers. The function of management came to be seen as a profession with an ethic of responsibility for the stakeholders affected by managerial action: first, employees, and later, for society as a whole. Already by the 1920s and 1930s, according to Reinhard Bendix, managers were beginning to see their work as eliciting cooperation through the skillful handling of subordinates, rather than simply through exercising arbitrary authority (Bendix 1973, 281–340, especially 300–301).

The influence of this stakeholder model peaked in the decades of American economic hegemony following World War II. A rising tide of professional managers saw themselves coordinating the resources and adjudicating the competing demands of different constituents—employees, suppliers, communities, government, and so forth—in an enlightened way. In a lengthy 1956 study, for example, Francis X. Sutton and three other Harvard scholars contrasted the "classic" American business creed, which according to them emphasizes economic rewards, self-interest, and egotism; the property rights exercised by both management and employees; and the contractual subordination of employees to management, and management to owners with a more recent "managerial" variant, which stresses the responsibilities of managers and service to a variety of stakeholders; the interdependence of management and employees in the firm conceived as a human society; and the professionalization and autonomy of management (Sutton et al. 1956, 33–65, 100–104, 114–35, 159–63, 254–55, 263, 281, 344, 356–57, etc.).

The "professionalization" of management had a profound impact upon the employment relation, in two relatively distinct ways. On the one hand, socially and ethically minded managerialists were claiming, as Drucker did, that management made employees effective in their work, by avoiding or overcoming adversarial relations with their employees. Chester I. Barnard, the widely influential management theorist, claimed that business enterprises were inherently cooperative, and that the work of executives was in large part to smooth the way of cooperation. The job of managers was to manage, as Drucker frequently asserted. Managing involved setting the terms of employment, designing the work that employees performed, and delegating whatever decision-making authority was necessary in order to enable employees to produce. Sound management required enabling and encouraging employees to contribute their full potential of intelligence, skill, and effort to attain the goals defined by management, for success here redounded to the benefit of everyone.

In a second stream of thought (from which Drucker demurred), ethical managerialism claimed to make employees happy as well as effective. This branch of the ideology has absorbed a succession of visions as to what constitutes the happiness of employees. During the 1940s and 1950s, industrial psychologists promoted "human relations," or the happy immersion of individuals in workgroups; during the 1960s and 1970s, humanistic psychologists advocated the self-realization of employees as individuals; and during the 1980s and 1990s, contemporary consultants of all stripes are pressing the satisfactions of mastery and control which accrue to the members of self-managing workteams.

Most recently, ethical managerialism has staked out a teaching function, correlating with Shriver's third stage. They have come to see themselves as teachers, coaches, and "listeners" engaged in brokering different points of view. They have taken on what one ethicist has termed the "ecclesiological" task of defining the moral culture and values of their corporations, all while empowering employees to take charge of realizing those values (Everett 1986). Well-known managerialist gurus like Tom Peters counsel managers to articulate and reinforce the basic values of their organizations, then to turn employees loose to achieve them (Peters and Waterman 1982). Some companies, the most celebrated of which is Johnson & Johnson, for decades have framed their relationship with employees and other stakeholders within an evolving code of strict moral accountability.

However much managerial ideology has evolved in a covenantal direction—and much progress is evident, from early social-Darwinist interpretations of the employment relation, to the exhortations to empower employees—the litmus test of its covenantal viability is how well it balances the principles of managerial prerogative, employee self-representation, and employee self-direction in pressing for genuine cooperation (see chapters 14–17).

17. For a far-ranging managerialist prescription which lies close to the covenantal ethic proposed here, see Kanter 1983.

18. Michael Keeley has developed the most cogent analysis of this bias, which he argues afflicts much of the social-scientific field of organization theory (Keeley 1988). His compact, lively, and well-informed argument—with one limitation noted later in this chapter—is an invaluable resource for ethicists seeking to engage critically the vast field of social-scientific thinking about organizations.

19. For an excellent example of how ethical managerialism seeks to transcend adversarial relations by eliciting cooperation from employees while retaining control, see Johnson 1995 .

20. These statistics were compiled from Fierman 1994, 31–32, and Uchitelle and Kleinfeld, 1996, 1, 14–16. For a more positive interpretation of current employment trends, see Markels 1995.

21. For the source of this influential image within organization theory, see March 1962 ; Cyert and March 1963 .

22. Kleinfield 1996. See Bennett 1990 for an extended treatment of this trend, as well as Hirsch 1986 for practical advice on how to cope with the destruction of the "psychological contract" between management and employees. For a detailed appraisal keyed to human resource managers, see Morrison and Robinson 1997.

23. Stackhouse and McCann 1991.

24. Some Christian ethicists endorse other forms of economic organization: the Mondragon cooperatives in Spain, for example (Cort 1995, Raines and Day-Lower 1986, 137). These robust enterprises have much to recommend them, and cooperatives may grow increasingly important where a legacy of historical experience renders them a plausible and attractive alternative to the business corporation (see, for example, Dauncey 1989). Yet without a massive withdrawal of legitimacy, which is not inconceivable, the corporation is likely to remain the overwhelmingly dominant form of economic organization in the United States (Scherer 1988, 43–66).

25. Keeley 1988, chaps. 5 and 6.

26. Herman 1991.

27. At present, business ethics has attracted principally philosophers and social scientists, who have sought to grasp how business enterprises ought to function from within the perspective afforded by their respective domains of knowledge. Philosophers have sought to attain moral impartiality by deploying such heuristic constructs as the "social contract," or "stakeholder theory," or "neutral, omnipartial rule-making," or some other combination of traditional deontological and utilitarian arguments (Donaldson 1982, Freeman 1984, Green 1994, DeGeorge 1995, Beauchamp and Bowie 1997, Velasquez 1991). Social scientists, for their part, have subjected the "ought" as well as the "is" of organizational practice to the norms of disinterested empirical research. They are developing hypotheses and models specifically for testing the moral values and tone of business enterprises (see, for example, Greenberg and Bies 1992). This movement towards moral objectivity is hardly complete. Philosophers especially have focused upon the rights of employees as individuals—which resonates well with the long-established preference of management to deal with employees as discrete individuals. Philosophers in business ethics have yet to take up the issue of collective organization by employees, and to engage the literature of dissent from managerial ideology (see, for example, Donaldson and Werhane 1993). Nevertheless, potent resources for establishing fairness lie at hand, in philosophical conceptions of deontological, utilitarian, and teleological moral reasoning.

28. Green 1994; Velasquez 1991.

29. Niebuhr 1963, chap. 1.

30. As Lovin explains the "ethical naturalism" assumed by Reinhold Niebuhr's Christian realism, "Practical choices are not made by ideals alone, whether they be the biblical ideal of a justice that protects the poor and the weak, or a socialist ideal of economic equality. . . . What we ought to do becomes clear as we set those aspirations in relation to the workings of social institutions" (Lovin 1995, 106).

31. This approach appears to have some affinities with the "ethological" approach Max Stackhouse argues is uniquely appropriate to analyzing corporations as

"covenantal communities" (Stackhouse 1995, 28–31). Of course, the term "thick prescription" trades on a similar term made famous by the cultural anthropologist Clifford Geertz. Just as "thick description" involves "uncovering the conceptual structures that inform [action]" or more specifically "setting down the meaning that actions have for actors" in given cultural settings, thick prescription here involves scrutinizing the gestures, tactics, and strategies of management and employees to see what moral concepts they (implicitly or explicitly) express—but with the intent (absent in cultural anthropology) to develop evaluative judgments and recommendations for action (Geertz 1973, 27).

32. Herman 1995 .

Chapter 2

1. Most discussions have tended to enlarge upon appropriate theological principles for a more Christian political economy, usually taking up public-policy issues such as unemployment, just wages, and poverty, or to explore what might be termed the spiritual psychology of personal vocation in business. For examples of the former, see Benne 1981, Wogaman 1986, Meeks 1989, Hinze 1991, or the prime example of church teaching on economic matters in the U.S: the 1986 pastoral letter on the economy by U.S. Roman Catholic bishops (National Conference of Catholic Bishops 1986). For examples of texts centered on personal vocation, see Diehl 1987, Haughey 1989, and Childs 1995. A few texts helpfully have focused upon the modern business corporation, but more to assess its social value and legitimacy than to explore its internal operations, or specifically the employment relation. For contrasting perspectives, see Novak 1981 and Stackhouse 1987.

2. Levering 1988.

3. *Business Week* 1984.

4. Chewning et al. 1990.

5. Chewning et al. 1990, chaps. 1 and 2.

6. See, for example, their discussions of managerial politics, leadership, power, accountability, motivation, and communication (chaps. 8, 11–15).

7. McCoy 1985, 225–26; see also chap. 1.

8. McCoy 1992.

9. Williams and Murphy 1992, 18.

10. McCann and Brownsberger 1990.

11. The idea of interactivity between management and employees first entered management thought some seventy years ago, through the Gestalt psychology and process philosophy of Mary Parker Follett, an early organization theorist (Follett 1940, chap. 9). Niebuhr's paradigm of human responsiveness captures the dense "interweaving," in Follett's terms, of managerial and employee expectations and

action. For some subsequent accounts of how the shape and style of management evolved in response to feedback (often resistance) from employees, see the next chapter.

12. Chewning et al. 1990, 27–28.

13. McCoy 1985, 223–24.

14. Williams and Murphy 1992, 20–22; McCoy 1985, 236–38; Nash 1993, 38–48.

15. McCoy 1992, 67–68.

16. McCoy and Baker 1991.

17. In the words of management philosopher Michael Keeley, ethical managerialists mistakenly conflate the "goals for" the enterprise as articulated by management with the "goals of" the enterprise as a whole (1988, 107–8).

18. Andolsen 1989, 169, see also 79–80.

19. Bloomquist 1990, chap. 2.

20. Raines and Day-Lower 1986, chaps. 2, 3.

21. These ethicists may have been too kind, if anything. Secular critics have blasted the moral failures of management from several perspectives. Economists, historians, and journalists, often but not necessarily partisan to labor, have charged management with frittering away the economic advantages enjoyed by U.S. corporations during the post–World War II boom (Bowles, Gordon, and Weiskopf 1983; Bluestone and Harrison 1982). Others have documented, often with biting sarcasm, how management has abused the trust of stockholders and society at large by destroying whole industries through short-sightedness and greed (Bernstein 1990, Holland 1989, Hoerr 1988, Juravich 1985, Lieberman 1988). Such texts, largely ignored by Christian ethicists, provide helpful leverage in gaining constructively critical distance from managerial ideology.

22. MacIntyre 1984, 30, 74; Bellah et al. 1986, 45.

23. Sturm 1973, 352, 332–38.

24. Pemberton and Finn 1985, 199–200.

25. Once again, there is ample evidence to support these ethical appraisals. Social scientists and veterans of organizational struggle have indicted management for fostering a stultifying bureaucratic conformity, and for crushing the legitimate aspirations of employees for meaningful work (Garson 1975, Grenier 1988, Mills 1991). Indeed, by the 1980s, it even became fashionable for consultants and senior executives themselves to attack middle management for stifling creativity, encouraging bureaucratic bloat, and enforcing mind-numbing inertia (Hayes and Abernathy 1980, Judson 1982). What, then, remains of the potential for business enterprises to be moral communities? The prophetic voices sometimes round out their dissent from ethical managerialism with visions of authentic covenant-building, but their proposals make little room for reform by management. MacIntyre, Bloomquist,

Pemberton and Finn simply give up on business enterprise; they recommend that individuals withdraw from the domination of managerial values, removing themselves to create their own intentional, authentic communities (Pemberton and Finn 1985, chap. 9; MacIntyre 1984, 263; Bloomquist 1990, 101–13).

26. Rachleff 1993, 3–5.

27. Cavanagh and McGovern 1988, chap. 2; Cavanagh, Moberg, and Velasquez 1995.

28. Velasquez 1991; Green 1994.

29. Gustafson and Johnson 1988.

30. May 1983.

31. Krueger 1995, chap. 2.

32. Childs 1995.

33. Nash 1993, chaps. 4, 5.

34. By this criterion, the recent work of Oliver Williams seems a retreat from his early casebook, which sought to interpret dilemmas through a biblically informed narrative framework (Williams and Houck 1978). It may be that virtue theory is better suited to conceptualizing conflicts within the self than among agents.

35. Michael Naughton recently has outlined the differences among papal encyclicals, and used these teachings to evaluate recent managerial initiatives to reorganize work and compensation (Naughton 1992). The question is what might emerge when this already pluriform vision encounters secular fields of knowledge in a truly interdisciplinary conversation.

36. Kuhn and Shriver 1991, chaps. 2–9, 11.

Chapter 3

1. See, for example, Leo XIII's 1891 *Rerum Novarum,* sec. 15; Pius XI's 1931 *Quadragesimo Anno,* sec. 53; John Paul II's 1981 *Laborem Exercens,* sec. 15.

2. For a description of recent trends, see Markels 1995.

3. See in particular Raines and Day-Lower 1976; Bloomquist 1990, chap. 2; Childs 1995, chapter 2.

4. The idea of contingency has provided theorists with a way of explaining how organizational action is influenced from within and without. The internal structure of organizations is shaped by their markets (Lawrence and Lorsch 1967), by the technologies they use (Thompson 1967), by the pressures exerted by employees (Gouldner 1954, Crozier 1964), by the demands of external actors of all sorts (Pfeffer and Salancik 1978), and by the functions served at different levels (Parsons 1956)—to name a few of the more common categories of contingencies which theorists have examined. My model of contingency is rooted mostly in those

theories which emphasize individual choice and action. Particularly helpful has been the work of Thompson (1967, chap. 8) and of March and Simon (1958, chap. 3). The many postulates and hypotheses these theorists generate about the operation of technical rationality in organizational settings instantiate, although make no reference to, the idea of human will.

5. Langford 1971, chap. 1.

6. There appears to be a firm historical anchoring for both parts of this definition, according to Vernon Bourke's venerable study of human will (Bourke 1964). The first half reflects his discussion of will as "dynamic power," an emphasis evident somewhat in Augustine but mainly in the modern period, in Bacon, Hobbes, Kant, and, of course, Nietzsche (Bourke 1964, chap. 5). This understanding of will emphasizes aspects of choice and initiative, where will is seen as an originating energy. Rephrased in terms of Aristotle's metaphysics, my definition emphasizes will as an "efficient" rather than a "final" cause (Bourke 1964, 103). I choose this emphasis because the classical view of will as a rational appetite for good or evil expresses a teleology which seems overly cumbersome for interpreting the willed actions of management and employees. Interactivity, more than teleology, is the key for tracing the dynamics of their struggle. Hence the second part of my definition, "even against resistance," which is intended to accommodate the self-reinforcing spiral of resistance and counterresistance evident in labor history. To be sure, my definition does not assume conflict; it assumes only that discrete wills generate different projects, and that these may, but need not be, contradicted and opposed by each other.

7. These seemingly obvious claims have been explored and debated in a long series of classic texts in management. See Herman 1992 for a summary of the more salient claims made in this literature.

8. For one intriguing sociological analysis, see Burawoy 1979.

9. See Edwards 1979, chap. 7.

10. For a grim description in Sinclair's tradition, see Horwitz 1994.

11. The terms "will" and "struggle" call out for a theory of power to be articulated within a covenantal ethic. The exercise of power among human agents is commonly dichotomized within Christian ethics as expressing domination or enablement—either containing and frustrating or, as enlisting and enhancing, the capacities of agents to act. The normative bent of this dichotomy is directly relevant to a covenantal analysis, for management and employees have acted in ways to suppress or channel the agency of each other, while enhancing their own. Yet the form of relationship at issue—functional interdependence in business enterprises as tightly interlinked systems of human action—requires a further specification of the theory of power. Following what appears to be the mainstream in organization theory, I assume that power is possessed by either management or employees—or both, in varying degrees—when they control resources on which the other party is

dependent. This lies close to the "pluralist" perspective articulated by political scientist Robert Dahl (1957), but has received elaborate development in organization theory (Pfeffer and Salancik 1978). Such a vantage point encourages us to see who is dependent upon whom for what, and so provides a more flexible instrument for discerning the intertwining of cooperation and conflict rather than a precommitment to either domination or enablement as the primary lens through which to observe how power is exercised within business enterprises. That is not to say that domination is irrelevant to such description; organization theorists are keenly sensitive to how power institutionalized into hierarchies can obstruct or distort the "natural" flows of power to those who have the resources to solve organizational problems (see, for example, Salancik and Pfeffer 1977). The point is that a theory of power in business enterprises needs to account for the fact that power is far too fluid to be accounted for in terms of formalized systems of domination or simply as empowerment. For a systematic effort to encompass both dimensions of power in Christian ethics, see Hinze 1995.

12. For a fascinating and inspiring sociological study of the shapes such resistance took in the various departments of a large bank, see Smith 1990.

13. See H. R. Niebuhr 1963, 61–65, especially 62 for a definition.

14. This definition, original to this study, has two major intellectual roots: Niklaus Luhmann's analysis of trust, for the idea that social actors employ "devices" for coping with unreliability (Luhmann 1980), and H. L. A. Hart's theory of contract law, for the idea that individuals might use contracts to bind themselves as a means of inducing others to bind themselves (Hart 1961, chap. 3, especially p. 27).

15. Once again, the definition includes a borrowed element: H. Richard Niebuhr's claim that the core of covenant-making resides in the making and keeping of promises, to the point of unlimited commitment (Niebuhr 1954,131–33).

16. My 1988 dissertation argues that a series of classic texts since 1900 in management thought and organization theory sought to ground and understand the relationship between managements and employees strictly in exchange, minimizing or eliminating any element of "integration" around shared beliefs or goals. In so doing, the theorists were unable to explain on what grounds management and employees might have reason to trust each other (Herman 1988).

Chapter 4

1. One type explicitly binds only God. These "patron" covenants include the early Noachic (Genesis 8:21–22), the early Abrahamic (Genesis 15:1–5; both ascribed to the Jahwist), the later Noachic (Genesis 9:8–17) and the later Abrahamic (Genesis 17:1–22; both ascribed to the Priestly writer), and the Davidic (2 Samuel 7:8–16). The other type, here denominated "loyalty" covenants, bind primarily the

people: the Mosaic (Exodus 20:1–24:8), as renewed by Moses on the plain of Moab prior to the conquest (Deuteronomy 5–30), by Joshua at Shechem (Joshua 24:1–28), by King Josiah in Jerusalem (2 Kings 23), and by Nehemiah in the rebuilt Jerusalem (Nehemiah 9:38–10:31). No theological reasons for this dual line of covenant-building are given. But the lack of an exactly specified linkage between the two sets of obligations serves to resist a contractual interpretation of the relationship: God is not engaged in exchanging patronage for loyalty. For the varieties of covenants among human partners, see Mendenhall 1976, 716–17.

2. Genesis 31:36–55, Genesis 20, and Joshua 9:3–21, respectively.

3. 1 Samuel 18:1–5 and 20:1–42, especially vs. 30–32.

4. Jeremiah 18:1–6.

5. During the monarchical period, for example, God is portrayed as being restrained from destroying human beings variously by their timely repentance (2 Kings 18:9–18; 19:1–34), courageous interventions by their leaders (Exodus 32: 7–14, Deuteronomy 9:8–21), or—most significantly for this study—a binding covenantal promise (1 Kings 11:11–12; 2 Kings 13:23; Psalm 106:40–46). Yet the possibility of destruction, conveyed by authoritative threats, hovers over the community, right until the end of time.

6. Niebuhr 1941, 12–18.

7. Of the three Old Testament phases, the first is presented through the Jahwist and Elohist texts (most of Genesis, except the Priestly sections cited below, much of Exodus 1–24, and Numbers 11–14); the second through the texts shaped by the Deuteronomist (Deuteronomy, Joshua, Judges, and the "historical" books from 1 Samuel through 2 Kings, plus the pre-Exilic prophets, mainly Hosea, Amos, Isaiah 1–40, and portions of Jeremiah and Ezekiel); the third through Priestly texts (Genesis 1–2:4a; 5; 6:9–22; 9:1–17, 10, 17, 36; 46:6–27; Exodus 25 through Numbers 10, Leviticus, and other materials not relevant to this analysis).

8. God initially promises Abraham progeny and land (Genesis 15:1–5); Abraham responds with pointed questions aimed at clarifying who this God is (Genesis 15:2–3, 8); God tests Abraham's faith by postponing the secure delivery of both progeny and land; Abraham bargains with God for the survival of Sodom in order to determine whether God is just (Genesis 18:16–33); God tests Abraham's faith by demanding the sacrifice of Isaac (Genesis 22:15–18); and so forth. Moses similarly responds to God's promises and demands with questions of his own (Exodus 3:11, 13; 4:1, 10, 13) until God's patience is exhausted.

9. The specific covenants, of course, are very different. The covenant with Abraham binds God to create and sustain the nation of Israel, while the covenant announced to Moses at Sinai binds the people (with their thrice-repeated consent) to faithfulness and responsible behavior (Exodus 19:7–8; 24:3, 7). For a vivid evocation of the struggle, see Psalm 78.

10. For example, Numbers 20:1–13. For a compact combination of discipline and promises, see Deuteronomy 8:2–10. The Deuteronomist sees nothing wrong with miracles, even though they are hardly less coercive than punishment in eliciting the absolute trust God demanded (Deuteronomy 4:32–40). The punishments range from inflicting disease and death, to stranding the people for years in the desert (Numbers 12:1–15; 16:1–35).

11. In effect, both sides are engaged in determining the character and reliability of each other (Exodus 32:7–14 or Deuteronomy 9:15–29). In the most remarkable negotiation, Moses cannily points out that if God wipes out the people of Israel, the surrounding nations will conclude that this God lacked the power to deliver on the promises made to Israel (Numbers 14:12–19).

12. Amos, Hosea, and the pre-Exilic portions of Isaiah, Jeremiah, and Ezekiel unanimously condemn Israel for failing to abide by the Sinai covenant. See Hosea 4:1–11; 6:7–10; Amos 3–4; Isaiah 24:4–6; Jeremiah 11:1–13; Ezekiel 16:8–29.

13. The prophets view other nations, particularly the Assyrian empire which eventually conquered Israel, as divinely selected tools of punishment (Isaiah 10:5–11; Jeremiah 1:14–19). To stave off such destruction, the prophets voice hot deterrent threats (Isaiah 5:25–30; Amos 7:1–3), as does the Deuteronomist through the curses which accompany blessings (Deuteronomy 28:15–46). When the Assyrian armies finally conquer Israel, they are viewed as carrying out God's punitive will (2 Kings 17:7–18). God's punishment also works within, as David is beset with a series of disasters interpreted by the author of 1 Samuel as retribution for his "taking" of Bathsheba and murder of Uriah (2 Samuel 13–19, viewed in light of 2 Samuel 12:11–12; see also 2 Samuel 7:8–16 for a lucid explanation of how God combines promises and discipline).

14. Hosea 11:8–9; Amos 7:23; Ezekiel 18:19–32.

15. As modeled and led by their kings, of course. The kings repent, whether for personal or corporate sins, but with different results. Saul receives no mercy (1 Samuel 15:24–25, 30); David's punishment is moderated (2 Samuel 12:13); Josiah and Hezekiah effectively defer punishment for Israel until after their deaths (2 Kings 18–20, see 20:19; 2 Kings 22–23:30, see 23:26–27).

16. 1 Kings 8:31–40; Samuel 13:8–15; Psalm 51. Some sacrifices are successful (2 Samuel 24:15–25); some are not (1 Samuel 13:8–14; 15:22–23; Isaiah 1:11–17).

17. Isaiah 54:7–8; see 40:1–11; 41:8–13 for reassurances to bolster the confidence of the people.

18. Compare the Priestly (Genesis 9:12–17; 17:1–27) versions of the Noachic and Abrahamic covenants with the Jahwist versions (Genesis 8:21–22; 17:1–27).

19. Leviticus 17–26; Psalm 119.

20. Consider Nehemiah 13:15–31 in light of Nehemiah 9:6–37. The dialectic also is visible in "Third Isaiah": chaps. 56–66.

21. John 5:31–47; 9:24–41; 12:34–43; Romans 2:17–24.

22. Matthew 9:35–38; John 6:53–58; 10:1–18; Hebrews 9:11–22. The theme of divine self-sacrifice is hardly unique to the New Testament; see the third and fourth "servant songs" of Isaiah 50:4–11; 52:13–53:12.

23. Matthew 4:18–22; 9:37–38; 10:7–16; 28:19–20. The fatherhood of God is expressed in such passages as Matthew 6:1–18; 25–33. All Synoptic references are to the Gospel of Matthew, except where parallels are unavailable or other Gospel passages are relevant.

24. Matthew 5:17–48; Luke 6:20–26; 16:19–31; Acts 10:9–48.

25. Matthew 20:29–34; 21:22; also see Luke 11:5–13; 18:1–8.

26. Of the Synoptic gospels, Mark appears most skeptical of the ability of disciples to understand Jesus' witness (Mark 4:13; 6:52; 8:14–21; 9:32; etc.); the "messianic secret" has been the object of much study. John, in contrast, envisions a perfect unity of understanding and will between God, Jesus, and the community of the chosen (John 15:1–17; 17: 1; John 2:18–25; 4:7–21).

27. Jeremiah 18:6–10.

28. Romans 3–9. This unilateral model informs the classic biblical-theological discussion of the covenant theme by Walther Eichrodt. "The covenant lays claim to the whole man and calls him to a surrender with no reservations" (Eichrodt 1961, 1:45) Eichrodt emphasizes the theme of surrender when explaining the fear, faith, and love in which "man's personal relationship with God" is denominated (Eichrodt 1961, 2:268–301; e.g., 2:278, 282–83, 291, etc.). This surrender should not be confused with a servile fear of God or with an impotent passivity towards others; according to Eichrodt, living in covenant with God involves "intense spiritual activity, and audacious risks," founded upon "unshakeable confidence and willing obedience, humble renunciation of one's own way and unconditional adherence to the goal of God's leading"(2:282, 272). So Eichrodt helpfully appears to affirm that God wants the active engagement of human wills in the "horizontal" work of building up covenantal relations, a viewpoint which is quite biblical (Deuteronomy 10:12–22, for example). The major problem with his spiritually rich description is that it is dualistic; his model presupposes that human agents are either in a state of rebellion requiring surrender or, having surrendered, have become heroically aligned with the will of God. Much of the biblical narrative, particularly the later portions, assume that such conflict and cooperation are deeply intertwined. This more complex view is more helpful in developing a covenantal ethic for management and employees.

29. This qualified freedom can be defined more precisely by using Albert O. Hirschman's well-known economic analysis of how dissatisfied individuals respond to organizations in "decline" (Hirschman 1970). He distinguishes three options: exercising "voice" or influence within the organization, as opposed to the more traditional options of leaving ("exit") or silent conformity ("loyalty"). God's covenanted people

lack the capacity to "exit," while always retaining the capacity to resist. Exit also is not available for God, by divine choice. At the other end, God wants more than a coerced "loyalty," which would stifle the voluntary self-entrustment which God seeks from the people. (The people, in contrast, are denounced by the prophets for assuming God is bound to them through such a narrow loyalty.) In effect, it appears that "voice" is the principal means through which both sides seek to influence each other.

30. Mark 7:24–30.

31. Ezekiel 18.

Chapter 5

1. Lovin 1995, 106–7.

Chapter 6

1. In chapters 6 and 7 I use the terms "employer" and "worker" because nineteenth-century business enterprises were generally small and often run by their owners. From chapter 8 on, "management" and "employee" are juxtaposed, to reflect the emergence of management as a stratum in the ever larger and more bureaucratic corporate enterprises of the twentieth century. See Bendix 1974, chap. 4.

2. These labor-oriented histories offer a rich although obviously biased resource of information about the strategies and tactics of both sides. I was unable to find histories of strategies and tactics for managing labor written from a managerial point of view.

3. The tactics of individual resistance merit a separate treatment extending beyond the scope of this study. For a fascinating introduction, see Burawoy 1979.

4. Commons et al., *History of Labor in the United States,* vols. 1, 2 (1921) and 3 (Lescohier and Brandeis 1935). This early history is summarized by Selig Perlman in a 1922 textbook (Perlman 1922). This material of course is wildly out of date, and so of little use to labor historians today. My purpose calls for then-contemporary accounts, better to capture the flavor of the strategies and tactics as they were deployed at the time. As a result, I have used sources from the particular era under discussion, where possible. While I have not explicitly drawn data about managerial or labor initiatives from recent histories (such as Montgomery 1987 for the late nineteenth and early twentieth centuries) or sociological studies (such as Bendix 1974 or Edwards 1979 for the twentieth century), my interpretation has been developed with such texts in the background. It should be further noted that I use all the sources in this study as primary sources. That is, I use them strictly for the reportage of events, and ignore historiographical debates about interpreting these events. While this procedure is naive and perhaps impermissible for historians oper-

ating within their guild, it appears sufficient for the purpose of making broad claims about the moral content of the struggle between management and employees.

5. Perlman 1922, chap. 13. This history is narrated in Commons et al. 1921, 1:493–535, 564–74, and 2:13–84, 332–55 and 430–38.

6. Commons et al. 1921, 1:493–510.

7. Ibid., 1:127, 467.

8. Ibid., 2:110–12, 430–38; Rayback 1959, 97–98, 114.

9. Relevant sections of Commons et al. include 1:185–332, 424–37, 536–63, and 2:85–175, 439–70.

10. Ibid., 1:616–20; 2:203–51, 269–300.

11. Ibid., 2:204–6.

12. Ibid., 439–70.

13. Commons et al. use the term sparingly. The relevant sections include: 1:25–184, 335–471, 575–616, and 2:175–91, 301–31, 356–429, 471–537.

14. Ibid., 1:61–107.

15. Ibid., 1:109.

16. Ibid., 1:155.

17. Ibid., 1:125–26, 418.

18. Lescohier and Brandeis 1935, chap. 3, 386.

19. Commons et al. 1921, 1:407.

20. Ibid., 1:401–3; 2:29–33, 57, 64.

21. Ibid., 2:47.

22. Ibid., 2:195.

23. Ibid., 2:181–85.

24. Ibid., 2:185–91.

25. Ibid., 2:197.

26. Ibid., 2:363–65.

27. Ibid., 2:445, 483.

28. Ibid., 2:306–8, 326.

29. Ibid., 2:308.

30. Ibid., 2:422–23.

31. Ibid., 2:427.

32. Ibid., 2:386.

33. Ibid., 2:496–97.

34. Ibid., 2:504–9.

35. Ibid., 2:502–3.

36. Forbath and Becker 1992.

37. Perlman and Taft 1935, 66–69.

38. Commons et al. 1921, 2:530.

39. Ibid., 2:531.

40. Perlman and Taft 1935, chap. 13.
41. Ibid., 491.
42. Fantasia 1988, 42–43.
43. Lovin 1980.

Chapter 7

1. H. R. Niebuhr 1942, 1943.
2. H. R. Niebuhr 1962, 59–73.
3. Rauschenbusch 1912, 194–95.
4. See Simmons and Mares 1983; Piore and Sabel 1984.
5. Hirschman 1970, 30. This problem may be avoided in modern experiments in worker-owned enterprises. Worker-owners have to come to terms with whatever management they install. Exit, as a result, may be followed by "reentry" of a sort, as workers struggle to strike a balance between retaining control and ceding it to the management they have hired.
6. Bellah 1986, chap. 2.
7. Leo XIII, *Rerum Novarum,* secs. 11–12; John Paul II, *Laborem Exercens,* sec. 14, National Conference of Catholic Bishops 1986, secs. 114–16. See also the 1980 statement of the Lutheran Church in America, which emphasizes the obligations of stewardship conferred by the holding of property (Lutheran Church in America 1980, 433–34); a new statement by the Evangelical Lutheran Church in American is in process. The United Church of Christ in a statement later in the 1980s does not include property among basic human rights, but acknowledges the enviable productivity of corporations and presses for economic democracy, which implies some legitimation of property rights as control over economic resources (United Church of Christ 1987, 458, 464–66).

Chapter 8

1. Commons et al. 1921, 2:522. Given that the U.S. population included 58 million workers in 1900 and expanded to 72 million by 1910, the significance of this gain should not be overstated (Lescohier and Brandeis 1935, 35).
2. Commons et al. 1921, 2:24. According to Commons et al., this period of relative calm derived less from the success of tactics employed by either side than from a shift of power within industry. A fundamental change occurred as the enterprises of the nineteenth century became the corporations of the twentieth. Throughout the nineteenth century, manufacturers were dependent upon merchants who controlled the distribution and sales of their products—and effectively pressured manufacturers to reduce wages to their workers. By 1898, manufacturers

gained control of what now is termed marketing and distribution, and so were in a position to "assume obligations with reference to wages and other working conditions" (Commons et al. 2:525). For a thorough description of this transformation, see Chandler 1977, chaps. 7–11. In effect, the principle of managerial prerogative became more widely effective. But the "honeymoon" didn't last; it quickly expired in those industries where companies were combined into "trusts." The monopolistic power of trusts soon was turned against workers as well as customers.

3. Commons et al. 2:326.

4. Wolman 1936, 138–39.

5. Commons et al. 2:520.

6. Regarding the AFL's exclusion of women, see Kessler-Harris 1982, 99, 152–57, 202–4, 268 and 305; regarding African-Americans, see Moody 1988, 59, 73.

7. Wolman 1936, 113.

8. Perlman and Taft 1935, 410.

9. Montgomery 1979, 97.

10. Ibid., 20.

11. Ibid., 97.

12. Quoted in ibid., 108.

13. Wolman 1936, 26, 34, 113.

14. Brandes 1976, chap. 13.

15. Ibid., 121–22.

16. Perlman and Taft 1935, 409.

17. Ibid., 351–52.

18. Brandes 1976, 127, 143.

19. Ibid., chaps. 4 and 5.

20. Ibid., chaps. 6–8, 10–12.

21. Ibid., 28.

22. Ibid., chap. 4.

23. Ibid., 140.

24. Ibid., 139–40.

25. Ibid., 18, 83–84.

26. Ibid., 137–41. The only exception was provided by African-American workers, who, already accustomed to paternalistic treatment, were flattered to be consulted by management.

27. Perlman and Taft 1935, 336–41.

28. Brandes 1976, 123–26, 129–33; Perlman and Taft 1935, 351,352, 593–95.

29. Brandes 1935, 128–29.

30. R. Niebuhr 1926a, 1926b, 1927b.

31. Brandes 1935, 135–42.
32. Ibid., 143–44.
33. Nadworny 1955.
34. As quoted in Nadworny 1955, 149–50.
35. Jacoby 1983.

Chapter 9

1. H. R. Niebuhr 1989, chap. 4, especially 50–53.
2. Ibid., 109.
3. This enlarged understanding of freedom is suggested by Reinhard Bendix's classic study of how "managerial ideologies" (convictions employers held about their relations with workers) evolved from the late nineteenth into the early twentieth centuries. Bendix draws from the publications of employer associations to argue that advocates of the early twentieth-century open-shop movement asserted the absolute right of employers to run their enterprises as they saw fit. To this end, they deployed crude coercive tactics, which rested upon a nineteenth-century ideology that celebrated individual striving of successful entrepreneurs (Bendix 1974, 270). Workers by implication were failures in the social-Darwinian struggle. But in the years after World War I, as businesses were becoming large bureaucratized corporations, the ideology changed. Managers (no longer owners or employers) began to define themselves as skillful handlers of subordinates, engaged in eliciting cooperation rather than fostering competition (Bendix 1974, 300–301). They began to focus attention upon workers as creatures whose feelings and attitudes needed to be understood so as to elicit greater productivity from them (Bendix 1974, 287–98).
4. John Paul II 1991, 14–21.
5. Rauschenbusch 1907, 419–30; 1912, 380–400.
6. Rauschenbusch 1912, 178; see 156–79.
7. H. R. Niebuhr 1989, 110.
8. Lovin 1980.
9. Ibid., 12.

Chapter 10

1. R. Niebuhr 1920, 590.
2. Ibid., 1920, 592.
3. Perlman and Taft 1935, 595.
4. For an account of the first such trip, see Fox 1987, 77–79.
5. Eddy 1927, 103–19.

6. Ibid., 115–18.
7. R. Niebuhr 1927a.
8. R. Niebuhr 1920, 591.
9. Fox 1987, 75–77.
10. R. Niebuhr 1926a, 1355.
11. R. Niebuhr 1931, 19–20; 1935, 112–113; Fox 1987, 76–77.
12. R. Niebuhr 1933, 203–4.
13. R. Niebuhr 1952, 232, 238.
14. Ibid., 1926a, 1926b, 1927b; see Fox 1987, 95, 109–10.
15. R. Niebuhr 1927c; see also Fox 1987, 97–98.
16. R. Niebuhr 1957 [1929], 132–33, 1926a, 1355.
17. R. Niebuhr 1935, 66; 1943, 70–76.
18. R. Niebuhr 1953, 240–43.
19. R. Niebuhr 1943, 48.
20. Ibid., 85, 87; 1935, 62–68.
21. For a psychologically persuasive account of covenanting as a growing sense of obligation not dischargeable through contractual stipulations, see May 1983.

Chapter 11

1. Bernstein 1970.
2. Ibid., 222–97.
3. Ibid., 491.
4. Ibid., 478–79, 490–91; Fantasia 1988, 44, 47.
5. Fantasia 1988, chap. 4.
6. Bernstein 1970, 519–51.
7. Moody 1988, 19.
8. Bernstein 1970, 500, 679–80.
9. Ibid., 466–470.
10. Fantasia 1988, 44, 46.
11. Hunt 1938, 398.
12. Moody 1988, 18–19. A helpful compact history is provided by Kochan, Katz, and McKersie 1986, 30–37.
13. Schatz 1983, 170–74.
14. Slichter, Healy, and Livernash 1960, 1.
15. Fitch 1957, 11.
16. Kuhn 1961, 6.
17. Slichter, Healy, and Livernash 1960, 752.
18. Kuhn 1961, 1.

19. Slichter, Healy, and Livernash 1960, 210, 625, 804. This text is a virtual encyclopedia of well-organized information about every facet of the employee-management relationship under collective bargaining during the 1950s.

20. Ibid., 1.

21. Daykin 1959.

22. Slichter, Healy, and Livernash 1960, 148–52, 186, 237, 278, 280.

23. Moody 1988, 65. According to the union figures Moody cites, the hourly wages of unionized workers in major industries rose an average of 80 percent between 1950 and 1965, or approximately 30 percent faster than the rate of inflation.

24. Slichter, Healy, and Livernash 1960, chap. 11.

25. Wolman 1936, 138–39.

26. Kessler-Harris 1982, 99, 152–57, 202–4, 305; Moody 1988, 59, 73.

27. Kessler-Harris 1982, 268–69; Moody 1988, 21; chap. 3.

28. Kuhn 1961, chap. 5, offers a catalogue of these tactics and a nuanced discussion of how they work.

29. Slichter, Healy, and Livernash, 1960, 670–671; Kuhn 1961, 177.

30. Roy 1952; Hammett et al. 1957, 133; Burawoy 1975.

31. Moody 1988, 18.

32. Ibid., 85–94.

33. The term is used loosely, of course. See Bluestone and Harrison 1982, 133–135.

Chapter 12

1. Boulding 1953.

2. Ibid., 214–18; 245–54.

3. R. Niebuhr 1953, 229–33.

4. Ibid., 233.

5. Boulding 1953, 251; see also 217.

6. R. Niebuhr 1953, 240–43.

7. Ibid., 238.

8. Chester Barnard vividly sketches the self-control or “responsibility” required of executives, and the idea of internalized restraint is a staple feature of classic manuals for managers. Barnard 1964, chap. 17.

9. Even Boulding acknowledged, in reply to Niebuhr, that some governmental regulation is needed (Boulding 1953, 245).

10. Astute analysts buttressed by game theory argue that “tit for tat” is the most effective strategy. However necessary it might be, such a strategy is still antithetical to a covenantal spirit.

11. R. Niebuhr 1953, 240–43.

12. Allen 1984, 292–93, 256–60, 42–45, 17, etc.

13. Joshua 24:20–22; see also Joshua 24:27.

14. Joshua 24:18b, 21, 24; Exodus 19:7–8; 24:3, 7.

15. Deuteronomy 27:14–26; see also Deuteronomy 5:22–33 for the self-binding which follows upon the delivery of the Decalogue, and Nehemiah 10: 28–11:2 for a later episode of collective self-binding.

16. 2 Kings 22–23.

17. Matthew 23:23–24; Luke 11:42.

18. 2 Samuel 11:27b–12:9.

19. Matthew 13:28–32; 21:33–46.

20. See, for example, Allen 1984, chaps.1 and 2.

21. Matthew 23: 13–36; Luke 11:37–52.

Chapter 13

1. The covenantal benefit lies in the structures which organize adversarial discussions around points of agreement as well as of difference, and which bind management and employees to commit themselves, as a matter of internal as well as external coercion, to respect the principles of self-representation and managerial prerogative, respectively. There are utilitarian benefits as well, although that is a matter of hot debate. Economists Richard B. Freeman and James L. Medoff argue, through detailed statistical analysis, that "American unionism . . . [is] a plus on the overall social balance sheet" even if a "minus" for any particular corporation (Freeman and Medoff 1984, chap. 16, especially 248). The question of the overall social value of collective bargaining lies far beyond the scope of this study, which is concerned only to describe and evaluate the strategies and tactics which management and employees use to shape the thinking and action of each other.

2. For a forthright statement of this managerial aim, see Freedman 1988—an article on behalf of the Conference Board, an educational association which serves and speaks for management.

3. Perhaps the most complete social-scientific study is Thomas A. Kochan, Harry C. Katz, and Robert B. McKersie's systematic and detailed analysis of how changing management strategy has undermined the collective bargaining system set up in the 1930s (Kochan, Katz, and McKersie 1986). Chapters 13 and 14 utilize aspects of their "multilevel" analysis. In keeping with my method of relying upon contemporary accounts and appraisals as primary sources, I draw upon recent journalism, particularly feature articles in the *Wall Street Journal* for narratives and trends. And since the strategies and tactics are initiated by management, I draw upon the literature of opposition to establish the benchmarks for covenantal adequacy for these initiatives.

4. McConville 1980, 61–62; Davis 1986, 131.

5. McConville 1980, 66–67.

6. For a description of how the consultants set up anti-union campaigns, see Georgine 1980.

7. DeMaria 1980.

8. Fantasia 1988, 56.

9. Ibid., 56.

10. Religious Committee for Workplace Fairness, *Restoring the Balance: Toward Justice for Working People* 1991.

11. Fantasia 1988, 66.

12. Kochan, Katz, and McKersie 1986, 50; Milbank and Bounds 1993. The numbers are approximate. Other sources put the percentage at 11.9 in 1991 and 11.5 in 1993 (Suskind 1992; Salwen 1993a). But by 1995, union membership was registering small gains (Zachary 1995).

13. Zachary 1995.

14. Fantasia 1988, 61.

15. Milbank and Bounds 1993.

16. Salwen 1993a; Tomsho 1993.

17. Milbank and Bounds 1993.

18. Shellenbarger 1994. Sadly enough, the law has been ignored or flouted in key respects by 5 to 22 percent of 300 recently surveyed firms.

19. Zachary 1995. See also Salwen 1993d.

20. Kochan, Katz, and McKersie 1986, 70; 66–76.

21. Stillman 1980, 76; Bluestone and Harrison 1982.

22. Suskind 1992.

23. Zachary and Ortega 1993; Ehrbar 1993.

24. Zachary and Ortega 1993.

25. For a manual of how to "reengineer," see Hammer and Champy 1995.

26. Uchitelle 1994.

27. Keller 1992.

28. Ehrbar 1993.

29. For some recent journalistic assessments, see Fuchsberg 1993; White 1996; Markels and Murray 1996.

30. Zachary and Ortega 1993.

31. Lublin 1993.

32. Ibid.

33. For an example of the genre, see Tarr and Juliano 1992.

34. Noer 1993, chap. 12.

35. Thomas 1995.

36. Uchitelle 1994.

37. Zachary 1995.

Chapter 14

1. Dunlop 1988.

2. This chapter draws from the primarily journalistic accounts of partisans, opponents, and newspaper reporters. Helpful works by partisans include: Simmons and Mares 1983; Zwerdling 1980; and Sherman 1994. Helpful works by opponents include: Parker 1985; Wells 1987; and Fantasia et al. 1988. For contemporary reportage, I rely primarily upon first-page feature articles in the *Wall Street Journal.*

3. Jenkins 1974.

4. Zwerdling 1980, 41–52; 117–34.

5. Fantasia et al. 1988, 482–83

6. Zwerdling 1980, 19–29.

7. For an anecdotal history, see Simmons and Mares 1983, chap. 6; for a more jaundiced history, see Grenier 1988, 3–19.

8. Grenier 1988, chaps. 4–6.

9. Ibid., 189.

10. *Business Week* 1981, 86; Simmons and Mares 1983, 102. Yet another estimate is higher: 44 percent of all companies with more than 500 employees had QC programs by 1982. Lawler and Mohrman 1985, 66.

11. Parker 1985, 85.

12. Naj 1993.

13. Ibid.

14. Lawler and Mohrman 1985, 68–69.

15. Kochan, Katz, and McKersie 1986, 35–37, 62–65.

16. For the contrast between QC and QWL programs, see Simmons and Mares 1983, 112–13.

17. A rate of 35 percent of all companies, involving an average of 30 percent of employees in each company (Gordon 1992, 60). For the smaller figures, see Lublin 1992.

18. Gordon 1992, 63.

19. Reid 1990; Rosow, chaps. 6–10.

20. Parker 1985, 24–26. For a more compact discussion, see Wells 1987.

21. Parker and Slaughter 1988.

22. Naj 1993.

23. Parker 1985, chap. 3.

24. Reisman and Compa 1985.

25. Interestingly enough, both cases involved the same union: the United Autoworkers. This is no accident, in that the UAW has pressed for cooperation with management far more visibly than any other union. It might be argued that the Saturn and Caterpillar examples are irrelevant, since large unions in manufacturing industries represent the past rather than the future of an economy focused increas-

ingly upon services and information. Indeed, the relevance of large unions to strategies of cooperation with management is very much in question. Yet in a realm of human activity so permeated with the contingencies which management and employees present to each other, the future is likely to be conditioned heavily by the suspicions and loyalties which both sides bring forth in negotiating their relations with each other.

26. The following account of Saturn relies principally upon a vivid and sympathetic but not celebratory journalistic account (Sherman 1994).

27. Ephlin 1986, 144.

28. Sherman 1994, chap. 17, esp. 207.

29. Ibid.

30. Ibid., 200.

31. Ibid., 274.

32. Ibid., 269–71.

33. Ibid., 322–23.

34. Ibid., 269–78.

35. Ibid., 309–14.

36. Goodman 1980, 490.

37. Rauschenbusch 1912, 311–23; 419–29.

38. Parker 1985, 91–94; see also Fantasia 1988, chap. 6, for a richly textured argument on the merits of strikes and other such actions for building community among workers.

39. The GM management has not been so scrupulous outside Saturn. It pitted union-organized plants against each other, encouraging them to break ranks with the UAW in order to stave off closures (McCann 1992).

Chapter 15

1. For a classic theoretical discussion of this linkage between managerial directives and employee compliance, see Barnard 1964 [1938], 167–71 or Simon 1976, chap. 2.

2. Kochan, Katz, and McKersie 1986, 147–49.

3. Leo XIII, *Rerum Novarum,* secs. 15–17.

4. Pius XI, *Quadragesimo Anno,* secs. 83–84.

5. Ibid., secs. 44, 49, 54, 101.

6. John XXIII, *Mater et Magistra* sec. 92, see also 91–96.

7. John Paul II, *Laborem Exercens,* secs. 12–15.

8. John Paul II, *Centesimus Annus,* sec. 43.

9. Stanley Hauerwas rightly questions whether human work can bear the enormous theological value which John Paul II invests in it (Hauerwas 1983,

44–51). Yet it weakens his own argument to argue that work is nothing more than an instrumentality for survival, on the unsupported assertion that "most work is not intrinsically fulfilling." Work need not be exalted as "co-creation" with God to have deep theological significance. And exactly how much work can be redeemed by cooperative reorganization remains to be seen. Surely the self-managing teams at Saturn find more value in the objective dimensions of their work than do the workers on more traditional GM assembly lines.

10. John Paul II, *Laborem Exercens,* secs. 11–15.

11. Piux XI, *Quadragesimo Anno,* 69; John XXIII, *Mater et Magistra,* secs. 23, 91–96; John XXIII, *Pacem in Terris,* secs. 1–34; John Paul II, *Centesimus Annus,* sec. 32.

12. Personal communication from Daniel L. Petree, Chair of the Business and Economics Department, Concordia College, August 1996.

Chapter 16

1. The UAW represented some 14,000 of Caterpillar's 38,000 (in 1994) workers (Rose 1994a).

2. Rose and Kotlowitz 1992; Mills 1991, 452.

3. Kelly 1993, 7.

4. Farney 1993.

5. *Business Week* 1994, 36.

6. Rose 1994b.

7. Rose and Kotlowitz 1992.

8. Kelly 1993, 7.

9. Rose and Kotlowitz 1992.

10. Kelly 1993, 7; Mills 1991, 453. The older, unionized workers were to retain their high wages (averaging $19 per hour in 1993), while new hires were to be paid $10 per hour (Rose 1994b). Management also cut back expensive overtime pay by putting workers on a "flexible" schedule that made them available to work on weekends or for ten hours a day.

11. Rose and Kotlowitz 1992.

12. Kelly 1993, 7.

13. Rose and Kotlowitz 1992.

14. Mills 1992, 452.

15. Wagner 1994, 312–30; for an extensive and thoughtful analysis, see Kochan, Katz, and McKersie 1986, chap. 6.

16. MacIntyre 1984, 188–92.

17. Rose and Kotlowitz 1992.

18. Kurt Vonnegut illustrates the power of these values in an early satire on the General Electric Corporation. Hordes of workers displaced by the complete auto-

mation of the factories rise up—led by an erstwhile pastor—smash the machines of their oppression, and immediately set to work patching the pieces back together (Vonnegut 1974).

19. O'Brien 1993.

20. Rose and Kotlowitz 1992.

21. Ibid.

22. Rauschenbusch 1912, 169–79.

23. Salwen 1993b.

24. Hauerwas 1983, 48.

Chapter 17

1. Renewed conflict hardly exhausts the alternative futures available. Labor scholars and others have offered a striking range of predictions about the management-employee relation. Gordon, Edwards, and Reich (1982) assume that management will increase control over workers, while Hirschhorn (1984) anticipates that management will become increasingly dependent upon employees, due to the skills new technologies will require and that employees will have learned. Piore and Sabel (1984) predict the reemergence of craft industries in decentralized industrial districts; Charles Heckscher (1988) projects that managers themselves will develop their own craft-based unions; and for Kochan, Katz, and McKersie (1986), future directions in labor-management simply defy prediction.

2. Stackhouse and McCann 1991.

3. The only other alternative is for management to absorb the perspective of employees so thoroughly that no such negotiations are necessary—an aspiration which seems paternalistic, and liable to abuse in any case. The models of practical reasoning put forward by philosophically minded business ethicists seem vulnerable to this temptation to the extent that they do not explicitly call for dialogue and consultation rather than unilateral decision-making.

4. Dunlop 1988.

5. Salwen 1993c.

6. Barnard 1964 [1938], 3–7.

Works Cited

Allen, Joseph L. 1984. *Love and Conflict: A Covenantal Model of Christian Ethics.* Nashville: Abingdon.

Andolsen, Barbara Hilkert. 1989. *Good Work at the Video Display Terminal: A Feminist Ethical Analysis of Changes in Clerical Work.* Knoxville: University of Tennessee Press.

Barnard, Chester I. 1964 [1938]. *The Functions of the Executive.* Cambridge: Harvard University Press.

Beauchamp, Tom L., and Norman E. Bowie. 1997. *Ethical Theory and Business,* 5th edition. Upper Saddle River: Prentice-Hall.

Bellah, Robert N. 1986. *Habits of the Heart: Individualism and Commitment in American Life.* New York: Harper and Row.

Bendix, Reinhard. 1974. *Work and Authority in Industry.* Berkeley: University of California Press.

Benne, Robert. 1981. *The Ethic of Democratic Capitalism: A Moral Reassessment.* Philadelphia: Fortress.

Bennett, Amanda. 1990. *The Death of the Organization Man.* New York: William Morrow.

Bernstein, Aaron. 1990. *Grounded: Frank Lorenzo and the Destruction of Eastern Airlines.* New York: Simon and Schuster.

Bernstein, Irving. 1970. *Turbulent Years: A History of the American Worker, 1933–1941.* Boston: Houghton Mifflin.

Bloomquist, Karen L. 1990. *The Dream Betrayed: Religious Challenge of the Working Class.* Minneapolis: Fortress.

Bluestone, Barry, and Bennett Harrison. 1982. *The Deindustrialization of America: Plant Closings, Community Abandonment and the Dismantling of Basic Industry.* New York: Basic.

Boulding, Kenneth E. 1953. *The Organizational Revolution: A Study in the Ethics of Economic Organization.* New York: Harper & Brothers.

Bourke, Vernon J. 1964. *Will in Western Thought: An Historico-Critical Survey.* New York: Sheed and Ward.

Bowles, Samuel, David M. Gordon and Thomas E. Weisskopf. 1983. *Beyond the Waste Land: A Democratic Alternative to Economic Decline.* Garden City: Anchor Press/Doubleday.

Brandes, Stuart. 1976. *American Welfare Capitalism.* Chicago: University of Chicago Press.

Burawoy, Michael. 1979. *Manufacturing Consent: Changes in Labor Process Under Monopoly Capitalism.* Chicago: University of Chicago Press.

Business Week. 1981. "The New Industrial Relations." *Business Week* (May 11): 84–98.

———. 1984. "Who's Excellent Now? Some of the Best-seller Picks Haven't Been Doing So Well Lately." *Business Week* (November 5): 76.

Cavanagh, Gerald F., and Arthur F. McGovern. 1988. *Ethical Dilemmas in the Modern Corporation.* Englewood Cliffs: Prentice-Hall.

Cavanagh, Gerald F., Dennis J. Moberg, and Manuel Velasquez. 1995. "Making Business Ethics Practical." *Business Ethics Quarterly* 5 (1995): 399–418.

Chandler, Alfred D. 1977. *The Visible Hand: The Managerial Revolution in American Business.* Cambridge: Harvard University Press.

Chewning, Richard C., John W. Eby, and Shirley J. Roels. 1990. *Business Through the Eyes of Faith.* San Francisco: HarperCollins.

Childs, James M., Jr. 1995. *Ethics in Business: Faith at Work.* Minneapolis: Fortress.

Commons, John R., et al. 1921. *History of Labor in the United States,* vols. 1, 2. New York: Macmillan. (For vol. 3, see Lescohier and Brandeis 1935.)

Cort, John C. 1995. "Is Mondragon the Way?" In Max L. Stackhouse and Dennis P. McCann, eds., *On Moral Business: Classical and Contemporary Resources for Ethics in Economic Life:* 558–60. Grand Rapids: William B. Eerdmans.

Crozier, Michel. 1964. *The Bureaucratic Phenomenon.* Chicago: University of Chicago Press.

Cyert, Richard M., and James G. March. 1963. *A Behavioral Theory of the Firm.* Englewood Cliffs: Prentice-Hall.

Dahl, Robert A. 1957. "The Concept of Power." *Behavioral Science* 2: 201–15.

Davis, John P. [1897] 1961. *Corporations: A Study of the Origin and Development of Great Business Combinations and of Their Relation to the Authority of the State.* New York: Capricorn.

Davis, Mike. 1986. *Prisoners of the American Dream.* London: Verso.

Dauncy, Guy. 1989. *After the Crash: The Emergence of the Rainbow Economy.* New York: Bootstrap Press.

Daykin, Walter L. 1959. "Arbitrators' Determination of Management's Right to Manage." In J.K. Louden and J. Wayne Deegan, eds., *Wage Incentives:* 188–205. New York: Wiley.

De George, Richard T. 1995. *Business Ethics,* 4th edition. Englewood Cliffs: Prentice-Hall.

DeMaria, Alfred T. 1980. *How Management Wins Union Organizing Campaigns.* New York: Executive Enterprises Publishing Company.

DePree, Max. 1989. *Leadership Is an Art.* New York: Dell.

Diehl, William E. 1987. *In Search of Faithfulness: Lessons from the Christian Community.* Philadelphia: Fortress Press.

Donaldson, Thomas, and Patricia H. Werhane. 1993. *Ethical Issues in Business: A Philosophical Approach,* 4th edition. Englewood Cliffs: Prentice-Hall.

Drucker, Peter F. 1954. *The Practice of Management.* New York: Harper & Row.

———. 1974. *Management: Tasks, Responsibilities, Practices.* New York: Harper & Row.

Dunlop, John T. 1988. "Have the 1980's Changed U.S. Industrial Relations?" *Monthly Labor Review* 111 (1988): 29–33.

Eddy, Sherwood. 1927. *Religion and Social Justice.* New York: George H. Doran.

Edwards, Richard. 1979. *Contested Terrain: The Transformation of the Workplace in the Twentieth Century.* New York: Basic Books.

Ehrbar, Al. 1993. "Re-engineering Gives Firms New Efficiency, Workers the Pink Slip." *Wall Street Journal* (March 16): 1.

Eichrodt, Walther. 1961. *Theology of the Old Testament,* vols. 1–2. Philadelphia: Westminster.

Ephlin, Donald F. 1986. "United Autoworkers: Pioneers in Labor-Management Partnership." In Jerome M. Rosow, ed., *Teamwork: Joint Labor Management Programs in America:* 133–45. New York: Pergamon.

Everett, William Johnson. 1986. "OIKOS: Convergence in Business Ethics." *Journal of Business Ethics* 5: 313–25.

Fantasia, Rick. 1988. *Cultures of Solidarity: Consciousness, Action and Contemporary American Workers.* Berkeley: University of California.

Fantasia, Rick, Dan Clawson, and Gregory Graham. 1988. "A Critical View of Worker Participation in American Industry." *Work and Occupations* 15: 468–88.

Farney, Dennis. 1993. "To End an Impasse: Workers at Caterpillar Hope Against Hope Clinton Will be True." *Wall Street Journal* (July 26): 1.

Fierman, Jaclyn. 1994. "The Contingency Work Force." *Fortune* 129 (January 24): 30–36.

Fitch, John W. 1957. *The Social Responsibilities of Organized Labor.* New York: Harper & Row.

Follett, Mary Parker. 1940. *Dynamic Administration: The Collected Papers of Mary Parker Follett,* Henry C. Metcalf and L. Urwick, eds. New York: Harper & Row.

Forbath, William E., and Craig Becker. 1992. "Labor." In Kermit L. Hall et al., eds., *The Oxford Companion to the Supreme Court of the United States.* New York: Oxford University Press.

Fox, Richard Wightman. 1987. *Reinhold Niebuhr: A Biography.* San Francisco: Harper & Row.

Freedman, Audrey. 1988. "How the 1980's Have Changed Industrial Relations." *Monthly Labor Review* 111: 35–38.

Freeman, R. E. 1984. *Strategic Management: A Stakeholder Approach.* Boston: Pitman.

Freeman, Richard B., and James L. Medoff. 1984. *What Do Unions Do?* New York: Basic Books.

Fuchsberg, Gilbert. 1993 "Why Shake-Ups Work for Some, Not for Others." *Wall Street Journal* (October 1).

Garson, Barbara. 1975. *All the Livelong Day: The Meaning and Demeaning of Routine Work* . New York: Penguin Books.

Geertz, Clifford. 1973. *The Interpretation of Cultures.* New York: Basic Books.

Georgine, Robert. 1980. "From Brass Knuckles to Briefcases: The Modern Art of Union-Busting." In Mark Green and Robert Massie, eds., *The Big Business Reader: Essays on Corporate America:* 89–104. New York: Pilgrim.

Goodman, Paul S. 1980. "Realities of Improving the Quality of Work Life: Quality of Work Life Projects in the 1980s." *Labor Law Journal* 31: 487–94.

Gordon, David M., Michael Reich, and Richard Edwards. 1982. *Segmented Work, Divided Workers: The Historical Transformation of Labor in the United States.* New York: Cambridge University Press.

Gordon, Jack. 1992. "Work Teams: How Far Have They Come?" *Training* (1992): 59–65.

Gouldner, Alvin W. 1954. *Patterns of Industrial Bureaucracy: A Case Study of Modern Factory Administration.* New York: The Free Press.

Green, Ronald M. 1994. *The Ethical Manager: A New Method for Business Ethics.* New York: Macmillan.

Greenberg, Jerald, and Robert J. Bies. 1992. "Establishing the Role of Empirical Studies of Organizational Justice in Philosophical Inquiries into Business Ethics." *Journal of Business Ethics* 11: 433–44.

Grenier, Guillermo J. 1988. *Inhumane Relations: Quality Circles and Anti-Unionism in American Industry.* Philadelphia: Temple University Press.

Gustafson, James M., and Elmer W. Johnson. 1988. "Efficiency, Morality, and Managerial Effectiveness." In John R. Meyer and James M. Gustafson, eds., *The U.S. Business Corporation: An Institution in Transition:* 193–209. Cambridge: Ballinger.

Hammer, Michael, and James Champy. 1995. *Reengineering the Corporation: A Manifesto for Business Revolution.* New York: Harper.

Hammett, Richard S., Joel Seidman, and Jack London. 1957. "The Slowdown as a Union Tactic." *Journal of Political Economy* 65: 126–34.

Hart, H. L. A. 1961. *The Concept of Law:* Oxford: Clarendon Press.

Hauerwas, Stanley. 1983. "Work as Co-Creation: A Critique of a Remarkably Bad Idea." In John W. Houck and Oliver F. Williams, eds., *Co-Creation and Capitalism: John Paul II's "Laborem Exercens."* Washington, D.C.: University Press.

Haughey, John C. 1989. *Converting Nine to Five: A Spirituality of Daily Work.* New York: Crossroad.

Hayes, Robert, and William Abernathy. 1980. "Managing Our Way to Economic Decline." *Harvard Business Review* 58: 67–77.

Hecksher, Charles. 1988. *The New Unionism: Employee Involvement in the Changing Corporation.* New York: Basic Books.

Herman, Stewart W. 1988. "Exchange and Integrative Trust Between Employee and Organization: An Analysis of Organization Theory Through the Agency Theory of H. Richard Niebuhr and Reinhold Niebuhr." Dissertation: University of Chicago.

———. 1991. "Furthering the Conversation Between Philosophy and Organization Theory." *Business Ethics Quarterly* 1: 121–32.

———. 1992a. "The Modern Business Corporation and an Ethics of Trust." *Journal of Religious Ethics* 20: 111–48.

———. 1992b "The Potential for Building Covenants in Business Corporations." In Max L. Stackhouse and Dennis P. McCann, eds., *On Moral Business: Classical and Contemporary Resources for Ethics in Economic Life:* 514–520. Grand Rapids: William B. Eerdmans.

Hinze, Christine Firer. 1991. "Bridge Discourse on Wage Justice: Roman Catholic and Feminist Perspectives on the Family Living Wage." In D.M. Yeager, ed., *Society of Christian Ethics Annual:* 108–32.

———. 1995. *Comprehending Power in Christian Social Ethics,* Atlanta: Scholars Press.

Hirsch, Paul M. 1987. *Pack Your Own Parachute: How to Survive Mergers, Takeovers, and Other Corporate Disasters.* New York: Addison-Wesley.

Hirschhorn, Larry. 1984. *Beyond Mechanization.* Cambridge: MIT Press.

Hirschman, Albert O. 1970. *Exit, Voice and Loyalty: Responses to Decline in Firms, Organizations, and States.* Cambridge: Harvard University Press.

Hoerr, John P. 1988. *And the Wolf Finally Came: The Decline of the American Steel Industry.* Pittsburgh: University of Pittsburgh Press.

Holland, Max. 1989. *When the Machine Stopped: A Cautionary Tale From Industrial America.* Boston: Harvard Business School.

Horwitz, Tony. 1994. "9 to Nowhere: These Six Growth Jobs are Dull, Dead-End, Sometimes Dangerous." *Wall Street Journal* (December 1): 1.

Hunt, Frazier. 1938. *One American and His Attempt at Education.* New York: Simon and Schuster.

Jacoby, Sanford M. 1983. "Union-Management Cooperation in the United States: Lessons from the 1920s." *Industrial and Labor Relations Review* 37: 18–33.

Jenkins, David. 1974. *Job Power: Blue and White Collar Democracy.* Baltimore: Penguin.

John XXIII. 1963 [1961]. *Mater et Magistra* (Christianity and Social Progress). In William J. Gibbons, S.J., ed., *Seven Great Encyclicals:* 217–74. New York: Paulist Press.

———. 1963 [1961]. *Pacem in Terris* (Peace on Earth). In William J. Gibbons, S.J., ed., *Seven Great Encyclicals:* 287–326. New York: Paulist Press.

John Paul II. 1981. *On Human Work (Laborem Exercens).* Boston: St. Paul Editions.

———. 1991. *On the Hundredth Anniversary of Rerum Novarum (Centesimus Annus).* Washington, D.C.: United States Catholic Conference.

Johnson, Elmer W. 1995. "Shaping Our Economic Future: Dignity in the Workplace." In Max L. Stackhouse and Dennis P. McCann, eds., *On Moral Business: Classical and Contemporary Resources for Ethics in Economic Life:* 650–53. Grand Rapids: William B. Eerdmans.

Judson, Arnold S. 1982. "The Awkward Truth About Productivity." *Harvard Business Review* 60: 93–97.

Juravich, Tom. 1985. *Chaos on the Shop Floor: A Worker's View of Quality, Productivity and Management.* Philadelphia: Temple University Press.

Kanter, Rosabeth Moss. 1983. *The Change Masters: Innovation for Productivity in the American Corporation.* New York: Simon and Schuster.

Keeley, Michael. 1988. *A Social-Contract Theory of Organizations.* Notre Dame: University of Notre Dame Press.

Keller, John J. 1992. "Some AT&T Clients Gripe That Cost Cuts are Hurting Service." *Wall Street Journal* (January 24): 1.

Kelly, Kevin. 1993. "Labor's Metamorphosis? The High Stakes at Caterpillar." *Commonweal* 120 (January 15): 7–8.

Kessler-Harris, Alice. 1982. *Out to Work: A History of Wage-Earning Women in the United States.* New York: Oxford University Press.

Kleinfield, N. R. 1996. "The Company as Family, No More." *The New York Times* (March 4): 1.

Kochan, Thomas A., Harry C. Katz, and Robert B. McKersie. 1986. *The Transformation of American Industrial Relations.* New York: Basic Books.

Krueger, David A. 1995. *Keeping Faith at Work: The Christian in the Workplace.* Nashville: Abingdon.

Kuhn, James W. 1961. *Bargaining in the Grievance Settlement: The Power of Industrial Work Groups.* New York: Columbia University Press.

Kuhn, James W., and Donald W. Shriver, Jr. 1991. *Beyond Success: Corporations and Their Critics in the 1990s.* New York: Oxford University Press.

Langford, Glenn. 1971. *Human Action.* New York: Doubleday-Anchor.

Lawler, Edward E., III, and Susan A. Mohrman. 1985. "Quality Circles After the Fad." *Harvard Business Review* 63: 65–71.

Lawrence, Paul R., and Jay W. Lorsch. 1967. *Organization and Environment: Managing Differentiation and Integration.* Boston: Harvard University Graduate School of Business Administration.

Leo XIII. 1963 [1891]. *Rerum Novarum* (The Condition of Labor). In William J. Gibbons, S.J., ed., *Seven Great Encyclicals:* 1–29. New York: Paulist Press.

Lescohier, Don D., and Brandeis, Elizabeth. 1935. *History of Labor in the United States, 1896–1932,* vol. 3: *Working Conditions and Labor Legislation.* New York: Macmillan.

Levering, Robert. 1988. *A Great Place to Work: What Makes Some Employers So Good (And Most So Bad).* New York: Random House.

Lieberman, Ernest D. 1988. *Unfit to Manage: How Management Endangers America and What Working People Can Do About It.* New York: McGraw-Hill.

Lovin, Robin W. 1980. "Covenantal Relationships and Political Legitimacy." *Journal of Religion* 60: 1–16.

———. 1995. *Reinhold Niebuhr and Christian Realism.* Cambridge: Cambridge University Press.

Lublin, Joann S. 1992. "Trying to Increase Worker Productivity, More Employers Alter Management Style." *Wall Street Journal* (February 13).

———. 1993. "Survivors of Layoffs Battle Angst, Anger, Hurting Productivity." *The Wall Street Journal* (December 6): 1.

Luhmann, Niklas. 1980. *Trust.* New York: John Wiley & Sons.

Lutheran Church in America. 1980. "Economic Justice: Stewardship of Creation in Human Community." In Max L. Stackhouse and Dennis P. McCann, eds., *On Moral Business: Classical and Contemporary Resources for Ethics in Economic Life* (1995): 430–34. Grand Rapids: William B. Eerdmans.

MacIntyre, Alasdair. 1984. *After Virtue.* Notre Dame: University of Notre Dame Press.

March, James G. 1962. "The Business Firm as Political Coalition." *The Journal of Politics* 24: 662–78.

Markels, Alex. 1995. "Critical Slot: Restructuring Alters Middle-Manager Role but Leaves It Robust." *Wall Street Journal* (September 25): 1.

Markels, Alex and Matt Murray. 1996. "Call it Dumbsizing: Why Some Companies Regret Cost-Cutting." *Wall Street Journal* (May 14): 1.

May, William F. 1983. "Moral Leadership in the Corporate Setting." In Wade L. Robison, Michael Pritchard, and Joseph Ellin, eds., *Profits and Professions: Essays in Business and Professional Ethics:* 183–213. Clifton, N.J.: Humana Press.

McCann, Dennis P. 1992. "The Old Habits of Adversarial Economics." *Christian Century* 109 (April 8): 356–57.

McCann, Dennis P., and M. L. Brownsberger. 1990. "Management as a Social Practice: Rethinking Business Ethics After MacIntyre." In D.M. Yeager, ed., *Society of Christian Ethics Annual:* 223–45.

McConville, Ed. 1980. "The Southern Textile War." In Mark Green and Robert Massie, Jr., eds., *The Big Business Reader: Essays on Corporate America:* 59–71. New York: Pilgrim Press.

McCoy, Charles S. 1985. *Management of Values: The Ethical Difference in Corporate Policy and Performance.* Boston: Pitman.

———. 1992. "Narrative Theology and Business Ethics: Story-Based Management of Values." In Oliver F. Williams and John W. Houck, eds., *A Virtuous Life in Business: Stories of Courage and Integrity in the Corporate World*: 51–72.

McCoy, Charles S., and J. Wayne Baker. 1991. *Fountainhead of Federalism: Heinrich Bullinger and the Federal Tradition*. Louisville: Westminster/John Knox.

Meeks, M. Douglas. 1989. *God the Economist: The Doctrine of God and Political Economy*. Minneapolis: Fortress.

Mendenhall, G. E. 1976. "Covenant." *Interpreter's Dictionary of the Bible*, Supplement: 714–23. Nashville: Abingdon.

Milbank, Dana, and Wendy Bounds. 1993. "Unions Display a Revival of Militancy." *Wall Street Journal* (July 8): 2.

Mills, D. Quinn. 1991. *Rebirth of the Corporation*. New York: Wiley.

Montgomery, David. 1979. *Workers' Control in America: Studies in the History of Work, Technology and Labor Struggles*. Cambridge: Cambridge University Press.

Montgomery, David. 1987. *The Fall of the House of Labor: The Workplace, the State, and American Labor Activism*. New York: Cambridge University Press.

Moody, Kim. 1988. *An Injury to All: The Decline of American Unionism*. New York: Verso.

Morrison, Elizabeth Wolfe, and Sandra L. Robinson. 1987. "When Employees Feel Betrayed: A Model of How Psychological Contract Violation Develops." *Academy of Management Review*: 226–56.

Nadworny, Milton J. 1955. *Scientific Management and the Unions, 1900–1932*. Cambridge: Harvard University Press.

Naj, Amal Kumar. 1993. "Some Manufacturers Drop Efforts to Adopt Japanese Techniques." *Wall Street Journal* (May 7): 1.

Nash, Laura L. 1993. *Good Intentions Aside: A Manager's Guide to Resolving Ethical Problems*. Boston: Harvard Business School.

National Conference of Catholic Bishops. 1986. *Economic Justice for All: Pastoral Letter on Catholic Social Teaching and the U.S. Economy*. Washington, D.C.: National Conference of Catholic Bishops.

Naughton, Michael. 1992. *The Good Stewards: Practical Applications of the Papal Social Vision of Work*. Lanham, Md.: University Press of America.

Niebuhr, H. Richard. 1962 [1941]. *The Meaning of Revelation*. New York: Macmillan.

———. 1942. "War as the Judgment of God." *Christian Century* 59 (May 3): 630–33.

———. 1943. "War as Crucifixion." *Christian Century* 60 (April 28): 513–15.

———. 1954. "The Idea of Covenant and American Democracy." *Church History* 23: 126–135.

———. 1963. *The Responsible Self: An Essay in Christian Moral Philosophy*. New York: Harper and Row.

———. 1989. *Faith on Earth: An Inquiry Into the Structure of Human Faith*. Richard R. Niebuhr, ed. New Haven: Yale University Press.

Niebuhr, Reinhold. 1920. "The Church and the Industrial Crisis." *The Biblical World* 54 (November): 588–92.

———. 1926a. "Henry Ford and Industrial Autocracy." *The Christian Century* 43 (November 4): 1354–55.

———. 1926b. "How Philanthropic Is Henry Ford?" *The Christian Century* 43 (December 9): 1516–17.

———. 1927a. "Business Is Business—Plus" (review). *The Christian Century* 44 (January 1): 15–16.

———. 1927b. "Ford's Five-Day Work Week Shrinks." *The Christian Century* 44 (June 9): 713–14.

———. 1927c. "The Effects of Modern Industrialism on Personality." *Student World* 21 (October): 299–305.

———. 1957 [1929]. *Leaves from the Notebook of a Tamed Cynic.* New York: Meridian.

———. 1931. "Property and the Ethical Life." *The World Tomorrow* 14 (January): 19–21.

———. 1933. "After Capitalism—What?" *The World Tomorrow* 16 (March): 203–205.

———. 1935. *An Interpretation of Christian Ethics.* New York: Harper & Row.

———. 1941. *The Nature and Destiny of Man,* vol. 1:*Human Nature.* New York: Charles Scribner's Sons.

———. 1943. *The Nature and Destiny of Man,* vol. 2:*Human Destiny.* New York: Charles Scribner's Sons.

———. 1946a. "Lessons from the Railroad Strike." *The Messenger* 11 (June 25): 6.

———. 1946b. "The American Labor Movement." *Christianity and Society* 12 (Winter): 6–8.

———. 1953. "Coercion, Self-interest, and Love." In Kenneth E. Boulding, ed., *The Organizational Revolution:* 228–44. New York: Harper & Brothers.

Noer, David M. 1993. *Healing the Wounds: Overcoming the Traumas of Layoffs and Revitalizing Downsized Organizations.* San Francisco: Jossey-Bass.

Novak, Michael. 1981. "A Theology of the Corporation." In Michael Novak and John W. Cooper, eds., *The Corporation: A Theological Inquiry:* 203–24.

O'Brien, Timothy L. 1993. "Company Wins Workers' Loyalty by Opening Its Books." *Wall Street Journal* (December20).

Parker, Mike. 1985. *Inside the Circle: A Union Guide to QWL.* Boston: South End.

Parker, Mike, and Jane Slaughter. 1988. "Management Stress." *Technology Review* 91 (October): 36–39.

Parsons, Talcott. 1956. "Suggestions for a Sociological Approach to the Theory of Organizations—I." *Administrative Science Quarterly* 1: 62–85.

Pemberton, Prentiss L., and Daniel R. Finn. 1985. *Toward a Christian Economic Ethic: Stewardship and Social Power.* Minneapolis: Winston.

Perlman, Selig. 1923. *A History of Trade Unionism in the U.S.*. New York: Macmillan.

Perlman, Selig, and Philip Taft. 1935. *History of Labor in the United States, 1896–1932,* vol. 4: *Labor Movements.* New York: Macmillan.

Peters, Thomas J., and Robert H. Waterman, Jr. 1982. *In Search of Excellence: Lessons from America's Best-Run Companies.* New York: Warner Books.

Pfeffer, Jeffrey, and Gerald Salancik. 1978. *The External Control of Organizations.* New York: Harper & Row.

Piore, Michael J., and Charles F. Sabel. 1984. *The Second Industrial Divide: Possibilities for Prosperity.* New York: Basic Books.

Pius XI. 1963 [1931]. *Quadragesimo Anno* (Reconstructing the Social Order). In William J. Gibbons, S.J., ed., *Seven Great Encyclicals:* 125–67. New York: Paulist Press.

Rachleff, Peter. 1993. *Hard-pressed in the Heartland: The Hormel Strike and the Future of the Labor Movement.* Boston: South End.

Raines, John C., and Donna C. Day-Lower. 1986. *Modern Work and Human Meaning.* Philadelphia: Wesminster.

Ramsey, Paul. 1980 [1950]. *Basic Christian Ethics.* Chicago: University of Chicago Press.

Rauschenbusch, Walter. 1964 [1907]. *Christianity and the Social Crisis.* New York: Harper Torchbooks.

———. 1912. *Christianizing the Social Order.* New York: Macmillan.

Rayback, Joseph G. 1959. *A History of American Labor.* New York: Macmillan.

Reeck, Darrell. 1982. *Ethics for the Professions: A Christian Perspective.* Minneapolis: Augsburg.

Reid, Peter C. 1990. *Well Made in America: Lessons from Harley Davidson on Being the Best.* New York: McGraw-Hill.

Reisman, Barbara, and Lance Compa. 1985. "The Case for Adversarial Unions." *Harvard Business Review* 63: 22–36.

Religious Committee for Workplace Fairness. 1991. *Restoring the Balance: Toward Justice for Working People.* Religious Committee for Workplace Fairness.

Rose, Robert L. 1994a. "Some Caterpillar Workers Strike Early as Company Braces for UAW Walkout." *Wall Street Journal* (June 22).

———. 1994b. "Plowing Ahead: UAW's Long Strike Fails to Crimp Output at Caterpillar's Plants." *Wall Street Journal* (October 4): 1.

Rose, Robert L., and Alex Kotlowitz. 1992. "Back to Bickering: Strife Between UAW and Caterpillar Blights Promising Labor Idea." *Wall Street Journal* (November 23): 1.

Rosow, Jerome M. 1986. *Teamwork: Joint Labor-Management Programs in America.* New York: Pergamon Press.

Roy, Donald. 1952. "Quota Restriction and Goldbricking in a Machine Shop." *American Journal of Sociology* 52: 427–42.

Salancik, Gerald R., and Jeffrey Pfeffer. 1977. "Who Gets Power—And How They Hold on to It." *Organizational Dynamics* (Winter): 3–21.

Salwen, Kevin G. 1993a. "Why Ms. Brickman of Sarah Lawrence Now Rallies Workers." *Wall Street Journal* (May 24): 1.

———. 1993b. "DuPont Is Told It Must Disband Nonunion Panels." *Wall Street Journal* (June 7): 2.

———. 1993c. "To Some Small Firms, Idea of Cooperating with Labor Is Foreign." *Wall Street Journal,* (July 27): 1.

———. 1993d. "What Us, Worry? Big Unions' Leaders Overlook Bad News, Opt for Status Quo." *Wall Street Journal* (October 5).

Schatz, Ronald W. 1983. *The Electrical Workers: A History of Labor at General Electric and Westinghouse, 1923–1960.* Urbana: University of Illinois Press.

Scherer, F.M. 1988. "Corporate Ownership and Control." In John R. Meyer and James M. Gustafson, eds., *The U.S. Business Corporation: An Institution in Transition:* 43–66. Cambridge: Ballinger.

Shellenbarger, Sue. 1994. "Many Employers Flout Family and Medical Leave Law." *Wall Street Journal* (July 26).

Sherman, Joe. 1994. *In the Rings of Saturn.* New York: Oxford University Press.

Shriver, Donald W., Jr. 1995. "Three Images of Corporate Leadership and Their Implications for Social Justice." In Max L. Stackhouse and Dennis P. McCann, eds., *On Moral Business: Classical and Contemporary Resources for Ethics in Economic Life:* 521–31. Grand Rapids: William B. Eerdmans.

Siker, Louke Van Wensveen, James A. Donahue, and Ronald M. Green. 1991. "Does Your Religion Make a Difference in Your Business Ethics? The Case of Consolidated Foods." *Journal of Business Ethics* 10: 819–32.

Simmons, John, and William Mares. 1983. *Working Together.* New York: Alfred A. Knopf.

Simon, Herbert A. 1976. *Administrative Behavior: A Study of Decision-Making Processes in Administrative Organization.* New York: The Free Press.

Slichter, Sumner H., James J. Healy, and E. Robert Livernash. 1960. *The Impact of Collective Bargaining Upon Management.* Washington D.C.: Brookings Institution.

Smith, Vicki. 1990. *Managing in the Corporate Interest: Control and Resistance in an American Bank.* Berkeley: University of California Press.

Stackhouse, Max L. 1987. *Public Theology and Political Economy: Christian Stewardship in Modern Society.* Grand Rapids: William. B. Eerdmans.

———. 1995. "Introduction: Foundations and Purposes." In Max L. Stackhouse and Dennis P. McCann, eds., *On Moral Business: Classical and Contemporary Resources for Ethics in Economic Life:* 10–34. Grand Rapids: William B. Eerdmans.

Stackhouse, Max L., and Dennis P. McCann. 1991. "A Postcommunist Manifesto: Public Theology After the Collapse of Socialism." *The Christian Century* (January 16): 44–47.

Stillman, Don. 1980. "The Devastating Impact of Plant Relocations." In Mark Green and Robert Massie, Jr., eds., *The Big Business Reader: Essays on Corporate America:* 72–88. New York: Pilgrim.

Sturm, Douglas. 1973. "Corporations, Constitutions, and Covenants." *Journal of the American Academy of Religion* 41: 331–53.

Suskind, Ron. 1992. "Threat of Cheap Labor Abroad Complicates Decisions to Unionize." *Wall Street Journal* (July 28): 1.

Sutton, Francis X., Seymour E. Harris, Carl Kaysen, and James Tobin. 1956. *American Business Creed.* Cambridge: Harvard University Press.

Tarr, Steven C., and William J. Juliano. 1992. "Leading a Team Through Downsizing." *HR Magazine* (October): 91–100.

Thomas, Emory. 1995. "Re-Engineer Cut Corporate Fat, Then Fell On His Own Budget Ax." *Wall Street Journal* (March 21)

Thompson, James D. 1967. *Organizations in Action.* New York: McGraw-Hill.

Tomsho, Robert. 1993. "Union 'Salts' Infiltrate Construction Industry." *Wall Street Journal* (November 18).

Uchitelle, Louis. 1994. "Job Losses Don't Let Up Even as Hard Times Ease." *The New York Times* (March 22): 2.

Uchitelle, Louis, and N. R. Kleinfield. 1996. "On the Battlefields of Business, Millions of Casualties." *The New York Times* (March 3): 1.

United Church of Christ. 1987. "Christian Faith and Economic Life." In Max L. Stackhouse and Dennis P. McCann, eds., *On Moral Business: Classical and Contemporary Resources for Ethics in Economic Life* (1995): 454–67. Grand Rapids: William B. Eerdmans.

Velasquez, Manuel G. 1991. *Business Ethics: Concepts and Cases,* 3rd edition. Englewood Cliffs: Prentice-Hall.

Vonnegut, Kurt. 1974. *Player Piano.* New York: Dell.

Wagner, John A., III 1994. "Participation's Effects on Performance and Satisfaction: A Reconsideration of the Research Evidence." *Academy of Management Review* 19: 312–30.

Walton, Clarence C. 1988. *The Moral Manager.* Cambridge: Ballinger.

Weinstein, Deena. 1979. *Bureaucratic Opposition: Challenging Abuses at the Workplace.* New York: Pergamon.

Wells, Donald M. 1987. *Empty Promises: Quality of Working Life Programs and the Labor Movement.* New York: Monthly Review Press.

White, Joseph B. 1996. "Re-Engineering Gurus Take Steps to Remodel Their Stalling Vehicles." *Wall Street Journal* (November 26): 1.

Williams, Oliver F., and John W. Houck. 1978. *Full Value: Cases in Christian Business Ethics.* San Francisco: Harper & Row.

Williams, Oliver F., and Patrick E. Murphy. 1992. "The Ethics of Virtue: A Moral Theory for Business." In Oliver F. Williams and John W. Houck, eds., *A Virtuous*

Life in Business: Stories of Courage and Integrity in the Corporate World: 9–27. Lanham, Md.: Rowman & Littlefield.

Wogaman, J. Philip. 1986. *Economics and Ethics: A Christian Inquiry.* Philadelphia: Fortress.

Wolman, Leo. 1936. *Ebb and Flow in Trade Unionism.* New York: New York Bureau of National Economic Research.

Zachary, G. Pascal. 1995. "Some Unions Step Up Organizing Campaigns and Get New Members." *Wall Street Journal* (September 1): 1.

Zachary, G. Pascal, and Bob Ortega. 1993. "Workplace Revolution Boosts Productivity at Cost of Job Security." *Wall Street Journal* (March 10): 1.

Zwerdling, Daniel. 1980. *Workplace Democracy: A Guide to Workplace Ownership, Participation and Self-Management Experiments in the United States and Europe.* New York: Harper & Row.

Index